Global NATO and
the Catastrophic Failure in Libya

Global NATO *and the*
Catastrophic Failure in Libya

Lessons for Africa in the Forging of African Unity

by HORACE CAMPBELL

Afterword by Ali A. Mazrui

MONTHLY REVIEW PRESS
New York

Library of Congress Cataloging-in-Publication Data

Campbell, Horace.

  Global NATO and the catastrophic failure in Libya : lessons for Africa in
the forging of African unity / by Horace Campbell.

    p. cm.

  Includes bibliographical references and index.

  ISBN 978-1-58367-413-0 (cloth : alk. paper) — ISBN 978-1-58367-412-3
(pbk. : alk. paper) 1. Libya—History—Civil War, 2011-2. North Atlantic
Treaty Organization—Armed Forces—Libya. 3. Regime change—Libya. 4.
Revolutions—Libya. 5. Intervention (International law) 6.
Neoliberalism—Libya. 7. Libya—Politics and government—21st century. I.
Title.

  DT236.C36 2013

  327.612—dc23

                        2013007503

Monthly Review Press

146 West 29th Street, Suite 6W

New York, New York 10001

www.monthlyreview.org

5 4 3 2 1

Contents

Abbreviations and Acronyms

ACOTA	African Contingency Operations Training and Assistance Program
ACRI	Africa Crisis Response Initiative
AFRICOM	United States Africa Command
AIG	American International Group
AQIM	al-Qaeda in the Maghreb
AU	African Union
BGS	British Geological Survey
bpd	Barrels per day
BRICS	Brazil, Russia, India, China, and South Africa
CFR	Council on Foreign Relations
CFTC	Commodity Futures Trading Commission
CIA	Central Intelligence Agency
CSIS	Center for Strategic and International Studies
EPSA	Exploration and Production Sharing Agreements
GCC	Gulf Cooperation Council
GWOT	Global War on Terrorism
IASB	International African Service Bureau
ICC	International Criminal Court
ICE	Intercontinental Exchange
ICIG	Istanbul Cooperation Initiative Group
IISS	International Institute of Strategic Studies
IMF	International Monetary Fund
LIA	Libyan Investment Authority
Libor	London Interbank Offered Rate
LIFG	Libyan Islamic Fighting Group
LSE	London School of Economics
MSU	Michigan State University

NATO	North Atlantic Treaty Organization
NGO	Non-governmental organization
NSC	National Security Council
NOC	National Oil Company/Corporation
NTC	National Transitional Council
NYMEX	New York Mercantile Exchange
OAU	Organization of African Unity
OPEC	Organization of the Petroleum Exporting Countries
psy-ops	psychological operations
R2P	Responsibility to protect
RECAMP	Reinforcement of African Peacekeeping Capacities Program
RUSI	Royal United Services Institute
TIA	Total Information Awareness
UAE	United Arab Emirates
USSR	Union of Soviet Socialist Republics

PREFACE

This book began as the February 17 uprisings exploded in Libya in 2011. At that moment, the world had been transfixed by the earthshaking events that had toppled the leadership in Tunisia and Egypt. Peter Hallward, a student of the Haitian Revolution of 1804, had remarked that "Egypt's popular revolution will change the world." Progressive forces internationally had been impressed by the new forms of political organizing that had birthed these revolutionary openings. Two years earlier, I had written *Barack Obama and Twenty-first Century Politics: A Revolutionary Moment in the United States*. In that book, I drew out the convergence of political, economic, ecological, and social contexts that gave rise to the new political alliance that was growing inside the United States. I identified the networks of peace and social justice forces that had been mobilized to defeat the neoconservatives. The book was intended to rethink the basic ideas of revolutionary politics for the twenty-first century.

I was in Nairobi, Kenya, when the first news began to emerge about the Benghazi demonstrations. The response of Gaddafi to these demonstrations was of great concern, but soon it became obvious that the forces of counterrevolution were busy seeking to exploit the political underdevelopment of the social forces in Libya. When Nicolas Sarkozy emerged as the champion of the "uprisings," it was instantly clear that the British and the French were up to mischief. Nicolas Sarkozy was no friend of progressive African movements, and his energetic support for the National Transitional Council led to caution from the international peace movement. The peace movement in the United States was divided over the question of the social character of the forces in motion in Libya. By the time of the push by Britain, France, and the United States for the passing of UN Resolutions 1970 and 1973, the jockeying among the military forces internationally was being played out so that all could see that the forces of NATO were not planning to intervene to protect civilians. Exactly a year earlier, I had written in the *Pambazuka News* (March 25, 2010) that the political leadership of Gaddafi was an obstacle to African unity. I had written this critique after Gaddafi had called for dividing Nigeria between Christians and Moslems.

Within the global peace and justice movement, I had taken the position that though Gaddafi should be opposed, it was equally necessary to oppose the NATO intervention. It was exactly one year after my contribution that I wrote opposing Gaddafi's massacre and foreign intervention in Libya. I had been traveling promoting my book during the period of the NATO bombing. I remember distinctly speaking to a small group of Angolan youths in Luanda in April 2011, saying that they ought to be careful in their form of opposition to the Angolan government. These youths had called for demonstrations to bring down the MPLA (Portuguese acronym for the Popular Movement for the Liberation of Angola) government. I cautioned them that Angola, like Libya, was well endowed with resources, and it would not take a big confrontation within Angola for the militarists to drum up some pretext to occupy Cabinda. I pointed to the long history of the work of the April 6 movement in Egypt and why political organizing had to be long and drawn out. As the NATO intervention turned into a stalemate, I was at one with the 200 African intellectuals who later wrote "An Open Letter to the Peoples of Africa and the World from Concerned Africans" on the intervention. At the time of the fall of Tripoli in August 2011, I was teaching in China at Tsinghua University in Beijing. I had been talking to my colleagues and students on the dangers of the NATO intervention and challenges for peace and justice forces globally. During my semester in China there was not a week when a major European leader was not traveling to China to seek financial assistance to bail out banks. I had been telling my Chinese colleagues in private that if China were to assist Europe, it should assist the European working class and not the banks and the capitalist class. My head of department had been interested in this argument, and he invited me to deliver a seminar on "Africa, China, and the European Union" at the Carnegie-Tsinghua Center. This was a memorable day in many respects because there were at least eight respondents to my presentation. Those representatives from the European Union downplayed the extent of the capitalist crisis, and there was only one respondent who agreed that China should rethink its alliance with the bankers in Europe and on Wall Street. Surprisingly, this person was a top official from the Export-Import Bank of China.

The date of the seminar, October 20, 2011, was memorable for another reason. As we were leaving the seminar, I joked with an official from Niger who had been part of the seminar, asking him if Gaddafi had escaped to Niger. When I returned to my office in the afternoon, we learned of the execution of Gaddafi. Immediately, after piecing together the news reports, I spoke to Firoze Manji of *Pambazuka* and called it a synchronized execution. My comments were published later as "The Assassination of Gaddafi." One week later I had written that the manner of the execution was an explicit attempt to humiliate Africa. Bearing in mind the way in which the Tanzanians had treated Idi Amin after his overthrow, I had been mindful of the secrets between Gaddafi and his European allies. I suspected then but did not know what was revealed later by the press in September 2012, that "Gaddafi was killed by a French secret serviceman on orders of Nicolas Sarkozy."

This book project started out as a modest monograph to challenge the claims of NATO that its intervention was a success. I had written one essay on NATO's catastrophic failure in Libya. The writing had been slow in Tsinghua because of the shortage of resources on Africa within Chinese universities. I had promised the monograph to the Africa Institute of South Africa by the spring of 2012. By that time, I had been calling on the peace movement to pay closer attention to the continued warfare in Libya. The monograph was completed in the summer of 2012, and by September I had begun working with other scholars, such as Vijay Prashad and Maximilian Forte, to better coordinate the opposition to the continued war in Libya. Collectively we collaborated on a small symposium to discuss the lessons learned in Libya. In that symposium, the members of the BRICS societies at the United Nations spoke at length on how the resolutions on Libya had stifled the Security Council and how the Libyan intervention and its aftermath had negatively affected the workings of the Security Council of the United Nations. It was there where we learned of new formulations that were being proposed by Brazil, China, and India with respect to the UN's doctrine of the "responsibility to protect." The representatives of India and South Africa at the Security Council had been very active on the international circuit calling for continued discussion on the lessons of the NATO intervention in Libya.

Younes Abouyoub had reached out to me last year for us to collaborate in the context of the Left Forum, 2012. This was a memorable session because of the lively debates, especially the contribution from the revolutionary women in the audience from Algeria. We collaborated again for a presentation hosted by the Hubert Harrison–Theodore W. Allen Society at the Brecht Forum in New York City on October 26. Then Younes participated via Skype from Tripoli and shared his front-row observations of the continued warfare and the helpless administrators who were supposed to be leading the transition.

The last two chapters of this book (preceding the Conclusion) were written in the aftermath of the fighting in Benghazi and the subsequent fallout that led to the resignation of David Petraeus as the Director of the Central Intelligence Agency of the United States. This was an agency that had been involved in the duplicity of supporting jihadists and then fighting against them. Together with the neoconservative forces, the intellectual environment in the United States had been polluted by the attempts of the militarists to "control the narrative."

Paula Broadwell has written for posterity that General Petraeus was a devoted fan of general Marcel Bigeard, the French colonial general who was famous for his support of colonialism and torture in Algeria. In this book, *All In: The Education of General David Petraeus,* we learnt that after reading a book about the colonial achievements of Bigeard, Petraeus admired "what it had to say about the cohesion of successful fighting units. Petraeus later wrote to Bigeard, beginning a correspondence that would continue intermittently until Bigeard's death in the summer of 2010, three weeks after Petraeus took command in Afghanistan. By then Bigeard had acknowledged Petraeus's accomplishment in Iraq and addressed him as a peer."

In short, Petraeus wanted the U.S. military to follow the racist and brutal strategies of the French in Africa.

The COIN strategy was also an affirmation of the need for perpetual warfare where the United States would be engaged in warfare in perpetuity in order to maintain global hegemony. The fall of Petraeus was a major boost to the morale of the peace and social justice forces two days after the historic convergence of the Obama ground operation with the new networks for peace and social justice. Barack Obama had dithered due to his focus on reelection and could not grasp the fact that compromise with the neoconservatives cannot solve the present economic crisis. Thus far the alliance that was mobilized to defeat the neoconservatives in the November 2012 electoral struggles has not yet found a new base for political organizing outside of electoral politics. The energies of the international chauvinist and militaristic forces will seek new ways to create mischief and in the process spread more wars. In the conclusion of this book, I share the call of Johan Galtung that the peace movement must become a new liberation movement. There are many lessons from the period of the solidarity campaigns of the anti-apartheid struggles that can inspire the new peace and justice forces. This book is written as one effort to link the global anti-imperialist movement in finding new ways to cooperate.

I want to thank the editors at Monthly Review Press who immediately saw the importance of this book for the international peace movement. I want to thank them as well for their enthusiasm in support of this project. The team at *Pambazuka News* was also very supportive. I want to particularly mention Zanna Rodriquez, who was steadfast in her efforts to ensure that this platform reached the wide constituency. There are so many others who contributed to the sharpening of this message. Marc Mealy and Wazir Mohammed were very close to the saga of the NATO war against the people of Libya, and I would like to thank them for sharing their energy so that this book could be completed. My partner, Makini, lived up to her name and held all of the family together while I was off in Africa and China.

We are in an exciting period. While the neoconservatives seek to confuse the young with arrogant ideas of white supremacy, millions of youths are looking for another mode of existence. The Occupy Wall Street movement served as the base for the progressives to electorally defeat the neocons. Mindful that it was in the midst of the dark days of fascism that revolutionaries such as George Padmore, C. L. R. James, W. E. B. Du Bois, and Paul Robeson stepped up to rally the anti-fascist forces, this book is written in that same tradition so that the forces of conservatism can be beaten back. I was aware that there were hundreds of thousands of youths in the military who were opposed to the imperial wars being fought. At the time of this writing, Bradley Manning stands out as an example of a youth who can both serve in the military and support the peace movement. There are hundreds of young persons who have joined the military seeking to escape the crisis of unemployment. This book is dedicated to the young people internationally who are struggling to break this imperial system so that humans can start on a new road that celebrates that we are all one. We are past the point where we have to imagine this.

*To the spirit and memory of Tajudeen Abdul Raheem
and all of those who continue to work for peace, unity, and
reconstruction while opposing fundamentalists globally.*

We must fight to save the euro.

—NICOLAS SARKOZY

The European experiment is of no use to us . . . the area known as North Africa should be Africanized. Either it will become a part of Africa or it will be an anomaly, and will therefore have no future.

As an inhabitant of North Africa, I have always rejected the Barcelona agreement which regards North Africa as part of the Middle East, with a vocation to integrate with Europe. This is a conspiracy against the integrity of Africa.

They have said to me the Barcelona agreement and cooperation with the European Union will be to Libya's advantage. They want to draw us in and to make use of us, through the Barcelona agreement, to dismember the African continent, stealing North Africa to make it join with the European Union. This is unacceptable. In any case, look at what has already become of the Barcelona agreement. It is in a comatose condition and could well disappear.

—MUAMMAR GADDAFI
speech in July 2001 at the opening of the African Union

If the Libyan war was about saving lives,
it was a catastrophic failure.

—SEUMAS MILNE

1 — INTRODUCTION
THE NATO INTERVENTION IN LIBYA:
A LESSON OF COLOSSAL FAILURE

When the Tunisian and Egyptian uprisings erupted in Africa in the first two months of the year 2011 with the chant, "The people want to bring down the regime," there was hope all over the continent that these rebellions were part of a wider "African Awakening." President Ben Ali of Tunisia was forced to step down and fled to Saudi Arabia. Within a month of Ben Ali's departure, Hosni Mubarak of Egypt was removed from power by the people, who mobilized a massive revolutionary movement in the country. Four days after the ousting of Mubarak, sectors of the Libyan people rebelled in Benghazi. Within days, this uprising was militarized, with armed resistance countered by declarations from the Libyan leadership vowing to use raw state power to root out the rebellion.

The first Libyan demonstrations occurred on February 15, 2011, but by February 21 there were reports that innocent civilians were in imminent danger of being massacred by the army. This information was embellished by reports of the political leadership branding the rebellious forces as "rats." The United States, Britain, and France took the lead to rush through a resolution in the United Nations Security Council, invoking the principle of the "responsibility to protect." This principle had been embraced and supported by many governments in the aftermath of the genocidal episodes in Rwanda, Bosnia, and Kosovo. UN Security Council Resolution 1973 of 2011 was loosely worded, with the formulation "all necessary measures" tacked on to ensure wide latitude for those societies and political leaders who orchestrated the North Atlantic Treaty Organization (NATO) intervention in Libya.[1] What was left out in the reporting on this resolution was that there had been provisions for mediation and a cease-fire.

In the following nine months, the implementation of this UN resolution exposed the real objectives of the leaders of the United States, France, and Britain. With the Western media fueling a propaganda campaign in the traditions of "manufacturing consent," this Security Council authorization was stretched from a clear and limited civilian protection mandate into a military campaign for regime change and the execution of the president of Libya, Muammar Gaddafi.[2] When, a week after Gaddafi's execution, Seumas Milne wrote in the UK newspaper *The Guardian*, "If the Libyan war was about saving lives, it was a catastrophic failure," he was communicating a conclusion that had been echoed by democratic forces all over the world, and repeated by concerned intellectuals who had written "An Open Letter to the Peoples of Africa and the World from Concerned Africans."[3] The themes of NATO's failure were repeated by Western newspapers that opined, "The Libya campaign, far from demonstrating NATO's abiding strength, rather exposed its manifold, and growing, weaknesses."[4] Think tanks and opinion framers such as the Royal United Services Institute (RUSI) of London and the Jamestown Foundation of the United States could not but comment on the clear failure of this highly publicized mission that was presented under the rubric of "humanitarianism." As a display of Western military strength and cohesion, the NATO operation was a failure and was understood to be so by the majority outside the orbit of the mainstream of the Anglo-American media.[5] Writers from Asia were linking the role of the U.S. Africa

Command (AFRICOM) to the new power grab in Africa, while there was massive opposition from Africa. In studying the catastrophic failures, African intellectuals have sought to highlight the illegal actions of NATO, calling for the International Criminal Court (ICC) to investigate and establish if war crimes were committed in Libya.

One year after the NATO forces embarked on their mission to carry out regime change in Libya, it is still pertinent to restate the principal ideas that came from Africa in the face of the present lawlessness, torture, and terror campaigns of competing militias. Amnesty International, by no means an organization unfriendly to NATO, issued a report in February 2012 detailing widespread torture in the prisons and makeshift detention facilities in Libya. This report documented savage practices that included beatings with whips, cables, metal chains, and wooden sticks, electric shocks, extraction of fingernails, and rape. Militia fighters conducted these attacks brazenly, in some cases abusing prisoners in the presence of human rights advocates.[6] Amnesty International has also reported the widespread persecution of innocent citizens by out-of-control militias. In January 2012, a report by a human rights group from the Middle East documented war crimes carried out by NATO in their eight-month operation for regime change.[7] No less a person than Navi Pillay, the United Nations High Commissioner for Human Rights, noted that "the lack of oversight by the central authority creates an environment conducive to torture and ill-treatment."

The more chilling aspect of this persecution is the racist attacks on those who are supposed to be "black" Africans. There are reports from numerous sources that, in addition to black Africans being detained en masse on the suspicion that they were mercenaries for Gaddafi, the town of Tawergha, previously a black African community, has been completely emptied and declared a "closed military zone" by the NATO-supported militia forces. Revenge and retribution is now being followed by separatist movements calling for either the dissolution of the present state or the establishment of a federal authority.

This reality of continued warfare and widespread torture of Africans demands a revisit of the position of the African Union (AU) that was articulated on March 10, 2011, at the 265th meeting of the Peace and Security Council of the AU. This "road map" was a five-point plan demanding:

> a ceasefire; the protection of civilians; the provision of humanitarian aid for Libyans and foreign workers in the country; dialogue between the two sides, i.e. the Gaddafi regime and the National Transitional Council (NTC); leading to an "inclusive transitional period" and political reforms which "meet the aspirations of the Libyan people."

The Scramble for African and Libyan Resources

One year after the UN resolution authorizing the use of force to implement the no-fly zone, the deployment of NATO military forces—coordinating with "special forces" from Qatar, under the umbrella of unlimited bombing campaigns—has left the international headlines. However, the reality of the destruction in Libya has not left the consciousness of Africans and those who support peace internationally.[8] In the open letter to the citizens of the world, the concerned African intellectuals expressed their pain and anger at the manipulation of the United Nations by the ruling elements in France, Great Britain, and the United States.[9] Drawing attention to the lessons from the wars against the people of Iraq and the statement by sectors of the neoconservative forces in the United States wishing for the "death of the United Nations," these intellectuals clarified the manipulation of information that preceded the passing of the United Nations Resolution 1973 of March 2011.

This attack on Africans in the midst of a depression is not new, and reminded African intellectuals of the context of the demise of the League of Nations. African scholars wanting to inspire a new appreciation of global history readily understand that it was during a capitalist depression that the League of Nations collapsed, after the European powers failed to intervene to halt the Italian invasion of Abyssinia, in

October 1935.[10] This failure of the League of Nations laid the foundations for the triggers of war that engulfed humanity in the tragic cycles of economic crises, fascism, war, genocide, and the dropping of an atomic bomb on Hiroshima and Nagasaki. In 2011, in the midst of another depression, international diplomacy had failed in Africa, and African intellectuals, like their predecessors of the International African Service Bureau (IASB) of the Depression years, were warning of the cascading forces for more war.[11] These African intellectuals reminded those who would listen that the UN Security Council had failed to prove that its authorization of the use of force under Chapter VII of the UN Charter was a proportionate and appropriate response to what had, in reality, developed into a civil war in Libya. They maintained:

> It is clear that the U.S. and its European allies are reverting to crude military means to re-colonize Africa. The independence that Africans fought so hard for must be defended. We cannot allow the second scramble for Africa to occur on our watch. We condemn the U.S., UK and France for the flagrant abuse of the UN Security Council and demand that the International Criminal Court investigate NATO to establish if war crimes were committed in Libya. We condemn the extra-judicial killing of Col. Gaddafi and call for an independent transparent international inquiry to establish the true facts surrounding it.

This book is written in the spirit of the international forces that are opposed to the present scramble for Africa and that are campaigning against the remilitarization of Africa. In the process of this analysis, we will elaborate on the insensate struggle among the Western powers for control over the continent's petroleum resources. African petroleum resources are caught up in a new transitional period, where the future of the top Western oil corporations is on the line. Even before the complete fall of Gaddafi's regime, one British scholar, David Anderson, had opined on "the fight for Libya's oil."[12] Waxing enthusiastically on the "significant pickings" in Libya, Anderson reflected on the opportunities for Europe's oil giants—Eni, Total, BP, and Repsol YPF—who are "perfectly positioned" to take advantage of these commercial opportunities. What was left out was the deep competition between European oil giants and the "Big Oil" firms from North America. In 2002, the African Oil Policy Initiative Group conducted a symposium titled "African Oil: A Priority for U.S. National Security and African Development." It was in this setting that former congressman William Jefferson said, "African oil should be treated as a priority for U.S. national security post–9/11. I think that . . . post–9/11 it's occurred to all of us that our traditional sources of oil are not as secure as we thought they were." Jefferson was reflecting one sector of the U.S. policy environment that fell under the sway of the alliance between big oil and big banks. The U.S. oil companies emerged as major international corporations after 1945 and influenced the U.S. government initiatives, wielding profound influence over the Pentagon, the State Department, the Department of Energy, the Department of the Interior, and other branches of the U.S. imperial system. In the era of financialization, these corporations became enmeshed in the Wall Street investment game and increased their influence over the U.S. political system at home and abroad. The relationship between the big oil companies, the U.S. political system, and the Wall Street oligarchs is described as the tripartite alliance in the U.S. political system.

After developing the tripartite alliance with the top Wall Street investment firms and riding on high oil and gasoline prices, the U.S. oil giants became the most profitable industry in the world. Six of the ten largest corporations in the world are oil companies. They are, in order, ExxonMobil, Royal Dutch Shell (Shell), British Petroleum (BP), Chevron, ConocoPhillips, and Total. These large corporations are at the core of what is called "Big Oil." According to the author of *The Tyranny of Oil*, Big Oil is experiencing a level of power that has only one historical precedent: that of the Standard Oil era. And, like Standard Oil, the companies appear willing to do anything to maintain their position.[13]

In our examination of the relationship between Goldman Sachs and the Libyan National Oil Company, we will draw attention to the challenge that Libyan independence posed to both oil imperialism and the dominance of NATO over the region of North Africa and the Mediterranean Sea. The oil companies never forgot that Libya's nationalization of oil in the 1970s was the precursor to Iranian nationalization in 1979 and Saudi Arabia's full takeover of Aramco in the mid-1980s.[14] Before the uprisings, Gaddafi had again raised the question of nationalizing Western oil companies. Numerous scholars have been explicit that Libya was enmeshed in the new geopolitics for energy resources.[15] These scholars can be distinguished from the spokespersons for Western corporations from universities and organizations such as the Atlantic Council or the Council on Foreign Relations in the United States. It is the very platform for the ideas of the "liberalization" and "freedom" that further exposes the worn-out intellectual apparatus of the West in the service of the tripartite alliance. Yet, as we will analyze in this book, the intelligentsia in the service of finance capital are in a losing battle at the intellectual level and on the ground in the actual competition to control the resources of Africa. After failing to compete in the marketplace with new rising powers, the military management of the international system is coming up against national oil corporations that are seeking new linkages with Brazil, China, India, and other emerging forces in the international system. Throughout the decade after international sanctions were lifted against Libya, the Gaddafi government skillfully used Exploration and Production Sharing Agreements (EPSA) with the Libyan National Oil Corporation to maintain a balance in its relationships among North American, European, Brazilian, Chinese, Russian, Turkish, Indian, and other corporate entities that were investing in Libyan energy markets. By the year 2009, the Chinese oil giant PetroChina overtook Exxon Mobil as the world's most valuable company. Though Exxon temporarily regained its position, the rapid growth of PetroChina, Sinopec, and the Brazilian state-owned Petrobras challenged the dominance of Big Oil and changed the international energy landscape. Libya was able to reflect on alternative sources of financing for its resources. By the end of 2010, China was the top investor in Libya.

The state-controlled Libyan Investment Authority (LIA) entered into the opaque world of financing energy markets before their corporate associates on Wall Street such as Goldman Sachs and the intellectuals who spoke on behalf of the oil companies realized that the neoliberal faction of the political leadership in Libya was too weak to deliver the economy and the Libyan reserves to the West. Gaddafi had kept the Western oligarchs at bay using a revolving-door mechanism. Moreover, the U.S. oil majors found Gaddafi's flirtation with non-European companies in Libya too threatening. Libya is a top producer of petroleum products, with less than 30 percent of its resources tapped. The leadership of this same Libya had become aggressive in its financial operations, while committing to the establishment of an African Monetary Union, an African Central Bank, and an African Investment Bank. After December 2010, the Central Bank of Libya took the controlling position in the Bahrain-based Arab Banking Corporation, which was owned by the Kuwait Investment Authority, the Central Bank of Libya, the Abu Dhabi Investment Authority, and other, smaller shareholders. (To date, few scholarly writings have linked the Libyan dominance in the Arab Banking Corporation to the tectonic events in Libya since February 2011.) Many of the political leaders in the Gulf Cooperation Council (GCC)—whose calling, since the 1970s, had been to recycle the resources of Arabia for the Western financial system—had been alarmed by the independence of the Libyan leadership in its thrust to move the Arab Banking Group out of its servile position to Western banking interests.

Taking Libya Out of Africa

This book will bring to light the interconnections between the resources of Libya, the NATO intervention, and the discrediting of the liberal discourses on African resources, including the discourses on human rights and the responsibility to protect. It is our intention to draw out the intensity of the Western preoccupation with Libya and the leading roles of Western intellectuals. In the Africanist establishment in the West, there are established experts on every African society. In the case of Libya, however, there were not only the country experts but also the intellectuals in think tanks, such as Chester Crocker (through the Atlantic Council), Joseph Nye, Michael Porter, Francis Fukuyama, Richard Perle, Bernard Lewis, Benjamin Barber, and Robert Putnam (through the Monitor Group), all of whom engaged in a sustained campaign to promote "reforms" in Libya and Africa.[16]

Saif al-Islam, one of Gaddafi's sons, had been schooled in the neoliberal discourse about "reforms" and had successfully ensnared leading Western intellectuals in a project to burnish the image of the Gaddafi government. The Monitor Group, a Boston-based, top consulting firm associated with the Harvard Business School, was seeking to catch up with the advance work of the London School of Economics (LSE), other British institutions of higher learning, politicians, and sectors of the energy industry. Anthony Giddens, one of the most cited sociologists of the Anglo-Saxon intellectual world and former director of the LSE, made many trips to Libya and brought in Tony Blair, the former prime minister, as an interlocutor to promote British interests in Libya "from strength to strength."

Joseph Nye (as one of the group of experts of the Monitor Group) has demonstrated, in theory and practice, that the international relations ideas about the soft power of the United States are part of the general "what is good for U.S. banks and corporations is good for humanity" toolbox. Institutions such as the Council on Foreign Relations (CFR) provide the necessary intellectual and policy network for the banks, the oil companies, and the barons of finance. However, the Libyan episode exposed the reality that the belief systems of "free markets" and "soft power" are tools of the neoliberal thrust of permanent war and the Americanization of the world. Richard Haass, president of the CFR, gave up the "soft power" façade and explicitly called for U.S. "boots on the ground." These realists of the U.S. foreign policy establishment poured invective against Libya by terming the people "tribalists." Anthropologists and other social scientists who are integrated into this ideation system were placed as front-line thinkers and writers for the military information operations against Africa. It then fell to the journals and information outlets of Western domination to saturate the media with "experts," to deny the possibility for citizens to understand Libyan society.

Concerned scholars who seek to understand the politics and culture of Libya from European language sources will find that U.S. and British intellectuals have sought to monopolize the interpretation of the political processes in Libya since the Gaddafi government came to power in September 1969. Country studies by research institutions were supplemented by books on oil and state building, with French and Italian intellectuals making their own contribution to a body of literature that took Libya out of Africa and reproduced ideas on the nature of tribal society in Libya.[17]

Tribal Libya, rogue state, terrorist state, and radical Islamist, all obscured the achievements of this society and highlighted the presumed divisions between Libya and Africa. A clear understanding of the historical processes of domination and resistance in Libya will highlight the regional differences between the areas formerly known as Cyrenaica, Tripolitania, and Fezzan. That these areas were not united under one political authority until 1951 is an important component of the nature of Libyan society. However, this regional differentiation does not take these peoples out of Africa—and it is important to restate that Libya is an African society with peoples who have an Arab identity. In the dominant Western literature, the Sahara is presented as a dividing line between North Africa and Sub-Saharan Africa, instead of an area marked by the exchange of ideas, peoples, and goods.[18] It is this tradition of division that renders the revolutionary changes in North Africa as part of an "Arab Spring."[19]

African scholars have instead drawn attention to the influence of the African revolutionary processes since the Algerian Revolution and the confluence of Pan-Africanism and Pan-Arabism in North Africa. Scholars such as Samir Amin have been able to analyze the historical foundations of the unity and diversity across this region while penetrating nationalism and the relationship to pre-capitalist formations in the Middle East and North Africa.[20] A great deal of trouble has been taken to identify the uprisings in North Africa as an Arab Spring, and this has been as conscious as the historic efforts to take Egypt out of Africa. The history of the Arabized Berbers in Libya is pertinent to the African relations with the region and is linked to the Pan-African Project of the

Jamahiriya, the term used to assert that Libya was a "state of the masses or a people's state."

An elaboration of the argument on the Pan-African linkages of the peoples of North Africa would carry us deeper into the past, which is outside the scope of this present analysis of the failures of NATO in an era of economic crisis. This orientation of the Libyan leadership had created disquiet within sectors of the Libyan populace, especially those in which cultural and intellectual orientation had predisposed people to cultural and ideological affinities with Western Europe. These social forces called themselves Arabs but were ideologically subservient to the Western ideas of the market. For centuries the region of North Africa had been viewed as a bridge between Africa, Europe, and Asia, especially the Levant. From the period of mercantilism to the rise of industrial capitalism, emerging European powers sought to invade and control North Africa. The Napoleonic campaign in Egypt was only one of the many expeditions to assert European domination after the emergence of capitalism on a world stage. After the decolonization momentum erupted, France and Britain attempted to seize the Suez Canal and this had precipitated war. Throughout the period of independence in this region, European powers associated control of it as vital to the security and economic well-being of Europe.

As the economic crisis in the Eurozone intensified, European leaders such as the French and Italian leaders were looking for ways to accumulate more capital from Africa.

Some scholars and liberal analysts have underplayed the depth of this capitalist depression, but Simon Johnson, former Chief Economist of the International Monetary Fund (IMF), has written of the "Quiet Coup" of the bankers in this depression. Paul Krugman wrote a book titled *End This Depression Now*, but in it failed to link the depression to the increased militarization in parts of the Middle East and Africa.[21]

Dispossession and expropriation of the resources of oppressed societies are now clear manifestations of the scramble for Africa in this moment of economic crisis.

Johnson, who wrote about the "Quiet Coup" in relation to the political power of the bankers and financiers in the United States, observed in *13 Bankers: The Wall Street Takeover and the Next Financial Meltdown* that the financial oligarchs cannot halt the rush to a new financial meltdown. The question is whether societies all over the world, especially in Africa, are ready for alternatives when this meltdown takes place. According to Johnson, "What we face now could, in fact, be worse than the Great Depression—because the world is now so much more interconnected and because the banking sector is now so big."[22] Samir Amin went further than describing the effects of this capitalist crisis by drawing attention to the polarization at the global level and deepening inequalities within societies. In the book *Ending the Crisis of Capitalism or Ending Capitalism?* Amin argued that "the global economic crisis has once again made people question the limitations of neoliberal globalization and, more generally, the limitations of capitalism."

These limitations have become apparent every day since 2008, when Lehman Brothers collapsed. In the years after that fateful event, the limitations of capitalism have been revealed in Western Europe, where the top European capitalist countries have undergone their deepest crisis since the 1930s. The long-term survival of the euro and the European Union is now in question. The big difference between the crisis today and that of the 1930s is that, in this period of independent African states, European powers could no longer use extra economic coercion such as "Plant More Crops" or other forms of coerced labor.[23] As Walter Rodney explained so clearly, as the Depression and war demanded austerity within Europe, the British colonial authorities within Africa were concerned with the need for "increased acreages of the conventional export crops and others which were deemed essential. It had already become standard practice to force Africans to grow more of the marketable crops at times of crisis in the global capitalist economy. This was a policy pursued in a somewhat disorganized form during the 1920s, and taken up very seriously when the Great Depression struck. The clearly stated objective of the Administration was to ensure that Africans maintained the total value of colonial production in spite of falling prices. The only way that this could be done was to exhort and ultimately coerce them to 'plant more crops' and hence the campaign of this name."

Formal colonialism had ended in Africa but European states such as France, Belgium, and Britain sought to maintain some of the former colonial relationships that Kwame Nkrumah had described as neocolonialism. France was particularly vulnerable to challenges to its special place in Africa and for forty years after the independence struggles, France was considered the gendarme of Europe in Africa.

It is against the reality of the NATO intervention in Libya that one can dissect the statement by French president Nicolas Sarkozy: "We will fight to save the euro."

Was the Libyan Intervention One Component of This Fight?

The changes in the international political economy have been so rapid that the Libyan intervention exposed the deep divisions within Europe and highlighted how sectors of French, British, and U.S. capital were resorting to brute force to remain competitive. The energetic participation of Qatar as core partner of NATO (through the Istanbul Cooperation Initiative, a group that functioned as a de facto NATO ally) clarified the ways in which proxy states are brought in as military partners in the new redivision of the world. One of the questions that will be posed in the Conclusion chapter of this study is whether these new relations, as manifest in the relations between the Istanbul Cooperation and the Mediterranean Dialogue initiatives, are sustainable in the medium term. Intellectually, the failures in Libya exposed the disinformation and military information operations of the West. Hugh Roberts captured this reality in his essay "Who Said Gaddafi Had to Go?":

> The intervention tarnished every one of the principles the war party invoked to justify it. It occasioned the deaths of thousands of civilians, debased the idea of democracy, debased the idea of law and passed off a counterfeit revolution as the real thing. Two assertions that were endlessly reiterated—they were fundamental to the Western powers' case for war—were that Gaddafi was engaged in "killing his own people" and that he had "lost all legitimacy," the

latter presented as the corollary of the former. Both assertions involved mystifications.[24]

Roberts maintained that a sober understanding of the Libyan intervention will only come to light by future work on those who manipulated the information. African intellectuals and policy makers have learned many lessons about the manipulation of humanitarianism. The duplicity of Western leaders was an eye-opener, and even allies of the United States such as Yoweri Museveni have written on the Libyan experience. His article "The Qaddafi I Know" clearly stated that, even though the Libyan leader was no saint, the West was wrong to intervene in African affairs.[25] In this short essay one could discern a "soul searching" of what it means to be an ally of the United States. For leaders such as Museveni, who had invested his own future with the U.S. military, the Libyan intervention was a revelation because Libya's leaders had worked overtime to rehabilitate themselves in the eyes of the United States and Britain—especially after the invasion of Iraq and the capture of Saddam Hussein.

The NATO operation exposed the reality that in the current depression there will be massive use of force by Western corporations to remain competitive. These corporate entities have decided to go beyond structural adjustment "reforms" and have taken a military stand in Africa. There were also commentators who perceived the Libyan intervention as a proxy war with China.[26] War and revolution in North Africa have opened a new period in the history of Africa.

For about a year after the execution of Gaddafi, the Western media and the academics presented the Libyan intervention as a major success. From the academic experts on Libya such as Dirk Vandewalle, this narrative of success was promulgated through journal essays with titles such as "After Qaddafi: The Surprising Success of the New Libya," in the November/December 2012 *Foreign Affairs*. What was intriguing about this narrative by Vanderwalle was that it continued the view that the Libyan intervention had been a success even after the death of the U.S. ambassador to Libya, Christopher Stevens, had been reported internationally. On Tuesday, September 11, 2012, Stevens and three others were killed in Benghazi. This episode brought into the open what had been hidden: that hundreds of militias were marauding and intimidating civilians. But because failure begets failure, the full scandal of the NATO enterprise in Libya and North Africa had to await the fall from grace of David Petraeus, who had joined the leadership of the Libyan intervention when he took over as Director of the Central Intelligence Agency in September 2011.

The interconnections between the resignation of David Petraeus and the failed attempts to rescue the ambassador brought out other aspects of the NATO intervention that culminated in the reported removal of General Carter Ham as commander of the U.S. Africa Command. It was announced on October 18, 2012, that he would be replaced by General Rodriguez. Eight days later, the U.S. Navy reassigned Rear Admiral Charles M. Gaouette, who has been the commander of the USS *John C. Stennis* Strike Group. Two weeks later, on November 9, 2012, General David Petraeus, a former four-star general in the United States Army, resigned from the directorship of the Central Intelligence Agency. These changes in the military apparatus were all related to the catastrophic failure of the hubris associated with perceived military power of the United States and the supposed inherent superiority of Western forms of cultural and economic organization. In this book, we will spell out how the ideas of neoconservatism and neoliberalism were discredited with the fall of the top generals from the military establishment. From the period of the assertiveness of the organization called the Project for a New American Century (PNAC), this group of what are now called neocons dominated the Bush administration, writing many books presenting goals to ensure U.S. military and economic dominance. In particular, Douglas Feith Jr.'s *War and Decision: Inside the Pentagon at the Dawn of the War on Terror* gave a ringside view of the manipulations that had been orchestrated to generate the climate for the military occupation of Iraq. The thrust of the analysis provided here is that if the Iraq war discredited neoconservatism, the fall of Lehman Brothers in 2008 discredited the ideas of neoliberalism.

Delusions about the invincibility of the U.S military had been promoted so loudly since the end of the Cold War that many of the top leaders of the political and military establishment believed their own propaganda. The amateurish behavior of David Petraeus and his colleague, General John Allen, exposed just how far the self-deception within the military apparatus had reached. Focusing on the failures is not based on gloating but part of an effort to strengthen the resolve of the peace and justice movement to challenge militarism and exploitation.

In the book *African Awakening: The Emerging Revolutions*, Samir Amin argues that the uprisings in Africa and the Middle East represent one sign of the new "storm zone" of repeated revolts in the countries of the South.[27] This book contends that the U.S. Africa Command and the objective of the conservative U.S. political forces are to preempt other revolutionary uprisings of the type and scale that removed the regimes in Tunisia and Egypt. This goal of the U.S. security establishment was explicitly outlined by the Center for Strategic and International Studies (CSIS) in Washington, D.C., at a major seminar on the implications of the uprising in Egypt.[28] Whether the uprisings in Egypt and Tunisia serve as one sign of the "storm zone" is a major concern for the Western oil companies, and despite its imitations, the African Union has understood that the war in Libya was an attack on Africans.

In this book, we will agree that the NATO intervention has served to speed up awareness in Africa that the African Union must be strengthened to be able to meet the political, diplomatic, and military requirements to resist external military missions such as that of NATO in Libya. We will also link this catastrophic failure to the failed ideas of Joseph Nye, Anthony Giddens, Lisa Anderson, and the international experts whose intellectual trajectory was to dismiss the project of African independence and African unity. What was striking about the advocates of liberal interventions was their silence when African migrant workers in Libya were being butchered by elements from the National Transitional Council (NTC).

The book will outline the disinformation that was unleashed to cover up the execution of Colonel Muammar Gaddafi and restate the argument that the manner of the killing and the destruction of the town of Sirte were aimed at the destruction of the ideas of African Unity. One does not have to agree with all of the ideas of Colonel Gaddafi, but there is one core idea—that of African freedom—that must be highlighted. From the work of Kwame Nkrumah to the stewardship of Nelson Mandela, there has been one overriding principle: Africans must dictate the pace and rate of the unification and freedom of Africa. If, according to sectors of the U.S. intellectual establishment, the U.S. war against the people of Vietnam reflected a "congenital moral failure of the American political system,"[29] this Libyan intervention and murder of Gaddafi will go down in history as a colossal failure of NATO and one that spurred the pace of the unity of Africa.

2—THE INDEPENDENCE OF LIBYA AND THE BIRTH OF NATO

The history of Libya has been intertwined for thousands of years with the social and economic transformations of Africa, Europe, and the Middle East. With a location in the north of the continent of Africa, the peoples of the region west of the Nile Valley were engulfed in the fortunes of trade, ideas, and religious expansion. Europeans along the Mediterranean coast interacted with the peoples of Libya for millennia, suffering major invasions from this region. Two of the more well-known forays from North Africa were by Hannibal and another by the Moors, who occupied the Iberian Peninsula as part of the wave of expansion after the seventh century. This invasion by the Moors emanated from Arabia, through Egypt to Morocco, and Arabized millions of the Imazighen people, called Berbers.[30] European scholars imposed concepts of hierarchy on the diverse populations of differing ethnicities that lived in the area that is now called Libya.[31]

The peoples who inhabit this territory were under the domination of the Ottoman Empire until industrial Europe reached the monopoly stage in the nineteenth century. Present-day Libya emerged out of two provinces of the Ottoman Empire—Tripolitania and Cyrenaica.

The third region, Fezzan, eluded complete occupation by the colonial powers. These provinces escaped events such as the French occupation of Algiers in 1830 and the financial domination of France over the area of what was to become Tunisia. After the Rothschild banking group helped Britain to consolidate its ascendancy in Egypt subsequent to the building of the Suez Canal in 1869, there was an unwritten Anglo-French convention that defined the British and Turkish spheres of influence in North Africa.

The Liberation Struggle

Like most present boundaries in Africa, Libya's current borders were carved out in the period of the imperial partitioning of Africa by European states. At the infamous Berlin Conference of 1884–1885, the region that is now Libya remained under Ottoman rule. Turkey was allowed to maintain nominal control over this region because the dominant imperial powers did not consider Turkish power a threat to monopoly interests in Europe.

Italy, which had recently been partially united, wanted to establish itself as a major world power in Africa but was soundly defeated by the Ethiopians at Dogali in 1887, and more decisively at Adowa in 1896. The Italians never gave up their goal of gaining colonial territory in Africa, and in 1911 invaded the area that is now called Libya. "By turning Cyrenaica into an armed camp, by arrests, deportations, confiscations and executions and by use of an overwhelming weight of modern military equipment, the Italians finally mastered the resistance and cornered the last, exhausted fighting bands of the Gebel Akhdar."[32]

In all African societies the people instinctively rose up to oppose foreign occupation, and Libya was no exception. Libyans of differing ethnic groups united to oppose Italian occupation, and a consciousness about being Libyan emerged in this anti-colonial period between 1911 and 1941. There was constant guerrilla resistance against the Italians, especially after Benito Mussolini's forces took power in 1922 and imposed fascist administrative structures in Libya. In order to snuff out rebellion, the fascists imported large numbers of Italian settlers and developed infrastructure to coordinate colonial control. Peoples from all regions rebelled against colonial fascism, with outstanding Libyans like Umar a Mukhtar waging guerrilla war against the Italians for more than twenty years. Like the coordinated hunt for Gaddafi eighty years later, Mukhtar was hunted down, captured, and hanged in one of the fascist concentration camps.

The Second World War sped up the processes of national consciousness and political organization that were then sweeping North Africa. Britain took control of the region after the Axis forces were driven from North Africa. With their monarchical traditions, the British supported one faction of the Libyans, the Sanussis, and installed their leader as King Idris. British intellectuals such as E. E. Evans-Pritchard functioned as colonial administrators, and through their anthropological writings sought to place the cultural modeling and categorizations of "primitive tribal" affiliations on Libya as on other African societies.[33]

The tide of nationalism had surged throughout the region in the decades between world wars. As fascist forces advanced across North Africa toward Egypt, many nationalists organized to break imperial domination of the region. The British doubled down to place puppet regimes across this area that was then, as now, considered geostrategically important for Europe. The British military controlled the society as a military zone, but the British plan for the rejuvenation of the British Empire after the Second World War came up against the realities of the changed international situation. Following the formation of the United Nations in 1945, the people of Libya were placed under UN Trusteeship, with Britain maintaining de facto political control, and over the period 1941–51 the provinces of Cyrenaica, Tripolitania, and Fezzan were united to become one kingdom. The independence of the United Kingdom of Libya was proclaimed on December 24, 1951— two years after the formation of a new military alliance, the North Atlantic Treaty Organization.

The strategic importance of Libya during the Second World War and the memory of the 1941 siege of Tobruk (a seaport city and peninsula on Libya's eastern coast, near the border with Egypt) were too fresh in the minds of the British for their military planners to give up control entirely, so the British decided to formalize their military presence in the country. The Libyan monarch signed a twenty-year treaty of friendship and alliance with Britain that included a clause for Britain to maintain military bases in Libya.

As the number one ally of Britain, the U.S. military was able to secure military base rights, signing an agreement with the Libyan king in 1954. The U.S. Air Force's Wheelus Air Base in Libya became known as "Little America" until the United States was asked to leave after Colonel Gaddafi seized power, on September 1, 1969. The United States has been scheming for a way back into Libya ever since.

NATO's Origins

When the North Atlantic Treaty was signed on April 4, 1949, most of the founding members were colonial overlords: Belgium, Britain, France, the Netherlands, Italy, and the United States.[34] The organization was dominated by the United States and constituted a system of "collective defense" whereby its member states agreed to mutual defense in response to an attack by any external party. The external party in question at that time was the USSR; NATO had been formed as an alliance ostensibly to defend Western Europe against the Soviet Union.

Charles de Gaulle pulled France out of the alliance in 1966, after it became clear that this military association was dominated by the United States and Britain (supporting their military industries). U.S. military industries had placed a lock on the market for military technology within NATO by implementing language in the treaty about the "standardization of allied military technology." In this case, the language meant that U.S. transnationals producing military equipment dominated NATO.

3—THE COLLAPSE OF THE SOVIET UNION AND THE EMERGENCE OF GLOBAL NATO

Historically, when an alliance is formed for a specific purpose—in this case, halting the spread of communism—it is folded when the mission is complete. Hence, after the fall of the Soviet Union in 1991, it was the expectation of many that the mission of NATO would be scaled down, as a "peace dividend." Instead, NATO expanded, adding new members seven times, and now it is composed of twenty-eight nations. Joining the original signatories were Greece and Turkey (1952); West Germany (1955; from 1990 as Germany); Spain (1982); the Czech Republic, Hungary, and Poland (1999); Bulgaria, Estonia, Latvia, Lithuania, Romania, Slovakia, and Slovenia (2004); and Albania and Croatia (2009). Most of the new members after 1991 were former members of the Warsaw Pact nations, with President George W. Bush pushing for NATO to expand farther east to include Georgia and Ukraine. The same George W. Bush mobilized NATO to fight wars in Afghanistan as Operation Enduring Freedom and in Iraq as Operation Iraqi Freedom, where member states of NATO worked as a "coalition of the willing."[35]

Protecting Finance Capital

Russia opposed the expansion of NATO, claiming that this was a military alliance to encircle Russia by extending its membership to include former members of the Warsaw Pact.[36] Even within the foreign policy establishment there were foreign service officers who believed that the expansion was a policy error of historic importance.[37] What these officers did not grasp, however, was that in the post–Cold War era the defense of the tripartite alliance at the apex of the U.S. economy required a transnational military force capable of intervening in any part of the world to protect "investments" and "free markets." Deregulation is a concept that flowed from this post–Cold War world, one that girded the neoliberal push and purported that the least regulated market is the benchmark for a highly democratic society.

NATO expanded under President Clinton to protect "globalized" capital, and it was in this period of expansion that NATO jumped from twelve members to sixteen, then to nineteen, then to twenty-six by 2004 and to twenty-eight members by 2009. Despite vocal opposition from Russia, the discussion of expanding NATO now proceeded to the idea of Global NATO.[38] The leaders of NATO slowly built up relations with Australia in the Pacific, and in the Middle East established the Istanbul Cooperation Initiative Group (ICIG). This brought in the six members of the Gulf Cooperation Council (GCC)—Bahrain, Kuwait, Oman, Qatar, Saudi Arabia, and the United Arab Emirates (UAE)—as allies of the United States after the start of the war against the people of Iraq.[39] This military agreement of 2004 cemented the links to the countries of this region, strengthening the 1994 agreement that had been termed the Mediterranean Dialogue initiative.[40] The initiative involved seven non-NATO countries of the Mediterranean region: Algeria, Egypt, Israel, Jordan, Mauritania, Morocco, and Tunisia. According to NATO, the Mediterranean Dialogue is based upon the twin pillars of political dialogue and practical cooperation. Vijay Prashad termed the members of the Gulf Cooperation Council "the Arab NATO."[41]

Africa remained outside the orbit of this globalized NATO because memories of the anti-apartheid struggles were too fresh in Africa, especially southern Africa. Soon after the end of apartheid, the government of the United States proposed an African Crisis Response initiative. Nelson Mandela was among the first to vigorously oppose this planned military force in Africa. For the next eight years, U.S. diplomatic efforts were geared toward ensnaring individual states into a military network dominated by the United States. Hiding behind the guise of humanitarian relief, in 2004 the United States announced the formation of the African Contingency Operations Training and Assistance program. The ostensive purpose of ACOTA was to train military trainers and equip African national militaries to conduct peace support operations. Less than four years later, the United States launched a new initiative, the U.S. Africa Command (AFRICOM). This new military force for Africa was rejected by even the most servile allies of the United States. There was only one country that, in public, promised basing privileges for AFRICOM. This was Liberia. The sentiment at the popular level in Africa restrained the political leaders from publicly entering the kind of "political dialogue and practical cooperation" that had ensnared the leaders of North Africa in the Mediterranean Dialogue.

Global NATO evolved as an umbrella for the protection of Wall Street and the international economic system dominated by the U.S. oligarchy. Richard Holbrooke was the perfect symbol of the political dialogue and practical cooperation needed to strengthen the relationship between militarism and Wall Street. Holbrooke had been pivotal in the networks woven among members of the foreign policy establishment and financial elite in the Council on Foreign Relations. Though the centrality of the CFR was partially dethroned by the Heritage Foundation and the conservative think tanks after the rise of Ronald Reagan, Wall Street barons such as Maurice Greenberg of American International Group (AIG) worked hard to become accepted into this establishment of the Northeast.[42] In the years 1981–93, Holbrooke advised Lehman Brothers, before he was drafted by the Clinton administration to be a top diplomat in Europe, negotiating the issues of the Balkan wars and an expanded NATO. After the defeat of the Clinton team in 2001, Holbrooke became the vice chairman of Perseus LLC, a leading private equity firm. Between February 2001 and July 2008, he was a key figure of the foreign policy establishment on the CFR and a member of the Board of Directors of AIG. AIG was at the center of the innovative financial projects that emerged from the era of mortgage-backed securities and credit default swaps.[43] The new enlarged NATO coincided with the expansion of the neoliberal operations of Wall Street and the new forms of finance capital that engulfed the world up to the time of the financial crisis of 2008. Throughout the 1980s AIG had supported the production of books and articles on the merits of deregulation and the importance of the global services economy.[44] The concentration and centralization of capital had given rise to the new political power of bankers, financial institutions, and oil companies that did not respect borders. Global NATO corresponded to the explosion of the new business model of Big Oil and Wall Street. This model was one where, according to Simon Johnson, a former Chief Economist of the IMF,

> business as usual now means inventing tradable, high-margin products using their market power to capture fees based on trading volume, taking advantage of their privileged position to place bets on their proprietary trading accounts, and borrowing as much money as possible (in part by engineering their way around capital requirements) to maximize their profits.[45]

This business is of interest to us for, as we will show later, the Libyan Investment Authority was ensnared in the opaque world that was informed by the belief in the inviolability of the free market. The narrative of "markets" concealed the real nature of power in "democratic societies" and provided the conditions for sub-prime lending, mortgage-backed securities, collateralized debt obligations (CDOs), and credit default swaps. Thus when NATO spokespersons argued that NATO was composed of democratic states (involving "a concert of democracies"), it is possible to grasp the meaning that these are countries where the political power of finance capital is manifest in the mantra of the "efficient market hypothesis." This doctrine was promoted by Stanley Fischer of the IMF, who argued: "Free capital movements facilitate a more efficient global allocation of savings, and help channel resources into their most productive uses, thus increasing economic growth and welfare, providing benefits that would outweigh the risks."[46]

The efficient market hypothesis had been promoted vigorously in Africa, where many economists accepted that developing countries should abandon restrictions on the flow of capital and open their economy to foreign money. Those states that did not adhere to this mantra felt the full weight of the political and military power of the international financial oligarchy. The political power of the IMF to undermine the sovereignty of African societies has been documented extensively, and scholars are now concentrating on how the IMF facilitated capital flight from Africa.[47]

In his book *The Liberal Virus: Permanent War and the Americanization of the World,* Samir Amin studied the relationship between militarism and neoliberalism and was able to penetrate the discourse of "free markets" and grasp its practical implications for international politics. From books by Amin, Yash Tandon, and others it has become possible to understand the relationship between the military management of the international system and the increased role of NATO. It has also been possible to grasp the unleashing of propaganda warfare against the citizens of the world, to launch missions such as the war in Kosovo in 1999. Humanitarianism became the cover for the new military management of the international system, as human rights was used as a pretext to sell war.[48] Africans could see through the duplicity of the humanitarian imperialism of NATO in the genocide in Rwanda and the NATO operations in the Balkans. In 1994, the United States took the lead in opposing the United Nations intervention to stop the genocide in Rwanda. In 1999, NATO bombed Kosovo for over seventy-nine days as it gave itself a new mission to expand U.S. military power—right up to Moscow's doorstep.

NATO Spreads Its Reach

Gingerly, given that Charles de Gaulle had left NATO in 1966, Nicolas Sarkozy rejoined it in 2009. The dollar's dominance as reserve currency had been a source of contention for France after the United States devalued the dollar in 1971 and undermined the principles of the 1944 Bretton Woods agreement. France had been working within Europe to challenge the dollar and the United States government on a world scale.

After the First World War, Britain and France took the lead in dividing up the territories of the former Ottoman Empire—and its oil resources—from Algeria to Iran. After the Second World War, however, Total Oil Company, the French inheritor of Compagnie des Petroles, was cut out of the redivision of North Africa and the Middle East. Weakened by war and divided politically, France could not be a dominant force within NATO or Europe. The 1956 Suez Crisis and the American response signaled the demise of British and French influence and the advent of the American age of dominance, along with the dollar as the currency of world trade. The operating principle within NATO was that France was to be a junior partner. General Charles de Gaulle resented the Anglo-American dominance and opted for the development of an independent military capability.[49] When the European states recovered, in the 1970s, France worked with the Germans to develop a currency and trade zone that would eventually become the European Union.

France intervened in Afghanistan as an independent military partner, and was initially critical of the U.S.-led "Coalition of the Willing" in Iraq. After the vigorous defense of U.S. capital in Iraq, with reactions from Americans about "freedom fries" during the Iraq war, French military planners retreated and decided to throw in their lot with the military sector of the U.S. establishment. With French acquiescence, the rationale of the militarists for a global role for NATO began to take shape and the idea of Global NATO was debated in military journals. One of the writers on this concept was Ivo Daalder, the U.S. Permanent Representative on the Council to NATO since 2009. Daalder was an ambassador with an understanding of the long history of financial and military cooperation among the Netherlands, the United Kingdom, and the United States. In an era when capital was truly transnational and the tripartite allies had no loyalty to any particular state, international capitalists wanted a new military force that was mobile and well equipped for the new scramble for African resources.

The call for a global role for NATO also came from NATO Secretary-General Anders Fogh Rasmussen, who pressed NATO leaders to expand their horizons beyond NATO's traditional focus on the North Atlantic region. A musing by defense specialists alerts us to the thinking:

> The concept of a Global NATO is used above all in connection with two *leitmotifs*—on the one hand the idea of the alliance becoming a global strategic actor (functional globalization) and on the other the notion of a NATO whose membership is in principle global (institutional globalization). The two dimensions can, however, scarcely be separated from one another but instead are intertwined.[50]

The discussion around the idea of the "institutional globalization of NATO" maintained that the security threats to capitalism were global and that NATO should consider itself as a "concert of democracies" keeping the order internationally. Within these journals, the idea was floated that NATO should be expanded to include Australia, Japan, New Zealand, South Korea, and possibly Brazil. After encircling Russia, the new posture was for the encirclement of China.[51]

The rationale was simply that the "operational level of NATO is the entire globe." In 2002, NATO declared that "to carry out the full range of its missions, NATO must be able to field forces that can move quickly to wherever they are needed, sustain operations over distance and time, and achieve their objectives."[52]

Despite the lofty positions of the strategic planners, NATO was bogged down in Afghanistan. Failure here, and the war of attrition, led to fatigue in the West, with numerous headlines calling for NATO to admit defeat and leave Afghanistan.[53] The prolonged crisis of capitalism inside the Western world meant that citizens had no appetite for an expanded imperial role.

That is, until Gaddafi—by promising to kill the citizens of Benghazi, whom he called "rats" and "vermin"—gave NATO the excuse it needed to seek to operationalize the idea of Global NATO.

4—MUAMMAR GADDAFI AND THE ELUSIVE REVOLUTION

Gaddafi came to power as the leader of Libya after a *coup d'état* removed King Idris on September 2, 1969. This bloodless coup was orchestrated by the Union of Free Unionist Officers under the leadership of its chairman, then Captain Muammar Gaddafi. King Idris's rule was replaced by that of a "Revolutionary Council," but Gaddafi emerged from the ranks of the free officers and over the following years asserted his authority to become the new head of state.[54] In the forty-two years that Gaddafi was in power, the politics of the society went through many twists and turns but remained relatively stable. After studying the Libyan experiment, Ruth First, the South African revolutionary historian, termed it "the elusive revolution."[55] This term is now most useful in grasping the zigs and zags of the Gaddafi regime over four decades, which can be said to have gone through four periods:

1969–1977: Period of the Revolutionary Command Council, or the period of elusive revolution

1977–1988: Period of confrontation with the Western states, including the 1986 bombing of Libya by Ronald Reagan

1988–2001:   Period of sanctions and isolation, and Gaddafi's
             move to embrace African diplomatic interventions
2001–2011:   Reopening to the West and the end of Gaddafi

During the first period, 1969–1977, society was governed by the
Revolutionary Command Council. Radical initiatives occurred, such
as the nationalization of oil companies and banks, and the expulsion
of the United States from Wheelus Air Base. The Libyan leadership
attempted to emulate the Pan-Africanism and Pan-Arabism of Gamel
Abdel Nasser, but within one year, in September 1970, Nasser passed
away and the Libyans had no model to anchor their experiment in
radical nationalism. Nonetheless, the elementary claims at recovering
national wealth were seen as threatening by the imperial forces, and by
1977 the U.S. Department of Defense listed Libya as a potential enemy
of the United States.[56] There was no doubt that Libya was no longer
simply an outpost for Western companies. However, the contradictory
postures, alliances, and partnerships that were proposed left Libya isolated because of the personalized nature of diplomacy under Gaddafi.
As one author summed up this period:

> Pushing his policies of anti-Zionism, anticommunism, and
> anti-imperialism, Qadhafi became something of a champion of
> reawakened Arab pride, an exemplar to many young Arabs of com-
> mitment to Arab Unity and of sincere and dedicated endorsement
> of the Palestinian cause. . . . Such widespread admiration was nev-
> ertheless relatively short-lived. It was not long before Qadhafi had
> begun to antagonize other Arabs with his disregard for diplomatic
> convention and his inflexible insistence on the absolute righteous-
> ness of his own policies and philosophies.[57]

After proposing a series of schemes to unite with Egypt, Morocco,
Tunisia, and Syria, the Gaddafi regime became isolated. This was especially the case with the Palestinians, in whose internal matters Gaddafi
attempted to dictate.

UN Sanctions and the "Conversion" of the Regime

While representing himself as a revolutionary, Gaddafi exposed his lack of understanding of international politics and his own ideological limitations in his alliance with Idi Amin of Uganda and by providing military and financial support to Amin when Uganda attacked Tanzania. Throughout the first twenty years of the Gaddafi regime, the Libyan government was embroiled in the internal politics of Chad, supporting differing factions and deepening the involvement of the Libyan forces in prolonged military scraps in the Aouzou dispute. (The Aouzou dispute refers to the small strip of land at the border between Chad and Libya that was claimed by both countries. This strip runs for some 600 miles in length and 90 miles at its broadest point and 50 miles at its narrowest. After the independence of Chad, French troops had remained in the disputed strip until 1985. After 1987 there were a number of skirmishes between Chad and Libya over this strip, until 1990 when both countries agreed to submit the dispute to binding arbitration by the International Court of Justice.) In 1994 the ICJ ruled that the strip belonged to Chad. Later that year Libya officially returned the area to Chad. These military wrangles, which have been journalistically termed the "Toyota War," diverted the attention of the African freedom struggle and gave legitimacy to French military intervention in Central Africa.[58] Gaddafi's infatuation with self-styled rebel leaders and organizations brought a steady traffic of individuals such as Charles Taylor making pilgrimages to Libya. (What Gaddafi did not know was that, during his relationship with Charles Taylor, this future president of Liberia was working as a U.S. intelligence asset.)[59] Through the organization al-Mathaba, the Libyan leadership proclaimed itself to be at the forefront of anti-imperialism, but Gaddafi's Green Book—the theoretical basis for this revolutionary posture—was as contradictory as the policies of Gaddafi.

On March 2, 1977, with the Declaration of the Establishment of the People's Authority, Libya was renamed the Socialist People's Libyan Arab Jamahiriya. Luis Martinez, in the *Libyan Paradox*, traced the twists and turns of the forms of rule of Gaddafi, who took the title of "Guide," exploring the periods of sanctions and isolation, and the energetic period of Gaddafi's "conversion."[60] This was when, after September 11, 2001, Gaddafi and his sons worked hard to ingratiate themselves with the United States and Britain, and begged to make Libya an ally in the Global War on Terror. Shukri Ghanem and Saif al-Islam Gaddafi were two central figures in this paradoxical relationship with the West.

As one of the Western specialists on Libya, Martinez followed the impact of the sanctions imposed on the country after Libya was accused of responsibility for the 1988 Lockerbie air disaster. From the moment of the tragic bombing of Pan Am Flight 103 over Lockerbie, Scotland, there were conflicting reports from Western intelligence agencies on who was responsible. Shukri Ghanem, who had been the quintessential insider of the regime and one of the "reformers" in the fourth period, categorically denied that Libya had anything to do with the Lockerbie bombing.

Many Western scholars have not grasped the importance of Nelson Mandela's diplomatic efforts to end the sanctions against Libya. Mandela, who by 1994 had become the president of South Africa, acknowledged Libya's support for the anti-apartheid struggles. Although Mandela had himself been declared a terrorist by the racist white minority regime and by Western intelligence agencies, he successfully mediated between the governments of Britain and the United States for the lifting of the UN sanctions against Libya. The sanctions were lifted in 1999, after the Libyan government agreed to hand over "suspects" to be tried in Europe. Nelson Mandela shuttled between Britain and Libya until he reached a breakthrough, with Libya agreeing to the principal demand: handing over the Libyans accused of placing the bomb on Pan Am Flight 103. One of the compromises agreed in the negotiations was that the accused would be tried outside Scotland. Hugh Roberts has discussed at great length the sophisticated diplomatic maneuvers by the Libyan government after these negotiations, so that Libya could reenter the Western fold without accepting responsibility for the Lockerbie disaster. According to Roberts:

It was only in 2003–4, after Tripoli had paid a massive sum in compensation to the bereaved families in 2002 (having already surrendered Abdelbaset Ali al-Megrahi and Al Amin Khalifa Fhima for trial in 1999), that sanctions were lifted, at which point a new reforming current headed by Gaddafi's son Saif al-Islam emerged within the regime.[61]

Roberts is among the few scholars who penetrated the diplomatic push by the Gaddafi regime to end the sanctions without admitting anything in relation to the Lockerbie affair. It is worth quoting him at great length:

It is often claimed by British and American government personnel and the Western press that Libya admitted responsibility for Lockerbie in 2003–4. This is untrue. As part of the deal with Washington and London, which included Libya paying $2.7 billion to the 270 victims' families, the Libyan government in a letter to the president of the UN Security Council stated that Libya "has facilitated the bringing to justice of the two suspects charged with the bombing of Pan Am 103, and accepts responsibility for the actions of its officials." That this formula was agreed in negotiations between the Libyan and British (if not also American) governments was made clear when it was echoed word for word by Jack Straw in the House of Commons. The formula allowed the government to give the public the impression that Libya was indeed guilty, while also allowing Tripoli to say that it had admitted nothing of the kind. The statement does not even mention al-Megrahi by name, much less acknowledge his guilt or that of the Libyan government, and any self-respecting government would sign up to the general principle that it is responsible for the actions of its officials. Tripoli's position was spelled out by the prime minister, Shukri Ghanem, on 24 February 2004 on the *Today* programme: he made it clear that the payment of compensation did not imply an admission of guilt and explained that the Libyan government had "bought peace."[62]

The general line on Libya by Western scholars and analysts was that the Gaddafi regime had undergone a "conversion," but in *The Libyan Paradox* Martinez explains in great detail how Gaddafi feared for his life. As a scholar working from French sources, Martinez would have been aware of the evidence produced by French journalists of the plans by British intelligence and the Libyan Islamic Fighting Group (LIFG) to assassinate Gaddafi in 1996. This was only one of the many assassination plots that Gaddafi had survived after coming to power in 1969. In November 2002, the British newspaper *The Guardian* reported that "British intelligence paid large sums of money to an al-Qaeda cell in Libya in a doomed attempt to assassinate Colonel Gadhafi in 1996 and thwarted early attempts to bring Osama bin Laden to justice."[63]

The evidence of the complicity between the Saudi and Western intelligence agencies in supporting the LIFG revealed that the plans for military destabilization and the removal of Gaddafi were not new, nor did they suddenly arise after the February 15 uprisings in Libya. Brisard and Dasquie's *Forbidden Truth* has opened one window into the world of the relationships between actors such as the Carlyle Group, the oil companies, and Libya. Condoleezza Rice, as an executive of Chevron Oil Company, was enmeshed in the web of intelligence, finance and international politics that transcended Libya. In September 2008, while she was secretary of state, Rice visited Libya and articulated with clarity that the United States had no "permanent friends in Libya, only permanent interests."

Western scholars took time to study the investment of the Gaddafi family to end isolation, and particular interest was focused on Saif al-Islam, who had earned a doctorate at the London School of Economics.[64] Shukri Ghanem, Saif al-Islam, and Moussa Koussa were three of the more influential persons in the Libyan bureaucracy who promoted market reforms and were dubbed the "neoliberal forces" within the Libyan establishment. Gaddafi had promoted an ideological platform called the Third Universal Theory. In the 1970s, this theory drew heavily from the ideals of Arab nationalism as espoused by Nasser. Nasserism, anti-imperialism, and non-alignment were supposed to anchor this Third Way between socialism and capitalism.

Efforts to deepen these ideas at the political level through mergers with neighboring states came to naught, and after the intervention of Nelson Mandela to end the isolation of Libya, Gaddafi turned to African unity as the basis of his political legitimacy. Throughout the years of the Jamahiriya, the political culture in Libya never matured to the point where there was a coherent alternative to the inherited social and economic structures. Organizations such as the General People's Congress, which was supposed to be the harbinger for the establishment of a "regime of people's power" and "direct popular democracy" at the grass roots, never found a real base among workers, poor farmers, students, and patriotic businesspersons. Gaddafi's inner circle stifled genuine social engagement, while the Western-educated bureaucrats worked to bring Libya into the fold of "market reforms."

The connections and discussions between the Libyan leadership and Western liberal scholars created an ambivalent relationship that exposed the hollow ideological basis of the intellectual apparatus of the leadership. Libyan universities did not produce rigorous scholarship because of the sycophancy that was promoted nationally and internationally around the Gaddafi family. When Libya signed a multibillion dollar exploration and production deal with British Petroleum in 2007, BP promised to spend U.S.$50 million on education and training projects. The ambivalence toward Europe that was expressed in political rhetoric was not matched inside the educational system. Those with resources in Libya sent their children to schools in North America and Western Europe. The al-Mathaba was established as a vehicle for anti-imperialism, but this was hollow and depended on the whims and caprices of the "brother leader." In this situation, those who had been educated in elite Western universities dominated the bureaucracy and promoted Western-type democracy and neoliberal reforms so that Libya could enjoy better relations with the United States and Britain. Various scholars had identified Moussa Koussa, Saif al-Islam, Mahmoud Jibril, Shukri Ghanem, Aziz al Isawi, and Tarek Ben Halim as the neoliberal reformers inside the government of Libya.[65] These functionaries had been so thoroughly schooled in Western ideas about economics that despite the massive oil reserves of Libya their mantra remained that Libya needed to open up to the West in order to attract "foreign investment capital, create free trade zones and enhance the fledgling stock market."[66]

Despite the dominance of the "reformers," Gaddafi's zigzags in relation to his international policies frustrated Britain and the United States, who wanted to have a dominant say in the future of the Libyan economy. During the period of sanctions, European firms from Italy, Germany, Spain, Austria, and Turkey had done brisk business in the oil sector, but the Gaddafi family wanted to be accepted by the United States and went all out to ingratiate itself with Washington and the associated intellectual networks of U.S. capitalism. The al-Mathaba confraternity brought together selected anti-imperialist activists from Africa, the Caribbean, and North America, but many of these activists never challenged the ideas of monarchical dreams, which culminated in Gaddafi declaring himself "King of Kings."[67]

5—THE NEOLIBERAL ASSAULT ON LIBYA: LONDON SCHOOL OF ECONOMICS AND HARVARD PROFESSORS

Although Gaddafi publicly proclaimed himself a revolutionary, he was spending millions of dollars supporting centers for Libyan studies in Europe and the United States. Many of the Libyans who came out of Western institutions were loyal supporters of the most conservative sectors of the Anglo-Saxon culture. They studied and worked in North America and Europe, but they eschewed the politics of social justice. Britain held a special place in the consciousness of educated Libyans, and British leaders worked hard to emerge as interlocutors in Libya. While he was Britain's prime minister, Tony Blair had been one of the supporters of the new relationship with Libya after sanctions, and British petroleum companies supported the probes of the Foreign and Commonwealth Office. Blair was the first major Western leader to visit Libya, in 2004.

Out of these new relationships, Saif al-Islam Gaddafi repaired to London and entered the world of British royalty and financial circles. He earned a doctorate at the London School of Economics, titling his thesis *The Role of Civil Society in the Democratization of Global*

Governance Institutions: From "Soft Power" to Collective Decision-Making?
Handsome donations were made to the LSE, and Anthony Giddens
brought to bear his considerable intellectual influence to argue that,
under Gaddafi, Libya had been "radically transformed." This process of
transformation entailed commercial relations with entities such as the
Oxford Group, Ernst and Young, and the consultancy firm McKinsey
and Company. In 2007, British Petroleum signed the largest deal with
the Libyan Investment Corporation to "explore around 54,000 square
kilometres (km2) of the onshore Ghadames and offshore frontier Sirt
basins, equivalent to more than ten of BP's operated deepwater blocks
in Angola. Successful exploration could lead to the drilling of around
20 appraisal wells." In the signing statement, the BP public relations
section noted that "during this exploration and appraisal phase, BP
will acquire 5,500 km2 of 2D seismic and 30,000 km2 of 3D seismic
and will drill 17 exploration wells."[68] It was in the context of this massive deal that BP undertook to "spend $50 million on education and
training projects for Libyan professionals during the exploration and
appraisal period, and, upon success, a further $50 million from com-
mencement of production. The education and training programmes
will be designed and managed in partnership with the NOC [National
Oil Corporation]."

Numerous British institutions of higher learning then jumped on
this opening for the training of young Libyans, and thousands of Libyans
were sent to British universities. By August 2011, the UK *Times Higher
Education Supplement* reported that there were 2,800 Libyan students
in the United Kingdom.[69] As the war intensified, numerous officials
from British universities resigned when the extent of these institutions'.
relationships with the Gaddafi family was revealed. The emergence of
Anthony Giddens as one of the top interlocutors between the British
academy and the Libyan leadership was one good example of how the
top layers of Western academia had been ensnared by the neoliberal push
within the universities in the twenty-first century. Anthony Giddens is
one of the most respected sociologists in the Anglo-American academic
world. Giddens is the author or editor of forty books translated into over
forty languages. His first work, *Capitalism and Modern Social Theory*, has

been continuously in print for more than three decades. Several of his other books have become academic bestsellers. He has written the leading textbook in sociology, which has sold a million copies worldwide since it was first published in 1988. According to Google Scholar, he is the most widely cited sociologist in the world today. The fact that he was a frequent visitor to Tripoli before the war spoke volumes of the competition between universities on both sides of the Atlantic to gain access to funds from Libya.

Once the top cadre of the society was drawn into the "institutional transformation" that was the gospel of Giddens, this relationship with British universities was replicated all over Western Europe and the United States. Universities such as Michigan State University and Tufts University had strong ties to the training of Libyan officials for the Gaddafi regime. Moussa Koussa, one of the leading interlocutors for the regime, had completed his master's at MSU thirty years earlier. Through the Western links of leaders such as Gaddafi's son and Prime Minister Blair, the Libyan government paid handsome sums of money to promote "institutional changes" in Libya. One major firm that was involved was the Monitor Group, a consultancy firm associated with the Harvard Business School in the United States. The Monitor Group was awarded a contract to produce a makeover for Libya and to introduce Gaddafi "as a thinker and intellectual, independent of his more widely known and very public persona as the Leader of the Revolution in Libya." The firm was also supposed to produce a book, *Qadhafi, the Man and His Ideas*, based in part on interviews between the Libyan dictator and these visiting international influentials. The book supposedly would "enable the international intellectual and policy-making elite to understand Qadhafi as an individual thinker rather than leader of a state."

The *Harvard Crimson* and the UK's *Guardian* newspaper reported in 2011 that, between 2006 and 2008, the Monitor Group entered into a contract with the Gaddafi regime that was worth at least $3 million. The Monitor Group had promised the Libyan regime that it would secure a "regular flow of high-quality visitors" to Tripoli who would be selected for the appeal of their ideas and for "the strength of their influence in guiding U.S. foreign policy." The high-quality visitors read like a who's who in the field of international relations in the United States. The list of individuals who were engaged in the Monitor Group project included Francis Fukuyama, author of *The End of History*; Richard Perle, a prominent neocon who advised President George W. Bush in the buildup to the Iraq invasion; and American academics such as Benjamin Barber, Joseph Nye, and Robert Putnam.[70] The visit and writings of Joseph Nye are of particular interest, insofar as his actions and writings expose the link between ideology and militarism in the United States. Saif al-Islam properly thanked Joseph Nye for his inspiration in the writing of his thesis:

> I would also like to acknowledge the benefit from comments I received on early drafts of the thesis from a number of experts with whom I met and who consented to read portions of the manuscript and provide advice and direction, especially Professor Joseph Nye.

Students of international relations have in the past been captivated by the writings of Joseph Nye on "soft power." During the era of military information operations and humanitarian intervention, the ideas of soft power were promulgated to legitimize Western intervention. After the fall of the Soviet Union, soft power became chic as strategists found this new form of intervention superior to outright "boots on the ground" militarism. Nye outlined three ways in which the behavior of other actors can be influenced: they can be threatened, they can be bribed, and they can be co-opted. Soft power refers to the ability to get "others to want what you want." According to Nye, "Since our Western liberal values determine what we want or don't want, soft power indicates the ability to determine values, that is, determine what goals actors will strive to accomplish." A country's soft power is reliant upon the attractiveness of its culture, political values, and foreign policies, all of which Nye refers to as the resources of soft power.

Critical scholars have been able to penetrate this discourse to expose the extent to which the idea of soft power seeks to conceal the coercive mechanisms of empire. Within the field of international relations, ideas of soft power obscure the real power in international

politics.[71] Haiti and Libya were two graphic examples of how imperial forces mobilized soft power to undermine the sovereignty of these
societies. Peter Hallward, in his book *Damming the Flood: Haiti and the
Politics of Containment*, exposed the role of humanitarian agencies in
creating the conditions for the destabilization of Haitian society. The
book brings the reader face to face with how international non-governmental organizations were central to the containment of the Haitian
project of self-determination. Soft power, in this instance, worked hand
in glove with the deployment of militaristic forces.

Unlike Haiti, Libya was awash with foreign reserves and therefore
could expend billions on reconstruction projects that employed productive labor. It is in the failure to deploy the usual NGOs that it is
possible to grasp the significance of Joseph Nye's visits in the context
of the later NATO intervention. Future historians will be able to reflect
on whether Nye's visits were part of the advanced reconnaissance necessary to grasp the inner workings of the Jamahiriya. Nye recounted
not only his meeting with bureaucrats of the Gaddafi regime, but also
the fact that he had sipped tea for three hours with Muammar Gaddafi
in 2007. He recounted Gaddafi's fascination with soft power:

> Where once he sought weapons of mass destruction, now he
> has abandoned his nuclear program. . . . Qaddafi, in other words,
> seems to have become interested in soft power—the art of pro-
> jecting influence through attraction rather than coercion. And the
> fact that he took so much time to discuss ideas—including soft
> power—with a visiting professor suggests that he is actively seek-
> ing a new strategy.

From his writings after returning to the United States, Nye had been
successful in getting Libyan officials to uncritically accept his vision of
power. David Corn, in a lengthy article in *Mother Jones* magazine, wrote
of the visit of Joseph Nye: Months later, he penned an elegant description of the chat for *The New Republic*, reporting that Qaddafi had been
interested in discussing "direct democracy." Nye noted that "there is
no doubt" that the Libyan autocrat "acts differently on the world stage

today than he did in decades past." The article struck a hopeful tone: that there was a new Gaddafi. It also noted that Nye had gone to Libya "at the invitation of the Monitor Group, a consulting company that is helping Libya open itself to the global economy."[72]

Getting Libyans to "Want What You Want"

David Corn's article neglected to spell out the institutional relationships between scholars such as Joseph Nye, the "reform" agenda of the Bretton Woods institutions, and the military industrial complex. To the extent that the foreign policy establishment, through the Council on Foreign Relations in New York, acts as a sounding board for the financial, military, and oil interests, it is possible to locate the role of scholars such as Anthony Giddens and Joseph Nye in Libya and Africa. After the lifting of sanctions by the U.S. government, the regime in Libya went overboard to please U.S. and British interlocutors, conveying to these academics the willingness of Libya to open up the economy and negotiate new partnership and exploration agreements with U.S. petroleum companies. After 2003 the Libyan government entered into agreements with the IMF. A number of state-owned enterprises were privatized, and in 2004 Libya opened up fifteen new offshore and onshore blocks for exploration and production agreements. Eleven of the best licenses went to U.S. companies, including Occidental, Amerada Hess, and ChevronTexaco. Saif al-Islam employed the international vocabulary of neoliberal capitalism: deregulation, transparency, rule of law, efficiency, markets, and those formulations meant to inspire confidence in the Wall Street firms that were wooing the Libyan leadership.[73]

The "reforms" increased inequality and strengthened those social forces close to the ruling circles. Class differences deepened, leading to the alienation of the mass of the population. Trade unions did not benefit from the "reforms." Though Libya had opened up its economy and restored diplomatic relations, there had been no such progress with respect to trade union rights. There were, and currently are, no independent trade unions. All workers' organizations were closely linked to the government. Samir Amin summed up the contradictions of this opening up (or, as Luis Martinez termed it, the "conversion"):

> Operating in a still-archaic society Gaddafi could indulge in successive "nationalist" and "socialist" speeches with little bearing on reality, and the next day proclaim himself a "liberal." He did so to "please the West," as though the choice for liberalism would have no social effects. But it had and, as is commonplace, it worsened living conditions for the majority of Libyans. The oil rent which was widely redistributed became the target of small groups of the privileged, including the family of the leader. Those conditions then gave rise to the well-known explosion, which the country's regionalists and political Islamists immediately took advantage of.[74]

The same political Islamists who had been opposed by the West, the Libyan Islamic Fighting Group (LIFG), became the instrument for the completion of the task that had been undertaken through the penetration of the "liberal reformers." When the rebellion matured, the real alliance between the LIFG was sealed in the loose alliance that was to emerge and call itself the National Transitional Council (NTC). Western intelligence agencies had up-to-date information on the LIFG because its origins emanated from the Libyan veterans who had fought against the Soviet occupation of Afghanistan. Vijay Prashad termed this group of fighters "America's Libyans," and drew particular attention to the role of Khalifa Hifter, who had lived in the U.S. state of Virginia for two decades and returned to Libya in March 2011 to be part of the army that fought against the Gaddafi government.[75] The ease with which Hifter had settled in Virginia, and his elevation to the position of commander of the NTC's army after the rebellion, raised speculation about linkages to the Western intelligence infrastructure.

From Wikileaks cables we now know that the Western companies were playing a waiting game with the Gaddafi regime. Gaddafi's policy forced oil and gas corporations to renegotiate their contracts, so although there were openings, the Western companies lived with uncertainties. Between 2007 and 2008, major companies such as

Exxon Mobil, Petro-Canada, Repsol (Spain), Total (France), Eni (Italy), and Occidental (U.S.) were compelled to sign new deals with the National Oil Company, on significantly less favorable terms than they had previously enjoyed, and were collectively made to pay $5.4 billion in up-front "bonus" payments. A June 2008 cable exposed the fact that the Oasis Group, which included the U.S. firms ConocoPhillips, Marathon, and Hess, was reportedly "next on the block," despite having already paid $1.8 billion in 2005. The cable questioned whether Libya could be trusted to honor the new exploration and production-sharing (EPSA IV) contracts, or would again "seek a larger cut." It further discussed the broader implications of the EPSA IV contracts. Though the contracts were "broadly beneficial" for oil companies, which stood to make "a great deal more money per barrel of oil produced," the threat of forced renegotiation of contracts created a dangerous international precedent—a "new paradigm for Libya that is playing out worldwide in a growing number of oil producing countries."

The oil giants and the U.S. government were alarmed by threats Gaddafi made, in a January 2009 video conference to Georgetown University students, to nationalize the oil and gas industry. A January 2010 cable recounts that "regime rhetoric in early 2009 involving the possible nationalization of the oil sector . . . has brought the issue back to the fore."[76]

Western leaders, who were waiting for an opportunity to intervene in North Africa after the uprisings in Tunisia and Egypt, immediately intervened on the side of the political Islamists with the doctrine of "responsibility to protect."

6—UN Security Council Resolution 1973 and the Responsibility to Protect

In Libya under Gaddafi, political opposition took a religious form and one of the more well-known opposition organizations was the Libyan Islamic Fighting Group.[77] This organization included members who had aligned with the United States to fight against the Soviet Union in Afghanistan. Some of its functionaries were named as beneficiaries of Saudi funds in North Africa and the Middle East. According to George Tenet, former head of the Central Intelligence Agency, "One of the most immediate threats [to U.S. security] is from smaller international Sunni extremist groups that have benefited from al-Qaida links. They include . . . the Libyan Islamic Fighting Group."[78] Long before the United States had identified violent Islamist extremists, Gaddafi had been among the first leaders to warn of the dangers of violent extremism. In 1996, Libya became the first government to place Osama bin Laden on Interpol's Wanted List.[79]

In 1995, the LIFG launched a jihad against Gaddafi's regime and attempted to escalate their activities into a "pre-revolutionary situation."[80] With the backdrop of years of bloodshed in neighboring

Algeria, the people of Libya had no appetite for armed rebellions and the cycle of bombings and state repression. The most significant LIFG attack was a 1996 attempt to assassinate Gaddafi. LIFG members, led by Wadi al-Shateh, threw a bomb underneath his motorcade. The group also staged guerrilla-style attacks against government security forces from its mountain bases. The response of the regime to these forms of armed opposition deepened the alienation of the regime from the peoples in the east. An effort at administrative reorganization of the country in 1998 did not repair the weaknesses of Libya's governance structures. After 1998, the regime embarked on the "liberalization of the economy" and policies of decentralization, but there was never any question that the inner circle of the Gaddafi family would loosen its monopoly over the use of force. One of the most profound weaknesses of the regime—the general lack of coherence of Libya's armed forces— was now revealed. This was because the regime was apprehensive about the "collaboration between Islamist rebels and the security forces."[81]

After September 11, 2001, Gaddafi ingratiated himself with the West and, in his "conversion," went overboard to cooperate with Western intelligence organizations to shut down the Islamists. The LIFG was banned worldwide (as an affiliate of al-Qaeda) by the UN 1267 Committee and was listed as a foreign terrorist organization. After the NATO intervention in Libya, British newspapers carried extensive details on the level of collaboration between Gaddafi and British and U.S. intelligence services. According to *The Guardian*:

> Papers discovered in Tripoli apparently show that MI6 gave Muammar Gaddafi's security service information on Libyan dissidents living in the UK. They also contain communications between British and Libyan security ahead of then-prime minister Tony Blair's desert tent meeting with Gaddafi in 2004. Britain is said to have helped the Libyan dictator with his speech-writing. The documents, discovered in the Tripoli offices of former head of Libyan intelligence Moussa Koussa, also show how the CIA worked with the Gaddafi regime on the rendition of terrorist suspects.[82]

From the *Christian Science Monitor* newspaper we also learned:

Nearly 300 pages of documents, copied by Human Rights Watch from the offices of Libya's external security service, provide unprecedented detail about how the CIA and Britain's MI6 worked closely to bring Libya "on side" and turn a brutal regime from foe into friend after Mr. Qaddafi in 2003 vowed to give up weapons of mass destruction, end support of militant groups, and take on Al Qaeda. Part of that effort was forcibly returning to Libya key opponents of the regime—including the Libyan who today commands anti-Qaddafi forces in Tripoli—despite knowing the conditions those suspects would face.[83]

The details of the exchanges between the Libyan government and the U.S. and British intelligence services are significant because these exchanges gave the West unprecedented information on the workings of Libyan intelligence capabilities. Gaddafi had enabled the imperial intelligence services by sharing information, financing their governments, purchasing junk equipment as weaponry, and cooperating with their intelligence agencies. Most important, these exchanges gave the West a clear understanding of the nature of the Libyan opposition.

The news about Gaddafis cooperation with British and U.S. intelligence services, along with their collaboration in relation to "enhanced interrogation techniques" (translated as torture), the exchange of information, and the secret transfers of opponents and "terror" suspects, clarified the extent of Gaddafi's cooperation with the West. Significantly, one of the "terrorists" who had been detained and rendered by Gaddafi, the LIFG leader Abdelhakim Belhadj, turned out to be a beneficiary of Western support against Gaddafi. He emerged as a prominent leader in the National Transitional Council in Tripoli, and at the time of this writing is the commander of NTC forces in the capital. These were the forces that the UN decided to protect in Libya.

A reconstruction of the chronology of the exchanges between the Gaddafi government and the West is essential because, just as the West rendered Belhadj to Gaddafi, so the West will change sides again. It is for this reason that the African scholarly community ought to study the chronology of Libya's disarmament and relations with the United States leading to the lavish praise of George W. Bush for Gaddafi.[84] Gaddafi had joined the "coalition of the willing" in the fight against terrorism and bent over backwards to open up oil exploration contracts for U.S. oil companies. In this way, the Gaddafi regime fully aligned itself with the United States in its Global War on Terrorism (GWOT).

The United States had intensified its activities in North Africa in the face of European trade and commercial activities. Jeremy Keenan, in *The Dark Sahara: America's War on Terror in Africa*, elaborated in detail the role of the U.S. military in supporting repressive governments under the guise of dealing with terrorism. Morocco, Algeria, Tunisia, Libya, Egypt, Mauritania, Mali, Niger, and Chad were able to strengthen their repressive apparatuses and to manipulate and use GWOT (for their own benefits and purposes). Of the states where the U.S. Africa Command became active, all except Egypt and Libya were former colonies of France, and in which French arms manufacturers had a lock on the arms market. These countries exploited this so-called war on terror by cracking down on almost all forms of opposition, especially minority groups, and almost any expression of civil society democratization. Keenan spelled out the reality that "with no terrorism (except state terrorism) in many parts of the region, notably in the Sahara-Sahel, before the launch of the GWOT, it has had to be contrived."[85]

As the United States exaggerated and fabricated the threat of al-Qaeda in the Maghreb, cooperation was extended to the political leaders who were being wooed to become part of the U.S. economic and military orbit. France had supported the political leader of Chad and continued to maintain a strong presence in that country, but Exxon Mobil used its financial and political muscle to produce oil in Chad with a pipeline through another client state of France, Cameroon. France was witnessing the diminution of its influence and seeing its political allies threatened and removed. When Ben Ali was faced with the uprising in Tunisia, he turned to the West to argue that the uprisings were led by Islamists. When the rebellion broke out in Libya, on February 15, Gaddafi correctly claimed that some of the forces of the opposition included Islamists. However, the same Western intelligence services that had cooperated with Gaddafi were now stoking the propaganda against him and mobilizing the media to argue that there was an imminent massacre of civilians in Benghazi. Within five days of the start of the rebellion, Benghazi was firmly controlled by opposition forces. "The rebels' advance continued and by the end of February the rebels had seized Libyan air force planes and Libyan navy ships."[86]

The Threat of Genocide: Facts and Fiction

Although the Western media carried stories that the Gaddafi air force was killing its own people, the Pentagon stated categorically that it could not confirm these stories. Within the debates at the UN, South Africans argued that there had been no jets used in attacks by Gaddafi against his own civilians. On March 1, 2011, U.S. Secretary of Defense Robert Gates and the Chairman of the Joint Chiefs of Staff, Admiral Mike Mullen, gave a press conference at the Pentagon where one reporter posed the question: "Do you see any evidence that he actually has fired on his own people from the air? There were reports of it, but do you have independent confirmation? If so, to what extent?" Secretary Gates responded, "We've seen the press reports, but we have no confirmation of that," and Admiral Mullen added, "That's correct. We've seen no confirmation whatsoever."[87] In March, Robert Gates and the Pentagon were against the intervention and were willing to state that the Pentagon itself had "no confirmation whatsoever" that jets and helicopters had been used to attack civilians.

Neither Colonel Gaddafi nor his son attempted to curb the international news that the Libyan army was about to commit genocide in Benghazi at a time when the militarized nature of the rebellion had transformed an uprising into a civil war. It was in this climate that the UN Security Council debated the resolutions on Libya. UN Security Council Resolution 1970 was passed on February 26, 2011:

Expressing grave concern at the situation in the Libyan Arab Jamahiriya and condemning the violence and use of force against civilians, deploring the gross and systematic violation of human rights, including the repression of peaceful demonstrators, expressing deep concern at the deaths of civilians, and rejecting unequivocally the incitement to hostility and violence against the civilian population made from the highest level of the Libyan government . . . [88]

This resolution was passed unanimously by the Security Council. In February, the real situation was still unclear and all members of the Security Council agreed that it was necessary to prevent a bloodbath in Libya. The resolution imposed sanctions on the Libyan regime and a travel ban on its top leaders. It was after this resolution that the French and British propaganda apparatus went into high gear to justify the use of the term "genocide" and encourage military intervention. Vijay Prashad noted correctly that

the "humanitarian intervention" from the Atlantic states and the Gulf Arabs attempted to wrest the dynamic from the rebellion from below and from the Arab spring, in general. That it has not been able to succeed fully is a testament to the deep springs of suspicion about imperialism that linger across West Asia and North Africa and to the faith of the people in their wanting control over their own lives. [89]

Gaddafi had linked himself to the anti-imperialist traditions in Africa without fully grasping the roots of Pan-Africanism and anti-imperialism. It was the anti-imperialism of the Global Pan-African Movement that would become the firmest force in opposition to the global intervention by NATO in Libya.

Efforts to persuade the African Union to support the call for military intervention did not succeed, but the Western media demonized the Libyan leader to the point that there was a general belief in the West that the Gaddafi regime was on the verge of committing genocide against its citizens. Samantha Power, who had ingratiated herself into the inner circle of the Obama administration, was the author of *A Problem from Hell: America and the Age of Genocide*. As a journalist without the rigorous historical training that could have given her a better understanding of the genocidal traditions of Western capitalism, dating from the time of the genocide of Native Americans, Power had been elevated to a professorship at Harvard University through her media exposure. She was one of the foremost spokespersons for Western military intervention, arguing that the U.S. policy toward genocide had been imperfect.[90] She set about fixing this as a member of the National Security Council (NSC) of the Obama administration.[91] As a crusader against genocide, she worked with Hillary Clinton at the State Department and Susan Rice at the United Nations to promote U.S. military intervention in Libya.

With active lobbying by the governments of Britain, France, and the United States, on March 17, 2011, the UN Security Council, acting under Chapter VII of the Charter of the United Nations, passed resolution 1973, from which we excerpt (for full text see appendix 3):

1. Demands the immediate establishment of a cease-fire and a complete end to violence and all attacks against, and abuses of, civilians;

2. Stresses the need to intensify efforts to find a solution to the crisis which responds to the legitimate demands of the Libyan people and notes the decisions of the Secretary-General to send his Special Envoy to Libya and of the Peace and Security Council of the African Union to send its ad hoc High Level Committee to Libya with the aim of facilitating dialogue to lead to the political reforms necessary to find a peaceful and sustainable solution;

3. Demands that the Libyan authorities comply with their obligations under international law, including international humanitarian law, human rights and refugee law and take all measures to protect civilians and meet their basic needs, and to ensure the rapid and unimpeded passage of humanitarian assistance.

Protection of civilians:

4. Authorizes Member States that have notified the Secretary-General, acting nationally or through regional organizations or arrangements, and acting in cooperation with the Secretary-General, to take all necessary measures, notwithstanding paragraph 9 of Resolution 1970 (2011), to protect civilians and civilian populated areas under threat of attack in the Libyan Arab Jamahiriya, including Benghazi, while excluding a foreign occupation force of any form on any part of Libyan territory, and requests the Member States concerned to inform the Secretary-General immediately of the measures they take pursuant to the authorization conferred by this paragraph which shall be immediately reported to the Security Council.

No-Fly Zone:

5. Decides to establish a ban on all flights in the airspace of the Libyan Arab Jamahiriya in order to help protect civilians;

6. Decides further that the ban imposed by paragraph 6 shall not apply to flights whose sole purpose is humanitarian, such as delivering or facilitating the delivery of assistance, including medical supplies, food, humanitarian workers and related assistance, or evacuating foreign nationals from the Libyan Arab Jamahiriya, nor shall it apply to flights authorized by paragraphs 4 or 8, nor other flights which are deemed necessary by States acting under the authorization conferred in paragraph 8 to be for the benefit of the Libyan people, and that these flights shall be coordinated with any mechanism established under paragraph 8;

8. Authorizes Member States that have notified the Secretary-General and the Secretary-General of the League of Arab States, acting nationally or through regional organizations or arrangements, to take all necessary measures to enforce compliance with the ban on flights imposed by paragraph 6 above, as necessary, and requests

the States concerned in cooperation with the League of Arab States to coordinate closely with the Secretary-General on the measures they are taking to implement this ban, including by establishing an appropriate mechanism for implementing the provisions of paragraphs 6 and 7 above;

9. Calls upon all Member States, acting nationally or through regional organizations or arrangements, to provide assistance, including any necessary overflight approvals, for the purposes of implementing paragraphs 4, 6, 7 and 8 above.

We have spelled out in great detail the contents of the resolution in order to emphasize that there was no provision for regime change in this resolution. The political justification for the no-fly zone had come from members of the Arab League, but the League meeting that supported the no-fly zone had been composed of the minority of its members. Most of those who called for the no-fly zone were involved in supporting the regimes in Yemen and Bahrain, whose leaders *were* killing their own people. The African Union correctly argued that the United Nations should follow the lead of the AU and the road map that had been developed at the meeting of the Peace and Security Council of the African Union on March 10, 2011.

There was much at stake for the African peoples in the challenges associated with the history of "humanitarian protection." Conscious of how militarism and humanitarianism had been refined by military strategists, African intellectuals and policy makers were conscious of militarists who considered Africa to be outside the "non-integrating gap." According to Thomas Barnett, author of *The Pentagon's New Map: War and Peace in the Twenty-First Century*,[92] the world was divided between the "functioning core" of economically developed, politically stable states integrated into global systems and the disconnected areas prone to warfare and terrorism.[93] The thesis of the book by Barnett followed the line of argument of Robert Kaplan, who had waxed about the "coming anarchy" in Africa.[94] Both Kaplan and Barnett represented one wing of the military/academic establishment that supported humanitarianism as one of the tools in the arsenal of Western militarism.

After the Rwanda genocide in 1994, and later the wars in the Balkans, African diplomats supported the principle of United Nations intervention based on the new international norm of "responsibility to protect." At the 2005 UN World Summit of the General Assembly, more than 170 heads of state and government accepted three interlinked responsibilities, which together constitute the principle of "responsibility to protect" (R2P):

> First, States accepted the responsibility to protect their own populations from genocide, war crimes, ethnic cleansing, and crimes against humanity. Second, States promised to assist each other in fulfilling their domestic protection responsibilities. And third, the international community took on a collective responsibility to react, in a timely and decisive manner, if particular States are manifestly failing to protect their populations from the abovementioned mass atrocity crimes.[95]

Long before the Libyan intervention, there had been differences between scholars from the Global South, who recognized the ways in which the UN principle was manipulated by Western countries and called R2P a role for kind-hearted gunmen.[96] As far back as 2007, scholars had warned that though the underlying idea was a noble one, the principle was open to manipulation: "It is thus fair to conclude that the concept currently encompasses a spectrum of different normative propositions that vary considerably in their status and degree of legal support."[97]

This elasticity was understood by long-term planners of the West, who had been surprised by the speed and thoroughness of the Tunisian and Egyptian revolts. These international strategists lost no time in pushing through the UN resolution, because, in the midst of the capitalist crisis, Libya's leader was threatening to nationalize Western interests.

One analyst of the Wikileaks cables drew attention to a 2008 cable that was particularly revealing:

The U.S. cultivated relations with certain figures in Gaddafi's regime, and secretly discussed the benefits of Gaddafi's removal from the scene. A July 2008 cable relates how Ibrahim el-Meyet, a "close friend" of Ghanem (and a source to "strictly protect") told the U.S. embassy that he and Ghanem "concluded that there will be no real economic or political reform in Libya until al-Gaddafi passes from the political scene," and this "will not occur while Gaddafi is alive."[98] These cables pointed to the reality that the West had a two-pronged strategy in Libya, one strategy to work closely with Gaddafi and another to work to build up information and resources to remove him.[99]

This strategy emanated from the importance that the West placed on Libyan oil. Experience elsewhere, especially in Haiti in the period prior to the removal of Aristide, had demonstrated that Western intervention had a greater chance of success once popular revolts were militarized. Hence, following the first demonstrations in Libya on February 15, the militarization of the opposition soon reached the point where the Western media could take sides in a political struggle inside of Libya. Far from protecting civilians, France had been in contact with the opposition forces in Benghazi through numerous assets on the ground, including the new activism of philosopher Bernard-Henri Lévy.[100]

Lévy credits both Nicolas Sarkozy and Hillary Clinton with the foresight to persuade others to join in this war: "I think this war was probably launched by two statesmen: Hillary Clinton and Sarkozy. More modestly, me."[101] In the same interview, Lévy acknowledged that the French military had drawn up plans for a military incursion into Libya before the events of February 2011. The UN Security Council resolutions that authorized an R2P-based intervention to protect Benghazi did not authorize outside powers to provide air support for the subsequent rebellion against Gaddafi.

African intellectuals and policy makers understood what was at stake in Libya. For African intellectuals on the left, such as those who wrote the open letter, the long-term implications of the UN mandate of responsibility to protect are worth considering in the context of the future need to protect the African population in Western Europe. The idea of the responsibility to protect was most needed in Rwanda in 1994 and later in Burundi. These were extreme cases when the idea of national sovereignty had to be set aside and foreign intervention became justifiable. Professor Patricia Daley studied the experiences of genocidal politics in Burundi and clarified the real meaning of humanitarianism. She defined humanitarianism as "an ethical interest in alleviating the suffering of human beings and the general human welfare of people. In times of crisis, as in war-torn situations, those with the necessary means should offer assistance to ameliorate the wretched conditions of their fellow human beings."[102]

Daley penetrated the humanitarian discourses of numerous European scholars and sought to move the understanding of genocide away from the analytical framework of ethnicity, which debased African lives, to one that taps into their emancipatory capacity for peace. She drew extensively from the work of the Nyerere Foundation and the investment that Julius Nyerere had made in the long-term search for peace in Burundi. Nyerere's notion of peace was the antithesis of the market economy–promoting "liberal peace" that was imposed on African societies by Western states and their NGOs. After Julius Nyerere's death, Nelson Mandela embraced the idea of the emancipatory capacity for peace by promoting ideas of truth and reconciliation. Throughout his tenure as president, Mandela sought to elevate the principles of Ubuntu from the philosophical levels about forgiveness and sharing to real politics of cooperation.

In fact, Nelson Mandela made this case at his first appearance as head of state at the Organization of African Unity (OAU). It was in this speech, in June 1994, that Mandela called for the end of genocide in Africa as part of an African renaissance:

> Even as we speak, Rwanda stands out as a stern and severe rebuke to all of us for having failed to address these interrelated matters. As a result of that, a terrible slaughter of the innocent is taking place in front of our very eyes. Thus do we give reason to the peoples of the

world to say of Africa that she will never know stability and peace, that she will never experience development and growth, that her children will forever be condemned to poverty and dehumanization and that we shall forever be knocking on somebody's door pleading for a slice of bread. We know it is a matter of fact that we have it in ourselves as Africans to change all this.

We must, in action, assert our will to do so. We must, in action, say that there is no obstacle big enough to stop us from bringing about a new African renaissance.[103]

Mandela committed the government of South Africa to end the scourge of genocide in Africa. From that moment, the momentum for the criminalization of genocide took root and the coming into being of the African Union presented a united front against genocide, crimes against humanity, and war crimes under domestic law. Africans were working hard to move the discussions about rampant violence in Africa from "tribalism" and ethnic hatred to grasping how the integration of Africa into global capitalist networks fanned the flames of violence and crude extraction of natural resources. It was the expectation of Africans that the mandate of responsibility to protect would be guided by a new understanding of the sources of weapons in Africa and the impact of Western alliances to the forces involved with genocidal economics.

This concept of "responsibility to protect" remained abstract, and the Western nations that led the invasion of Libya and execution of Gaddafi were cynical in the way in which they sought to act in the name of the "international community." In this instance, "international community" meant the interests of Western capital. Wall Street speculators, with the corporate media as the mouthpiece about the "international community," hid behind the diplomatic and political activities of the Gulf Cooperation Council (GCC), which was in the midst of a struggle with the Libyan leadership over the Arab Banking Corporation.[104]

7—LIBYA AND THE GULF COOPERATION COUNCIL

An IMF study of the banking sector in the Gulf Cooperation Council drew attention to the fact that Bahrain was the top banking center in the GCC and the Arab Banking Corporation was at the forefront of wholesale banking for the region. In the words of the study, "Bahrain also has a vibrant wholesale banking sector—the largest of which is the Arab Banking Corporation—which provides off-shore, investment banking, and project finance services to the rest of the region."[105] By December 2010, Libya had become the dominant shareholder of the Arab Banking Corporation, and Muhammad Layas, a confidant of the Gaddafi family, became the chairman of the Board of Directors of the Bahrain-based investment bank. Besides Libya, the other major investor in this bank was the Kuwait Investment Fund.[106]

Most of the political leaders of the GCC were monarchs who, at one time or another, registered fundamental differences with Gaddafi over international questions, especially the issue of Palestine. Indeed, Libya's turn to an energetic foreign policy in Africa had been in part due to Gaddafi's consideration that no major leader of the Arab world had intervened to defend Libya and bring it out of diplomatic isolation the way Nelson Mandela and the African states had done. After the formation of the African Union, Gaddafi threatened to pull out of the Arab League. It was only the strong intervention of Hosni Mubarak, who personally traveled to Tripoli, that kept Libya in the League.

The quarrel with Saudi Arabia was especially bitter, with the Libyan leader accusing the Saudi leadership of having a "pact with the American devil."[107] Qatar was the base for Western military and political operations in the GCC. As mentioned earlier, after the start of the war against the people of Iraq, NATO extended its reach into the Gulf region of the Middle East, through the Istanbul Cooperation Initiative that had been signed in the Turkish city in 2004. Under this initiative, Bahrain, Qatar, Kuwait, and the United Arab Emirates had elevated NATO's relations with the countries of the Mediterranean Dialogue to give legitimacy to NATO's planned military operations in North Africa and the Middle East. Slowly, the four prongs of Western control over North Africa and the Middle East were refined through the Istanbul Cooperation Initiative, the Mediterranean Dialogue, the U.S. Central Command, and the U.S. Africa Command. NATO was brought under the U.S. Central Command to fight against the people of Afghanistan. Egypt remained in the Central Command, while the buildup of private military contractors gave the West flexibility and plausible deniability in the planned interventions in this region. Qatar became a central location for the private contractors.

In 2008, the Emir of Qatar, Shaykh Hamad bin Khalifah Al Thani, visited Tripoli and sought to bring closer relations between Libya and these military formations. (Working through the "reformers" who dominated Libya's financial institutions, the West had been burrowing through Qatar, where relations had been developed between the Libyan Investment Authority and the Qatar Investment Fund.) Less than a year later, in March 2009, at the Arab League meeting in Doha, Gaddafi made quite an uncomplimentary speech about the King of Saudi Arabia over the objections of the Emir of Qatar.[108] The Emir represented himself as a reformer, while supporting the most conservative Islamists throughout the Middle East and North Africa. It was this monarch who was at the forefront of the war against the people of

Libya. Given his orientation, it was not coincidental that leaders such as the president of Sudan, Omar Bashir, were brought in as allies in the war against the people of Libya. The same Western leaders who had supported the indictment of Bashir before the International Criminal Court were now willing to cooperate with him in the military intervention in Libya.

As one of the core members of the GCC, Qatar formed the rump of the Arab League that passed the resolution calling for a "no-fly zone" to protect civilians in Libya. Of the twenty-two members of the Arab League, only eleven were present when it passed a resolution, on March 12, 2011, to support a UN no-fly zone over Libya.[109] Of the eleven members present, two—Algeria and Syria—opposed the resolution and nine supported it. Of these nine, six were members of the Gulf Cooperation Council and the other three were seduced by Saudi Arabia to support the resolution. The members who supported this "no-fly zone" were no paragons of democracy, and it was well-known that Saudi Arabia's record on human rights was no better than that of Libya. In fact, at the same time there was need to protect civilians in Bahrain and Yemen.[110] This Arab League resolution came two days after the African Union, on March 10, 2011, voted to reject foreign military intervention in Libya.

Protecting Civilians or Jockeying for Position

Once the Arab League passed its resolution, Al Jazeera was brought in to trumpet the view that it was the Arab League that had called for the no-fly zone, and the French and British were able to push through the UN Security Council resolution, on March 17, authorizing a "no-fly zone" over Libya. The Western members of Global NATO proceeded to interpret the resolution in any way they wished. Officially, as the text showed, the resolution was intended to give a green light for a limited intervention to protect civilians in Benghazi. However, no sooner was Benghazi secured than the military operation was expanded and became open-ended. The arms embargo was brushed aside, using

Qatar as a conduit for weapons supplies to the NATO special forces and the Qatar soldiers who were introduced as ground forces. Russia and China had abstained in the vote, and their efforts to reconvene the Security Council to debate the implementation of Resolution 1973 were dismissed.

There was good reason why NATO members did not want to discuss the implementation of the resolution. Numerous writers and commentators have drawn attention to the fact that ten times the numbers were slaughtered in Libya than those who were going to be protected. We quote extensively from *The Guardian* in this regard:

> All the while, NATO leaders and cheerleading media have turned a blind eye to such horrors as they boast of a triumph of freedom and murmur about the need for restraint. But it is now absolutely clear that, if the purpose of Western intervention in Libya's civil war was to "protect civilians" and save lives, it has been a catastrophic failure. David Cameron and Nicolas Sarkozy won the authorisation to use "all necessary means" from the UN Security Council in March on the basis that Gaddafi's forces were about to commit a Srebrenica-style massacre in Benghazi. Naturally we can never know what would have happened without Nato's intervention. But there is in fact no evidence—including from other rebel-held towns Gaddafi recaptured—to suggest he had either the capability or even the intention to carry out such an atrocity against an armed city of 700,000. What is now known, however, is that while the death toll in Libya when NATO intervened was perhaps around 1,000–2,000 (judging by UN estimates), eight months later it is probably more than ten times that figure. Estimates of the numbers of dead over the last eight months—as NATO leaders vetoed ceasefires and negotiations—range from 10,000 up to 50,000. The National Transitional Council puts the losses at 30,000 dead and 50,000 wounded.

> Of those, uncounted thousands will be civilians, including those killed by NATO bombing and NATO-backed forces on the ground. These figures dwarf the death tolls in this year's other most bloody Arab uprisings, in Syria and Yemen. NATO has not

protected civilians in Libya—it has multiplied the number of their deaths, while losing not a single soldier of its own.

For the Western powers, of course, the Libyan war has allowed them to regain ground lost in Tunisia and Egypt, put themselves at the heart of the upheaval sweeping the most strategically sensitive region in the world, and secure valuable new commercial advantages in an oil-rich state whose previous leadership was at best unreliable. No wonder the new British defence secretary is telling businessmen to "pack their bags" for Libya, and the U.S. ambassador in Tripoli insists American companies are needed on a "big scale."[111]

One African commentator, quoted in the same article from *The Guardian*, linked the issues of location, arms deals, oil, and competing Western interests in North Africa as the fundamental reasons for the Libyan intervention:

People who think that the West's intervention in Libya is just another oil grab are mistaken. Broadly speaking, for Britain military intervention is mainly about arms; Italy, natural gas; France, water; and for the U.S. [about] counter-terrorism and recon-struction contracts. Spreading democracy and saving the people of Benghazi form merely tangential benefits used to justify these ends. Lest we forget, NATO's bombardment began because Mr. Gaddafi threatened to do to Benghazi what Mr. Bashar al-Assad's forces are doing to various Syrian cities and NATO itself is poised to do in Sirte.

"History is a set of lies agreed upon," once remarked Napoleon Bonaparte. If left unchallenged the true motives behind what the French mainstream media have coined "Sarkozy's War" may be lost in the fog of war.

So what makes Libya so important to the West? Any real estate agent could tell you: location. Given that Libya sits atop the stra-tegic intersection of the Mediterranean, African, and Arab worlds, control of the nation . . . has always been a remarkably effective way to project power into these three regions and beyond.[112]

The concept of "responsibility to protect" is one of the set of lies that became central to the psychological warfare against citizens of the world to disguise the colossal failures of NATO in Libya. When the strategists orchestrated the UN Resolution, there was anticipation that the war against the Libyan regime would be quick and over within a month, but as the war dragged on, psychological operations were intensified. In April 2011, Jonathan Eyal, director of international security studies at the Royal United Services Institute in London, noted:

> Psychological warfare is being waged by Western governments in order to hasten the crumbling of the regime. The big hope for Western strategy is to avoid a drift into stalemate and avoid putting boots on the ground and hope it [the regime] collapses from within.[113]

For any psychological warfare operation to have credibility, there has to be some grain of truth in it, but the lies could not be agreed upon given the differing agendas of the French, the British, and the United States. There was one feature that united these NATO frontliners, and it was that the NATO intervention was based on struggles of the imperial forces in a moment of capitalist crisis.[114] The fierce competition between French and other Western forces for control over the future of Libyan oil was so intense that, after the Qatar and Western special forces entered Tripoli, Nicolas Sarkozy announced that he would visit Benghazi and Tripoli. Britain's David Cameron refused to be left behind, so he accompanied Sarkozy, on September 15, in the neo-colonial rush to Libya. Earlier in that week, Paolo Scaroni, the CEO of Italy's energy giant Eni, had been in Tripoli to discuss the resumption of Libyan gas exports. Turkish president Tayyip Erdogan had visited even earlier, as the varying Western powers competed for political influence, strategic positions, and profits. *The Guardian's* Simon Tisdall remarked: "In truth, like self-styled conquering heroes through history, the British and French leaders arrived in hot pursuit of victors' laurels that may, in time, produce a handy financial payback. This was, first and foremost, the Dave and Sarko spoils of war tour."[115]

"The race is on for Libya's oil, with Britain and France both staking a claim."[116] This was the headline in *The Guardian* on September 1, 2011 after the NATO-backed National Transitional Council overran Tripoli. Of the major resources for economic transformation and energy production, Libya possesses four. The first is a vast area of desert, which German solar companies have been surveying for future production of solar energy for Europe. The second major resource is water. Libya sits on the Nubian Sandstone Aquifer, which is an immensely vast underground sea of fresh water. The government of Libya has invested $25 billion in the Great Manmade River Project, a complex, 4,000 kilometers-long (approximately 2,485 miles) water pipeline buried beneath the desert that could transport two million cubic meters of water a day. The third resource is oil and gas, and this is what was mainly coveted by major Western countries.[116] Libya's fourth resource is the labor and mental faculties of its people.

8—LIBYAN RESOURCES

Prior to the major discoveries of fossil fuel by U.S. oil companies in the 1950s, Libya was considered a poor country whose economy was based on poor farmers and herders who were marginally integrated into the international capitalist system. So many tanks and artillery pieces had been deployed in the Second World War battles that the principal export was scrap metal. After the discovery of oil, the petroleum sector in Libya was dominated by British and U.S. oil companies. By 1957, there were about a dozen companies operating on some sixty different concessions in Libya. They included the seven majors—called the "Seven Sisters" of oil, or alternatively, Big Oil—and the French parastatal Compagnie Française des Petroles.[117] There was also Oasis, a consortium of three companies new to international petroleum exploration: Amerada Hess, Conoco, and Marathon.[118] Following the Libyan concession awards, the Oasis companies pooled their acquisitions. The Oasis Group (originally the Conorada Group) is a consortium composed of three U.S. "independent" oil companies: Amerada (now Amerada Hess), Continental (now ConocoPhillips), and Marathon. These companies had participated in independent biidding for concessions to produce oil in Libya as far back as 1955. Following the concession awards, the Oasis companies pooled their acquisitions. By 1965, when Libya opened a second round of concession bidding, Oasis was the number two producer of oil in Libya, bringing in more than 300,000 barrels per day. The energetic activities of these Western companies expanded Libya's petroleum sector so that by 1970, at the time of the revolution, Libya was exporting 3.3 million barrels of oil per day (bpd). After the 1969 revolution, the Libyan government partly nationalized the Oasis holdings with the government holding 51 per cent by 1973. It nationalized part of Oasis, amounting to 51 percent by 1973.

Mediterranean El Dorado

Once the revolution took place, in 1969, the Libyan government started to tax the oil companies, but their intransigence speeded the processes of nationalization and control by the Libyans. As Anthony Samson outlined in his book *The Seven Sisters: The Great Oil Companies and the World They Made:*

> It was not in the established oil countries of the Persian Gulf that the sisters faced their first critical showdown, but in Libya, the upstart oil producer on the edge of the Arab world in North Africa. For Libya broke up the ranks on both sides. It had let in the independents to challenge the sisters; and it was aloof from the cautious attitudes of the rest of OPEC. It was the outsider at both ends and by ignoring the rules it changed them.[119]

After the 1973 war between Egypt and Israel, the Libyan regime began to take an aggressive position in the Organization of Petroleum Exporting Countries (OPEC), and by 1979 the example of radical nationalization established by Libya had been followed by Iran, Saudi Arabia, and Kuwait. Over the fifteen-year period after the revolution in Libya, countries such as Iraq, Venezuela, Nigeria, Qatar, and the United Arab Emirates fully nationalized the holdings of the Western oil companies.[120] The leadership of Libya within institutions such as OPEC led to confrontations with the West, culminating in the 1977 ranking of Libya as number four in the list of potential enemies of the United States.[121] From this ranking, it followed that the differences between the countries expanded to the point where the Reagan administration bombed Libya in April 1986, in a clear effort to eliminate Gaddafi.[122]

From the era of the bombing to the Western-initiated sanctions over the Lockerbie flight, the question of the future of Libyan oil was followed closely by European oil companies, which moved in to profit from the standoff between the Libyans and U.S. companies.[123] Throughout the eighteen years of sanctions by the U.S. government, the Oasis Group maintained covert and overt linkages with the Libyan political establishment and worked through third parties or other institutions. The group's members—ConocoPhillips, Marathon Oil, and Amerada Hess—represented the "independent" oil companies that held leases on gas and oil reserves that were managed by Libya's National Oil Company.

While he still headed oil service giant Halliburton, Yahya Zoubir, in his analysis of *Libya in US Foreign Policy: From Rogue State to Good Fellow?*, correctly predicted that the U.S. government was working for the physical liquidation of Libya's leader. When the U.S. Congress passed the Iran-Libya Sanctions Act in 1996, the oil companies complained that non-U.S. companies would be the beneficiaries of this legislation. During that period, Richard Cheney—who was to become U.S. vice president in 2001—was the CEO of Halliburton. Cheney gave speeches denouncing the American policy on economic sanctions, describing it as counterproductive in many cases.[124] Some of the U.S. oil companies never left Libya. It was reported in U.S. papers that Halliburton had remained in the country, working through its international web of subsidiaries to evade U.S. restrictions on their operations in what they knew was the rich petroleum resources of Libya. In the book *The Crude Continent*, Duncan Clarke described Libya's resources as follows:

> Libya is well endowed with oil and gas resources, located close to European markets. Five major onshore sedimentary basins offer a

range of venture potential: Ghadames, Marzuk, Kufra, Marmarica and Sirte. In the offshore area are the Sabratah, Benghazi, and Bayda basins. The Sirte basin is by far the most prolific oil province, one of the largest in Africa. Even during sanctions it was the target and operations focus for many European players as well as state companies. The days of unlimited competition enjoyed by these companies have come to an end.[125]

Libya became heavily dependent on the hydrocarbon industry, which accounted for more than 95 percent of export earnings. By the middle of the 1990s, with information on massive new discoveries of petroleum in Libya, the U.S. oil companies renewed their efforts to return to what was seen as the Mediterranean El Dorado. It became known that Libya had one of the largest proven oil reserves in Africa and about 3.4 percent of the world's proved reserves—and most of it was unexplored. According to the *Oil & Gas Journal,* by 2010 Libya had total proven reserves of 46.4. billion barrels of oil, possibly the largest in Africa. "Close to 80 percent of Libya's proven oil reserves are located in the Sirte basin.... Libya's proven natural gas reserves as of January 1, 2011, were estimated at 54.7 trillion cubic feet."[126]

The analysis of Libyan resources is available in the mouthpiece of the petroleum industry, the *Oil & Gas Journal,* and from the platform of the industry, the U.S. Energy Information Administration. From the point of view of the energy importing states of Western Europe, Libya's oil sector enjoys two important advantages. First, the country is located on the opposite side of the Mediterranean Sea and close to European markets. Despite efforts to diversify Europe's energy mix, most European countries remain heavily dependent on imported oil. Geographical proximity means that Libyan oil is easy and cheap to import. This is related to the geopolitical point about location mentioned above. Second, unlike a large proportion of oil from the Persian Gulf region and elsewhere, Libya produces one of the highest-quality low-sulphur oils—light and sweet crude. Generally, this crude is the easiest to process and can be run by relatively "simple" refineries that may not be able to handle heavier or sourer substitutes. In short, Libya's importance to the oil market stems not only from its substantial production, but also from the light sweet quality of its crude grades.

By the beginning of the century, the liberal elements within the Gaddafi government had reached to the top echelons of the oil and banking sectors of the Libyan economy. It was in concert with these "liberal reformers" that the Gaddafi regime skillfully returned to the Western fold, after the UN sanctions were lifted in April 1999. Western oil companies competed vigorously to enter the Libyan energy markets, and the Libyan government used its resource as a tool of foreign policy. In the writings of one scholar, Ronald Bruce St John, Libya opened the door for American oil companies to return to Libya in December 2003:

> The U.S. government lifted some trade sanctions the following April, and restored diplomatic ties in late 2004. Virtually all remaining trade sanctions were lifted in September 2004. At that point the only sanctions still in place were certain export restrictions related to Libya's retention on the Department of State list of state sponsors of terrorism.... Improved commercial and diplomatic relations enabled U.S. oil companies to resume activities in Libya.[127]

This author then went on to explore how the government of Libya negotiated the Exploration and Production Sharing Agreements (EPSAs) with international oil firms. When the sanctions were lifted, Libya was producing only 1.5 million bpd and the objective of the government was to return to 3 million bpd by 2020. In the process, the Libyan government opened three rounds of EPSA IV, with the U.S. oil companies receiving the bulk of the concessions.

In addition to Exploration and Production Sharing Agreements, Libya also developed a bilateral model to stimulate foreign investment and to accelerate the development process. Its negotiations with Occidental Petroleum in 2003–2004 and Royal Dutch Shell 2004–2005 are two successful examples of the bilateral approach. More recently, British prime minister Tony Blair, during a May 2007 visit to Libya in which he said commercial relations between

Great Britain and Libya were going from "strength to strength," announced a $900 million contract returning British energy giant to Libya well over three decades after its assets were nationalized in 1971. The seven-year exploration and production agreements covered seventeen exploration wells, together with the acquisition of 30,000 square kilometers for survey.[128]

This skillful use of bilateral agreements under EPSA and Development Production Sharing Agreements meant that the government of Libya (although divided) maintained the initiative in its dealings with international oil companies. In May 2003, Libya's National Oil Company offered forty-three blocks in twenty-six areas. Some 120 international companies expressed interest in bidding:

> With nineteen successful bidders, the second round marked a greater diversity of winners. Italy's Eni took the largest number of permits. Other successful bidders included Exxon Mobil, the BG Group of the United Kingdom, China Petroleum and five Japanese companies. After a third bidding round for EPSA IV covering fourteen areas and forty-one blocks, twenty-three companies from fifteen countries bid for contracts in round three, with Russia's Tafneft taking three of the fourteen contracts offered, and Russia Garzpon taking one. Taiwan's state-owned China Petroleum Company, Canada's PetroCanada, and Germany's Winterhall also took one contract each.[129]

As Duncan Clarke noted in *The Crude Continent*, the openings from 2004 onward transformed the Libyan game. EPSA IV brought the cream of the oil industry to Libya, while the Libyan government widened the mix of the countries involved. "It has been a shrewd game, played by Libya with finesse and largely on its own terms. The outcome has been to establish the country as a major exploration destination not just in Africa but in the world."[130]

The one country that did not do well in this oil and diplomacy round was France. But if France was kept out of the Exploration and

Production Sharing Agreement, French water companies had their sights on the vast groundwater aquifers in Libya.

Libya's Groundwater Resources and the Great Manmade River Project

Less than six months after the execution of Muammar Gaddafi, the British Geological Survey (BGS) made known to the world what the Libyans already knew: Libya was sitting on the largest water reserves in Africa. *The Quantitative Maps of Groundwater Resources in Africa* declared to the world that "groundwater resources are unevenly distributed: the largest groundwater volumes are found in the large sedimentary aquifers in the North African countries Libya, Algeria, Egypt, and Sudan."[131] Of these, Libya possessed by far the largest volume of groundwater—99,500 cubic kilometers, compared to Algeria with 91,900 km3, Sudan with 63,000 km3, and Egypt with 55,200 km3.[132] These four countries form part of the vast underground sea of fresh water called the Nubian Sandstone Aquifer.

The Libyan state invested $25 billion in the Great Manmade River Project, a complex 4,000 kilometers-long water pipeline buried beneath the desert that could transport two million cubic meters of water a day. The objective of this, the largest engineering project in Africa, was to turn Libya—a nation that is 95 percent desert—into a food self-sufficient arable oasis. Prior to the publication of the BGS report, Western scholars and scientists had used the issue of "water scarcity" in Africa as psychological warfare to promote the privatization of water. Screaming headlines such as "Water map shows billions at risk of 'water insecurity'" were reproduced as international relations scholars wrote about water wars in the twenty-first century.[133]

Western transnational corporations such as Bechtel from the United States, Germany's RWE, and France's Veolia, Suez, and Lyonnaise des Eaux have been at the forefront of the call for the privatization of water resources. French companies such as Suez, Ondeo, and Saur control more than 45 percent of the world's water market. For these companies, Libya and the region of the Nubian Sandstone Aquifer should be within the French sphere of influence. The capitalist crisis had a severe impact on France and the ruling elements were looking for areas to shore up Frances "prestige."

Libya control of water resources (underground) undermines "water wars". Between oil and water, Libyan control of resources upset the balance of power and ability to control (foreign) policy.

9—France and Libya

At the moment of the Libyan intervention, French society was glued to a long-running scandal about the history of corrupt practices and the financing of elections in France by African leaders. For years there had been trials in France on the role of the French oil company ELF in Africa. ELF managers had been found guilty in one of France's biggest corporate crime trials. Former Elf Aquitaine executives were sentenced to five years in prison for using company money as bribes. In the 45,000 pages of documents for the trial there were reams of information on the role of ELF in Africa and how this oil company was an arm of the French foreign ministry.

Libya had kept ELF at arm's length, but in the era of the "conversion" of the Libyan leadership, Libya became part of the international oil-producing countries that assisted in the financing of the French presidential elections. Thus Libya joined the Republic of Congo, Equatorial Guinea, and Gabon as a supporter of the conservatives in France. At the outbreak of the NATO intervention, news came out of the millions of dollars spent by the Libyan leadership to finance the election of Nicolas Sarkozy. Days after Sarkozy became the foremost advocate of the rebellion in Benghazi, Saif al-Islam, the son of the Libyan leader said:

Libya funded the French election of Sarkozy. Soon thereafter, he advocated the rebellion in Benghazi — completely turning his back on stated loyalties.

Sarkozy must first give back the money he took from Libya to finance his electoral campaign. We funded it. We have all the details and are ready to reveal everything. The first thing we want this clown to do is to give the money back to the Libyan people. He was given the assistance so he could help them, but he has disappointed us. Give us back our money.[134]

This allegation against the French president was only one of the many scandals that had come to light about illicit funds, bribes, and kickbacks. French imperial activities in Africa had been the most pronounced of the former colonial European powers, and this imperial outreach transcended ideological divisions between left and right in France. Without Africa's wealth, France would be a minor power with about as much influence as Austria.

There were six major ways for the projections of the exploitative relationships between France and Africa. First, and most important, was the cultural and psychological posture based on the supremacy of Europe and the role of France as the base of enlightenment and civilization, including the revolutionary traditions of liberty, equality, and fraternity. Through cultural institutions of imperialism (especially through formations such as La Françafrique), the leading capitalists in France were able to entrench the politico-diplomatic, strategic, and economic interests of the top one percent of French society.

The second major form of domination, which reproduced the first, was the financial and commercial ties that protected French commercial operations in Africa. Third, there was the political alliance between the comprador elements in Africa and the French bourgeoisie. Through cultural institutions such as French schools and universities, the leaders of francophone Africa looked to Paris, disregarding the social needs of their own societies. Whether in dress, diet, speech, or marriage ties, the African leaders from former French colonies were known to be especially servile to the interests of France. This alliance reinforced the fourth mode, which was to ensure a steady supply of cheap and coerced labor from Africa, working at the bottom of the French economy. The largest numbers of such workers were from the North African states of

Algeria, Morocco, and Tunisia, and from Mauritania and the border societies of West Africa. The fifth form of domination was the supply of cheap raw materials, minerals, and food for France. All of these five forms of domination were sealed by the sixth, and possibly the most consistent: French military occupation and interventions in Africa.

From the period of the war against the people of Algeria up to the military intervention in Libya and Côte d'Ivoire, France stood out as the state that has intervened and been involved militarily in Africa more often than any other outside power. More than thirty years ago, Robin Luckham documented the multiple layers of "French Militarism in Africa."[135] Another British scholar, Anthony Clayton, wrote the important book, *France, Soldiers and Africa*, which dealt with France's military interventions in Africa, and from time to time British and U.S. academics wrote scathing critiques of the neocolonial heritage of France in Africa and the penchant for intervention by the French military.

This interventionist policy to support dictators such as Mobutu Sese Seko of Zaire had been covered up by discourses on "security agreements," "military cooperation," or defense pacts. France maintained a string of bases in the former colonies and performed direct support operations from these bases to those rulers who were in partnership with France. In the sixty-year period from the counterrevolutionary war against the people of Algeria up to 2011, France intervened more than 150 times in Africa.[136]

Throughout Africa, the scandals and corruption of France were only surmounted by the support of the French government for those who committed genocide in Rwanda. Chilling and unequivocal evidence from multiple sources details the complicity and participation of French military and political leaders in support of the 1994 genocide.[137] In the context of NATO's colossal failure in Libya, it is worth recalling that the support of France for genocide had been justified on humanitarian grounds. While the Clinton administration lobbied the UN to withdraw UN personnel from Rwanda at the moment of the real need to "protect civilians," France had organized support for those who were carrying out genocide under a supposedly "humanitarian mission" called Operation Turquoise. It was this support for the *génocidaires*, more than anything else, that would disqualify France from any role in protecting civilians from genocide. The complete disregard for, and dehumanization of, African lives was summed up by the remark of former president Mitterrand, who, in response to a journalist, said that "in countries like that genocide is not so important."[138]

Following the embarrassment of its support of the *génocidaires* in Rwanda in 1994, the French military establishment kept a low profile and sought to gain respectability for its military interventions in Africa by seeking international mandates, such as UN missions. French military activities in Africa after the Rwanda genocide were framed within the context of what was called the Reinforcement of African Peacekeeping Capacities (RECAMP) program. The RECAMP program was deliberately placed under the auspices of the UN and coordinated with the Organization of African Unity. Its avowed purpose was to increase the military capacity of African countries to engage in peacekeeping operations, should they wish.

In the face of the declaration of the United States to establish the Africa Crisis Response Initiative (ACRI), in 1996, France and Britain joined together in the December 1998 St-Malo summit. As early as the period of the war against the Algerian people, France and Britain had signed a series of military agreements, in Nairobi and Dakar, to preserve European interests in Africa. These two states overreached during the period of the nationalization of the Suez Canal, when they allied with Israel to attack Egypt. The rebuke of the United States was sobering, especially for Britain, because soon after the Suez debacle, President Eisenhower withheld financial support for Britain and there was a run on the pound. The British currency lost its position and became a junior supporting actor for the dollar in the international financial system.

Given its vulnerable position, Britain decided to act as a junior partner of the United States in Africa and worked effectively through officer training programs and the deployment of special forces such as the Special Air Services (SAS). During the 1990s, after Germany had united and the European Union seemed to be taking off as an alternative to the hegemony of the United States, Britain and France promised to set aside past rivalries and work together on African issues to protect European imperial privileges in Africa.[139] In December 1998, France and Britain issued the St-Malo Declaration, which laid the foundation for the creation of the European Security and Defense Policy (ESDP) as the military arm of the Common Foreign and Security Policy (CFSP) of the EU.[140] Under this declaration, the French and the British decided in St-Malo to enhance their "cooperation" in Africa.

U.S. strategic planners did not readily accept the legitimation of France for its interventionist policies, and foreign policy bodies such as the Council on Foreign Relations from time to time gave long treatises on the French military in Africa.[141] When the United States decided to be more competitive with the member states of the European Union by establishing ACRI (the precursor to the U.S. Africa Command), France objected.[142] In a study of the French response to the launch of AFRICOM, Niagale Bagayoko concluded, "With the launching of AFRICOM, the French officials are faced with a new challenge: keeping the American hard power as far as possible from what it still considers as France's exclusive sphere of influence. For this reason, AFRICOM may experience some difficulties in developing strong and constructive relationships with francophone African countries, still closely tied to France."

We have already drawn reference to the aggressive counter-terrorism operations in North Africa by the United States that ensnared the leaders of the countries of the Sahara. Slowly, in observing the unfolding of the hegemonic intentions of then U.S. Secretary of Defense Donald Rumsfeld and Vice President Dick Cheney, France sought to develop a new front through the United Nations to cooperate with UN peacekeeping forces in operations in the Democratic Republic of the Congo, all the while seething that Rwanda had left the umbrella of a francophone country to become an anglophone one. By the time AFRICOM was established, in 2008, France was cooperating fully with the United States while stepping up its cultural and commercial presence in Africa.

One golden opportunity for the French to put their image as defenders of those who committed genocide in Rwanda behind them came in the Republic of Côte D'Ivoire, when France sought a United Nations mandate to maintain and sustain its forty-year military presence in the country. In 2011, Laurent Gbagbo became another enabler of overt French intervention by his intransigence over vacating the Ivorian presidency. Sarkozy eagerly went in to "restore democracy."

For decades, France had mooted the idea of the Union for the Mediterranean (a multilateral partnership that encompasses forty-three countries from Europe and the Mediterranean Basin) to extend its power in North Africa. The United States, working through NATO, had kept its options in North Africa open through the establishment of the Mediterranean Dialogue. According to NATO's website in Brussels, "NATO's Mediterranean Dialogue was initiated in 1994 by the North Atlantic Council [and] currently involves seven non-NATO countries of the Mediterranean region: Algeria, Egypt, Israel, Jordan, Mauritania, Morocco, and Tunisia." The task of the Dialogue is to (a) contribute to regional security and stability, (b) achieve better mutual understanding, and (c) dispel any misconceptions about NATO among Dialogue countries.[143] Because the state of Israel was one of the seven countries involved in this Dialogue, the other six countries had to keep its existence out of the news media. Libya under Gaddafi had refused to be drawn into any Dialogue with Israel and steadfastly called for an African Union. France was threatened by the idea of a union of the peoples of Africa that was calling for total independence everywhere, including the Western Sahara and the home of Frantz Fanon in Martinique.

France had worked closely with the monarchy in Morocco to block the independence of Western Sahara because it coveted the wealth of the North African region. More important, French oil companies had been left behind after Gaddafi opened up Libya's petroleum sector to other Western firms. As noted above, the skill of the Libyan National Oil Company had ensured that no foreign oil company dominated the oil sector as the French did in countries such as Gabon. Before the lifting of sanctions, Italian oil companies had done a brisk business and they closely watched the operations of Total, the French oil company. Before Libya's oil production was made subject to the global opening,

Eni was Libya's largest foreign company, with 17 percent of oil/gas production.

In 2004, Gaddafi paid a visit to the European Commission in Brussels at the invitation of Romano Prodi, then president of the European Commission. Italy was a supporter of the French concept of the Mediterranean Union, and both countries were working together to bring Libya into the Euro-Med partnership that was being promoted by France. There had been disagreement inside the European Union on the question of Libya's invitation as far back as 1999, and in response to the dispute as to whether Gaddafi was ready for the privilege of joining the European-Mediterranean partnership, Gaddafi made his clearest statement with respect to the future of Libya and Western Europe:

> The European experiment is of no use to us . . . the area known as North Africa should be Africanized. Either it will become a part of Africa or it will be an anomaly, and will therefore have no future. As an inhabitant of North Africa, I have always rejected the Barcelona agreement which regards North Africa as part of the Middle East, with a vocation to integrate with Europe. This is a conspiracy against the integrity of Africa. They have said to me the Barcelona agreement and cooperation with the European Union will be to Libya's advantage. They want to draw us in and to make use of us, through the Barcelona agreement, to dismember the African continent, stealing North Africa to make it join with the European Union. This is unacceptable. In any case, look at what has already become of the Barcelona agreement. It is in a comatose condition and could well disappear.[144]

France opposed the idea of the African Union and kept open the possibility of Morocco becoming a member of the EU as a carrot to undermine the Union. France supported Moroccan occupation of the Western Sahara and doubled down in its security cooperation with states such as Morocco and Tunisia.

Even before the Italian, British, and U.S. oil corporations were competing with Russian, Chinese, Indian, and Turkish interests in

Libya, German industrial and financial power was stronger in Libya than that of France. The Germans had not been passive in the period of the promotion of the Euro-Mediterranean partnership. The German-led Desertec Industrial Initiative was being orchestrated to tap solar energy from the Sahara and supply Europe with 15 percent of its energy needs by the middle of the century. Hence, far from acquiescing to the French-led Mediterranean Union, Germany had been pursuing its own interests in North Africa and the Middle East, and these interests clashed with those of France. To articulate German interests, the German Institute for International and Security Affairs published a study on "German Middle East and North Africa Policy." It stated: "Well into the 1990s the Maghreb still occupied a marginal position in German foreign policy, with no sign of a clear formulation of German interests. However, in the past decade the region's importance for German foreign policy has grown steadily."[145]

France was not happy with this growth of German interest in North Africa. More important, the French felt slighted by the treatment of France in its negotiations over the compensation package for the victims of a French commercial airliner bombed over Niger in 1989. The crash killed 170 people, including 54 French citizens. In the negotiations, France had been in a hurry to come to an agreement with the Libyan authorities:

> The amount of financial compensation following the judgment of the Cour d'Assises in Paris was 211 million francs, of which 73 million had been reserved for those who had brought civil suits. This resulted in a figure of 35,000 dollars per victim. Unsurprisingly, the French government accepted this figure. For both the French and Libyan authorities, an end seemed now to have been put to the affair. . . . French public opinion became more inflamed when the Lockerbie families obtained a global sum quite out of proportion with that reached under the terms of the Franco-Libyan agreement: 2.7 billion dollars or 10 million dollars per victim. From then on, the French position changed, and—surprisingly—though France favored Libya's rehabilitation, France threatened to block the

PHILOSOPHER GO-BETWEEN

French intellectuals had simmered as they watched the access that their British and U.S. counterparts enjoyed in Libya. Bernard-Henri Lévy, the self-styled French philosopher who had been in close contact with the leaders of the "rebellion" in Benghazi, has written his own memoir on how he guided this rebellion. One reviewer who critiqued his book observed:

> Not content with priding himself on a good war, the author claims, pretty much, to have run it. He it was who arranged for France to recognize the National Transitional Council, he who saw to it that the rebels were properly armed, he who publicized the atrocities in Misrata after derring-do visits, he who drafted declarations and diplomatic communications for the Benghazi regime, and assured unity among the rebels by bringing mutually distrustful tribes together. And above all it was Lévy, the President's eminence, not so much grise as flauntingly ubiquitous, who guided his master's hand throughout.[147]

In this era of instant publishing we have the firsthand account as an unflattering portrait of Lévy, which revealed that "through reports in *Le Monde*, the countervailing perspective of the French bureaucracy has since emerged: They were planning a Libyan intervention all along, and Lévy's actions were a sideshow."[148] Just as, in the era of the seizure of Tunisia and other African lands, French bankers were fronts for politicians, so the picture has emerged of how this philosopher acted as an important go-between, linking Hillary Clinton to the "rebel leaders."[149] Even before the UN resolutions, he had traveled to Benghazi, building connections with the elements who later called themselves the National Transitional Council.

lifting of UN sanctions, if Libya failed to increase its compensation for the families of the victims.[146]

As Luis Martinez rightly pointed out, Libya had played hardball with the French and for them the matter of compensation was closed. However, after September 11, 2001, and the invasion of Iraq in 2003, the Libyans changed their stand and were eager to enter into good relations with the United States. France was adamant in its anger with the discrepancy, which implied that one U.S. citizen was worth $10 million while one French citizen was worth $35,000. France pressed until the Saif al-Islam Foundation came up with additional resources and Libya agreed to give each French family one million dollars each. By December 2007, relations between France and Libya had improved to the point where Gaddafi made a grand state visit to France, the first in thirty-four years. During that visit, Sarkozy worked hard to cement $4.5 billion in business agreements, over and above those worth $10 billion that had been signed earlier that summer (in July, Nicolas Sarkozy had flown to Tripoli to meet with Gaddafi and had signed agreements including a deal on building a French nuclear reactor in Libya).

As the self-declared gendarme of Europe in Africa, France was taken aback by the uprisings in Tunisia and Egypt in January 2011. Michele Alliot-Marie, Sarkozy's foreign minister, had spent her Christmas holidays in Tunisia, and when the uprisings began France offered support to Ben Ali, the leader of Tunisia, in the form of French security forces, who could provide expertise for a Tunisian police force that was beating and killing protesters. However, the removal of the Ben Ali dictatorship was too swift, and soon thereafter the Egyptian revolution changed the military balance in world politics. NATO panicked, and Sarkozy took the initiative to mobilize for the intervention in Libya. NATO's intervention in Libya served many purposes, but primarily that of securing more access to oil and water, while gaining a hold on its strategic location between three continents.

France worked closely with Lebanon and royal emissaries from Saudi Arabia to ensure the passage of the Arab League resolution on the no-fly zone. France was the first country in Europe to recognize the National Transitional Council (on March 10) as the government of Libya. French intelligence must have known that the president of the United States was preoccupied with the question of the capture of bin Laden and hence had delegated the question of Libya to sections of the National Security Establishment, which were divided on the course of action to take. While the UN Security Council was meeting in New York in March, the government of France convened a summit in Paris to organize "support" for the "rebels." At the end of the meeting on Saturday, March 19, President Sarkozy announced "without consultation" that French aircraft were in action over Benghazi. Within two hours, French aircraft were in action against Gaddafi's forces. At this time, both the United States and Britain were trying to ensure that they maintained good relations with other members of NATO, but France forced the issue of military intervention.

While the White House dithered, sectors of U.S. oil and banking that had been involved with the Libyan Investment Authority were calling for the involvement of their government. After the French leaped into action, the United States and Britain could not be left behind. Wall Street had too much at stake. Goldman Sachs had taken major risks with the money from the Libyan Investment Authority. U.S. oil companies had been spooked by the tenacity of the bilateral negotiations of the Libyan National Oil Company. France was also trying to cut the power of the Wall Street firms that had been at the forefront of the financialization of energy markets. Whereas the U.S. military was lukewarm to the idea of entanglement in Libya, the oligarchs of Wall Street had their own fish to fry in Libya.

10—LIBYA AND THE FINANCIALIZATION OF ENERGY MARKETS

The history of the financialization of energy markets followed the trail of the explosion of new financial products that were being invented by Wall Street in the aftermath of deregulation. During the period after the "Reagan revolution," there were a series of mergers and acquisitions, and financial institutions increased their influence and power over the political process. The general term of "financialization" describes the process when value can be generated mainly by financial instruments like derivatives, collateralized debt obligations (CDOs), and credit default swaps (CDSs), all of which are controlled by the financial sector. In the book *13 Bankers: The Wall Street Takeover and the Next Financial Meltdown*, Simon Johnson and James Kwak explored at great length the process by which financial institutions increased their political power in the United States through lobbying efforts, through the revolving door with Washington, and through the institutionalization of the idea that a large financial sector was the best thing for the U.S. economy.

13 Bankers was a call for drastic reforms of the financial services industry. This industry had in the past been one of the strong forces dominating the policy-making establishment in the United States. In this book, the authors spelled out the political and ideological power of the financial oligarchy, explaining how bankers influence policy making:

> The first was the traditional capital money, which wielded its influence already via campaign contributions and lobbying expenses. The second was human capital: the Wall Street veterans who came to Washington to shape government policy and shape a new generation of civil servants. The third and perhaps most important was cultural capital: the spread and ultimate victory of the idea that a large, sophisticated financial sector is good for America.[150]

Together, these powerful forces gave Wall Street a degree of political influence that no other payoffs to corrupt politicians could have bought. What the book neglected to mention was that by the time financialization captured the ideological space, the United States had been transformed from a military-industrial complex to a financial-military complex. We can grasp this decline in the importance of industries to the United States by the decline in importance of the industrial sector. By the time of the financial crisis in 2007–8, the concentration and centralization of capital reached the point where the financial services industry played a larger part in the U.S. economy than it did in 1950. In 1950, finance and insurance in the United States accounted for 2.8 percent of the U.S. Gross Domestic Product, according to U.S. Department of Commerce estimates. By 1960, that share had grown to 3.8 percent and by 1990 it had reached 6 percent. By 2010, finance accounted for 8.4 percent of GDP.

These bankers had been successful in influencing policies with the belief that efficient markets were the routes to prosperity. For three decades, the bankers and their think tanks had promoted the idea that countries had accepted the mantra that "developing countries should abandon restrictions on the flow of capital and open their economy to foreign money." Saif al-Islam and the "reformers" in Libya accepted this mantra and sought to enter the finance sector of the world economy by setting up their own financial vehicle, the Libyan Investment Authority.

In short, these Libyan "reformers" had accepted neoliberalism, and the LIA was the vehicle to support this new turn of the Socialist People's Libyan Arab Jamahiriya.

In the midst of the NATO operations in Libya, the British NGO Global Witness brought to the public the investment position for the LIA as of June 30, 2010, which stood at $53 billion. The information showed the diversity of Libyan assets held by major financial institutions, the place of hedge fund speculators, and the extent to which Libya had become a base for the provision of collateral for the oil and banks that had flocked to Libya after the establishment of the LIA.

In order to break down this dominant place of finance, it is essential to link this growth to a period of neoliberalism, in which, over several decades, financial leverage tended to override capital (equity) and financial markets tended to dominate over the traditional industrial and agricultural economies. The futures markets, hedge funds, and derivative products had blossomed, along with new instruments that were conjured by financial wizards called "quants." The increasing dominance of the finance industry in the sum total of economic activity could be measured in every area of the economy, but for this analysis we are specifically interested in the financialization of energy markets and the close alliance between the banks and the oil companies.

Investment Houses and Big Oil

The history of the power of Big Oil and the importance of Western oil cartels had been discussed at great length by politicians, policy makers, and sectors of the non-aligned movement. Throughout the period 1945–80 the power of the Seven Sisters and their dominance by the United States and Britain stimulated jealousy in Europe, especially among the French and Italians. The tag of "Seven Sisters" was in fact first popularized by Italian oil tycoon Enrico Mattei. The work by the Italians and the French to break into this circle of seven soon led to the acceptance of Italy's Eni and France's Total into the circle, to create a grouping of nine big and powerful Western oil companies:

Exxon (Esso), Shell, BP, Gulf, Texaco, Mobil, Socal (Chevron), the Compagnie Française des Petroles (CFP-Total), and Eni. Anglo-American capital could not fully manage the terrain of nationalism and militarism in North Africa and the Middle East, and the Italians and French brought added European diplomatic and political muscle to recover from the turbulent period of the OPEC embargos and the revolution in Iran.

In the book *The Tyranny of Oil,* Antonia Juhasz traces the power of the oil companies after the mergers brought back the kind of concentration that had existed before anti-trust legislation in the United States. During the Reagan revolution, the oil companies had grown stronger and had weakened any form of regulation by the U.S. government. Despite the spectacular failure of the energy company Enron, oil companies hired former Enron employees to deepen the processes of financialization. It was in this period that the teeth were pulled from the Commodity Futures Trading Commission (CFTC). In 1974, following the hearings in Congress subsequent to the OPEC embargo and rise in oil prices since 1973, Congress created the CFTC as an independent agency with the mandate to regulate commodity futures and option markets in the United States. The agency's mandate has been renewed and expanded several times, but in the era of liberalization and over-the-counter trading, the oil companies organized their own agency, the Intercontinental Exchange (ICE).

The extent of the link between the banks and the oil companies came to the fore during hearings in Congress after July 2008, when there was immense volatility in the price of oil and the role of the banks as crude oil speculators came to light.[151] "As the banks lost billions in the subprime mortgage debacle (largely caused by deregulation and market speculation) they are moving aggressively into energy trading." The hearings before the Senate revealed to U.S. citizens the extent to which the oil companies had worked to weaken the CFTC and establish ICE.[152] (ICE is now largely owned by BP, Shell, Total/Fina/Eni, Goldman Sachs, and Morgan Stanley.) In these hearings, U.S. lawmakers heard from Professor Michael Greenberger about how 35 percent of U.S.-based trading in West Texas Intermediate Crude (WTI) oil futures had shifted to "dark markets," completely unregulated, by agreement with Britain. These markets operated out of London and Dubai. As we will see later, this alliance between the emirates and the manipulators of the price of oil was the driving force for the NATO intervention in Libya.

The hearings had been called in the wake of the financial crisis of 2008, when open contracts for commodity-based financial derivatives—like commodity swaps traded at the New York Mercantile Exchange (NYMEX)—rose from $700 million to $3.3 billion. While NYMEX is an official institution that requires control of these speculations, over-the-counter trades of commodity derivatives not under scrutiny by the Securities and Exchange Commission (SEC) increased as well. After the Senate hearings, the senators acknowledged their impotence before the financial power of the alliance of Big Oil and the banks. Senator Carl Levin said, "The commodities futures markets have become an orgy of speculators, a carnival of greed."[153]

It was in this carnival of greed that the Libyan leadership entered. In the 1970s, Libya had been at the front of the nationalization of Western petroleum interests. Now, in the era of neoliberalism, Libya wanted to enter the game of energy trading and was swallowed by it.

The Libyan Investment Authority

In the period that Luis Martinez deemed the "conversion" of the Libyan leadership, the political reformers of Libya established a Sovereign Wealth Fund to diversify the holdings of foreign reserves and to effect greater control over the investment portfolio of the Libyan government. From the official Web page of the Libyan Investment Authority we learned that "the LIA . . . is a Libyan government organization established on August 28, 2006, by the GPCO [General People's Committee of Libya] to manage the value of Libya's oil revenues and to diversify the dependence of national income. It is a holding company that manages investment funds of the government coming from the oil and gas industry in various areas of the international finance market."[154]

At the outset, the Libyans were concentrating on the country they knew: Italy. Gaddafi made eleven visits to Italy, where the Italians promised to pay reparations and Gaddafi undertook to be the police for Europe in preventing would-be immigrants from crossing the Mediterranean. Soon after the establishment of the LIA, Libya took stakes of between 2 and 3 percent in the Italian bank UniCredit and in the Italian aerospace and defense company Finmeccanica. It also took a 7.5 percent stake in the Italian soccer club Juventus. Other notable investments included a 0.7 percent stake in Belgian financial group Fortis, a 3 percent stake in British publisher Pearson, and a 1 percent stake in the Russian aluminum company Rusal. By 2010, the LIA had amassed over $53 billion in assets held in different parts of the world. It was later estimated that the Libyan government held approximately $200 billion in investments throughout the world.[155]

The oligarchs of Wall Street ached to get their hands on the funds of the Libyan Investment Authority, and the tale of this "dalliance" remains one of the lesser-told aspects of the war against the people of Libya. One can read in the *Wall Street Journal,* the principal financial newspaper in the United States, how the LIA lost money, and the acrimonious fallout of these losses:

In early 2008, Libya's sovereign-wealth fund controlled by Col. Moammar Gadhafi gave $1.3 billion to Goldman Sachs Group to sink into a currency bet and other complicated trades. The investments lost 98% of their value, internal Goldman documents show. What happened next may be one of the most peculiar footnotes to the global financial crisis. In an effort to make up for the losses, Goldman offered Libya the chance to become one of its biggest shareholders, according to documents and people familiar with the matter. Negotiations between Goldman and the Libyan Investment Authority stretched on for months during the summer of 2009. Eventually, the talks fell apart, and nothing more was done about the lost money.[156]

Along with exiled Libyans, the suitors from the academic world had promoted the importance of free markets and investments, and their students in the Libyan bureaucracy entered the game even in the midst of information that the securitization of mortgages and the housing crisis had exploded. As documented in Charles Ferguson's *Predator Nation: Corporate Criminals, Political Corruption and the Hijacking of America,* the U.S. financial sector had become a rogue industry:

> Much of the new wealth of the U.S. financial sector was acquired the old-fashioned way—by stealing it. With each step in the process of deregulation and consolidation, American finance gradually became a quasi-criminal industry, whose behavior eventually produced a gigantic global Ponzi scheme—the financial bubble that caused the crisis of 2008. It was literally the crime of the century, one whose effects will continue to plague the world for many years via America's economic stagnation and Europe's debt crisis.[157]

Despite the evidence of the collapse of the Western financial system, academics and think tanks continued to promote the ideas of unregulated capitalism and that this crisis was a temporary recession. These believers accepted the refrain that the capitalist crisis was a temporary setback and that the dodgy trades would soon yield profits. From a *Wall Street Journal* article and investigations by Global Witness, we learned that

> Goldman soon carved out a new business with the Libyans, in options—investments that give buyers the right to purchase stocks, currencies or other assets on a future date at stipulated prices. Between January and June the Libyan fund paid $1.3 billion for options on a basket of currencies and on six stocks: Citigroup Inc., Italian bank UniCredit SpA, Spanish bank Banco Santander, German insurance giant Allianz, French energy company Electricité de France and Italian energy company Eni SpA. The fund stood to reap gains if prices of the underlying stocks or currencies rose above the stipulated levels.

But that fall, the credit crisis hit with a vengeance as Lehman Brothers failed and banks all over the world faced financial crises. The $1.3 billion of option investments were hit especially hard. The underlying securities plunged in value and all of the trades lost money, according to an internal Goldman memo reviewed by the *Journal*. The memo said the investments were worth just $25.1 million as of February 2010—a decline of 98%.[158]

The acrimony that followed has a direct bearing on the relationships between Wall Street and the Libyan leadership. Even after these losses, Goldman wanted to continue to engage with the LIA:

In May 2009, Goldman proposed that Libya get $5 billion in preferred Goldman shares in return for pumping $3.7 billion into the company, according to fund and Goldman documents. Goldman offered to pay the Libyan Investment Authority between 4% and 9.25% on the shares annually for more than 40 years, which would amount to billions of dollars more. Libyan officials prodded Goldman to recoup their losses faster. They also worried about whether it was wise to invest in Goldman given the collapse of Lehman and the resulting panic that swept global financial markets, the fund documents indicate. After four all-day meetings in July the two sides agreed to a rejiggered deal that would make back Libya losses in 10 years. Such a deal, which also could have left the fund with a Goldman stake, would have needed to be run past the Federal Reserve. That left both Goldman and fund officials worried about its viability.

Goldman changed its mind a week later, having second thoughts about the terms, according to a person familiar with the situation. That August, Goldman proposed some other options to Libya, including investing in other U.S. financial firms and in a "special-purpose vehicle" tied to credit-default swaps, a form of insurance against losses on loans and bonds. The Libyan Investment Authority decided that those options were too risky. Fund officials said they wanted to put the $3.7 billion into high-quality bonds. So

Goldman devised another special-purpose vehicle in the Cayman Islands that would own $5 billion of corporate debt, according to a Goldman document prepared for the fund.[159]

Goldman Sachs was trapped and had little room for maneuver, but the Libyans were the ones with the resources. With full knowledge that the financialization project was orchestrated through the financial sector in Dubai, the LIA moved to consolidate its position in the "dark markets" of the Emirates. Libya had entered into the opaque world of financing energy markets and, because it was awash with funds, could move internationally in ways beyond the control of Wall Street or London. After December 2010, the Central Bank of Libya took the controlling position in the Arab Banking Corporation based in Bahrain. The Arab Banking Corporation was owned by the Kuwait Investment Authority, the Central Bank of Libya, Abu Dhabi Investment Authority, and other shareholders with minor shares. Any move for making independent decisions in the Arab Banking Corporation threatened the web of speculators in the derivatives industry that depended on the recycling of petrodollars from the oil-rich nations of Kuwait, Libya, and the Emirates. Libya had gone for the jugular, by seeking to capture the base of the Intercontinental Exchange. After February 17, when the Libyans started to move to divest their funds from their overexposure to British and U.S. financial institutions, Libya's assets were frozen. This was prior to the ruse of protecting Libyans by Britain, France, and NATO.

11—The NATO Campaign

Very few reports have linked the Libyan dominance in the Arab Banking Corporation to the seismic events in Libya since February 2011. Those writers and analysts from Wall Street with links to the think tanks that Wall Street financed were front and center in the call for war. Although Samantha Power was pushing for war from within the National Security Council of the Obama administration, the military top brass and the Pentagon were not on board. The division within the national security establishment in the United States was on full display when Defense Secretary Gates told West Point officers in training, "In my opinion, any future defense secretary who advises the president to again send a big American land army into Asia or into the Middle East or Africa should 'have his head examined,' as General MacArthur so delicately put it."[160] Later, while the battle over the decision of a no-fly zone was being debated in the press, Gates again made the case against overt military involvement in Libya, warning that America should avoid another big, intractable land war like those under way in Iraq and Afghanistan. In his testimony before the House Appropriations Committee, he said:

> Let's just call a spade a spade, a no-fly zone begins with an attack on Libya to destroy the air defenses. That's the way you do a no-fly

zone. And then you can fly planes around the country and not worry about our guys being shot down. But that's the way it starts.[161]

The U.S. Treasury froze Libyan assets worth $30 billion, hoping to placate Wall Street and the forces in the United States that wanted full-scale military involvement. But the oil and banking lobby in the United States were not satisfied with half-measures. Helped by the maneuvering of Bernard-Henri Lévy and Hillary Clinton, Sarkozy decided to make the question of military intervention a *fait accompli*. France's Chief of Defense said that military operations would last a matter of "weeks" and he hoped not "months." The military leaders in the United States were declaring that if they were going to be involved, it would be in a limited manner. However, Sarkozy was not going to await the outcome of U.S. deliberations and political maneuvering. France acted and started bombing Libya even before an agreement was reached.

The war was launched on March 19, 2011, and officially ended on October 31. Through those seven months of warfare, NATO's forces could not explain their objectives to Africans or to the rest of the world. After the third day of bombing, when the tanks and air capabilities of the Libyan regime had been degraded, it was clear that the mission went beyond the UN Security Council mandate of "responsibility to protect."

By June 27, when the NATO bombings—150 sorties every day—were becoming counterproductive, the bank and oil forces became desperate and turned up the propaganda heat against Libya and Africa. It was an intensified operation, integrating psychological warfare and propaganda, which proved beneficial for NATO in relation to European and North American citizens, but alienated Africans and created a base of support for the Libyan government. The propaganda war to demonize and criminalize Gaddafi and his family took the form of an indictment by the International Criminal Court at the end of June, 100 days after the ineffective bombing campaign. This indictment was also meant to undermine the diplomatic efforts of the African Union and derail the African Union road map for peace talks.

The irony was that there was an ICC indictment against Gaddafi and his family for crimes against humanity, while NATO accepted the support of the President of Sudan, who had himself been indicted by the ICC in 2009.

Under the leadership of Jacob Zuma, the president of South Africa, the African Union had been vigorous in seeking a negotiated settlement. In June, Zuma met NATO Secretary-General Anders Fogh Rasmussen in Russia and pressed the case for the AU road map, calling for a cease-fire. By this time, Gaddafi had agreed to step aside in order to facilitate negotiations. NATO would not countenance the role of the African Union as a mediator. Rasmussen's response was that he was implementing the UN resolution—even though the objectives of the resolution had been achieved. For the backers of the war, when Tripoli was overrun by troops from Qatar and special forces from France and Britain, the objective became clear: the execution of Gaddafi.

In the following pages, we will analyze the stalemate, the psychological warfare against Libya, the preemption of the African Union mediating team, the takeover of Tripoli, and the execution of Gaddafi.

War in Libya: Europe's Confused Response

Within hours of the passing of the UN resolution on the "responsibility to protect," France launched air strikes against the forces of the Libyan government. [162] From the British military pundits we have this assessment of the actions of President Sarkozy on March 19:

> At the end of the meeting, however, President Sarkozy announced to the world's media and without consultation with either of the allies, who he had been with only minutes before, that French aircraft were in action over the city. Within two hours, French forces had engaged Qadhafi's tanks and armour in a dramatic series of attacks which halted the immediate advance of the government forces on Tripoli. [163]

This was the start of a confused military campaign that, despite the confusion, took thousands of African lives. According to the Royal

United Services Institute, this French attack was considered "grand-standing" because, as one British military media outlet stated, the attack was designed to force the hand of "Downing Street and Washington."

After the French attack at 6 p.m., U.S. and British submarines launched Tomahawk missiles at fixed targets throughout Libya at midnight.[164]

Within days, the German military announced that it was pulling forces out of the operation, then dubbed "Operation Odyssey Dawn," because there was disagreement as to who would lead the campaign. France had taken the lead to launch air strikes, but there was no guarantee that France could sustain a prolonged attack. The British news media carried the details of the protest by Germany, which demanded that the Libyan campaign be a European operation. The *Daily Mail* reported on March 23:

> Today the German defence ministry announced Berlin had pulled out of any military operations in the Mediterranean. A ministry spokesman said two frigates and two other ships with a crew of 550 would be reverted to German command. Some 60 to 70 German troops participating in NATO-operated AWACS surveillance operations in the Mediterranean would also be withdrawn, according to the ministry. Berlin isn't participating in the operation to impose a no-fly zone in Libya and abstained on the UN resolution authorising it.[165]

This information, three days after the start of the military operation, was an indication of the deep divisions. France wanted to limit NATO's role, and instead proposed a "war committee to oversee operations." For the French Foreign Minister, Alain Juppé, this committee would bring in foreign ministers of the participating states such as Britain, France, and the United States, as well as the small number of rulers who were speaking to the Arab League. The question of "who's in charge" was so blatantly and directly related to who would reap the fruits of this military engagement that the head of the Italian Senate's defense affairs committee, Gianpiero Cantoni, said that "the original French anti-Nato stance was motivated by a desire to secure oil contracts with a future Libyan government."[166] France had jumped the gun, and there was disagreement immediately as to the operational objectives. France wanted to maintain control and exclude Turkey, a competitor in the Mediterranean region and a state that France had campaigned to exclude from the European Union. Turkey wanted the operation to be limited, immediately criticizing France by saying that what had been sanctioned at the meeting in Paris, on March 18, had "gone beyond what had been sanctioned by the UN Security Council Resolution."[167] In this tussle, the Italian Foreign Minister, Franco Frattini, warned that "Italy would take back control of airbases it has authorized for use by allies for operations over Libya unless a NATO coordination structure was agreed to."[168] Italy understood that French leadership in the operation was a threat to its long-term interests in Libya.

Even while this bickering and fracturing was going on, however, bombs were raining down on Libyans. By the end of this unlimited bombing, in October 2011, 9,700 bombing missions had been carried out. In September, after the "capture of Tripoli," NATO's interim report stated that "since the beginning of the NATO operation (31 March 2011, 06.00GMT) a total of 26,323 sorties, including 9,658 strike sorties, have been conducted." This was an average of 150 air strikes per day against the people of Libya, killing hundreds—if not thousands— of people.[169]

In fact, from the pages of the International Institute of Strategic Studies (IISS) we learned that after the first two days, the objective of protecting civilians in Benghazi had been achieved:

> NATO aircraft rapidly secured air dominance by nullifying the regime's air force and ground-based air defences. On the first day, 19 March, the advance of regime forces toward Benghazi, the rebel capital—where Gadhafi had promised to wreak horrible revenge— was stopped. Attacks then targeted the regime's military capacity, including its armoured vehicles, artillery, short-range ballistic and surface-to-air missiles, command and control infrastructure, communications assets and munitions dumps.[170]

Once the objectives of the UN Security Council resolution had been achieved—that is, the restricted mandate to protect civilians— the objectives of NATO became confused, and driven by the unwritten plan to change the regime and execute Gaddafi. The International Institute of Strategic Studies noted: "The objectives of the nations involved were confused. Some countries participated with more than the mandate in mind—in other words, they sought Gadhafi's removal." A career officer of the British army, Chief of the Defense Staff, General Sir David Richards, questioned the legality of targeting and killing Gaddafi. For this questioning, he was rebuked and "slapped down" by British prime minister David Cameron, who opined that Gaddafi was a legitimate target for assassination. U.S. Defense Secretary Gates joined in this dispute, saying it would be "unwise" to target the Libyan leader, adding cryptically that the bombing campaign should stick to the UN mandate.[171]

While these disputations were being carried on in the media, Germany, Poland, Turkey, and Spain (frontline members of NATO) opposed the French action and had their own links to the Libyan leader. Germany had led the other allies within the European Union to oppose France's lead. France had successfully led the war in the first salvos, but like the Italians, the U.S. oil and banking forces did not want to wake up with France in the dominant position in Libya. Hence the political and military objectives of the Libyan war were confused. U.S. generals, with their eyes fixed on the quagmire in Afghanistan, were reluctant to enter into a protracted war, but Sarkozy forced their hands even before the debates inside the United States had been resolved. "The United States played a supporting role, but this involved the deployment of key military assets including intelligence, surveillance and reconnais-sance (ISR) platforms, and tanker aircraft, all of which were essential elements of alliance operations. The campaign therefore raised impor-tant questions about objectives, as well as about the nature and future of the NATO alliance."[172]

NATO started boming Libya on the night of March 19, 2011, after the passage of the UN Resolution 1973. European workers, faced with the capitalist depression in which the banks were calling on governments to impose austerity measures, were lukewarm toward the Libyan operation, so the invaders had to find novel ways for intervening. The intervention then took the form of bombings by NATO, disinformation campaigns, an alliance with Bashir from Sudan, on-the-ground special forces from the French and British commandos, and air and ground support from Qatar. The entire NATO operation in Libya depended on precision weapons, because there were no leaders who had the full support for ground troops.

We quote again from Western strategic reports:

The tactical air campaign was initially shaped to protect civilian lives, in accordance with the UN mandate. As such, it was a gradualist and coercive approach, and not one that was designed to remove Gadhafi from power rapidly. However, the latter goal appeared to be the implicit desire of the main countries involved— France, Britain and the United States. On 15 April, Cameron, Sarkozy and U.S. President Barack Obama wrote jointly in a newspaper article: "Our duty and our mandate under UN Security Council Resolution 1973 is to protect civilians, and we are doing that. It is not to remove Gadhafi by force. But it is impossible to imagine a future for Libya with Gadhafi in power."

Once the April 15 letter made it clear that the objective of the United States, Britain, and France was to remove Gaddafi, there were even more serious divisions within NATO as countries such as Poland refused to participate in this campaign. Of the twenty-eight members of NATO, the majority refused to participate in this military operation. Most members understood the reasons for Sarkozy's energy. Some voiced their opposition and reservations in private, but Polish prime minister Donald Tusk, in drawing attention to the inconsistencies and hypocrisy of leaders who earlier had feted Gaddafi, declared that the attack on Libya was for oil:

Although there exists a need to defend civilians from a regime's brutality, isn't the Libyan case yet another example of European hypocrisy in view of the way Europe has behaved toward Gaddafi in recent years or even months? That is one of the reasons for our restraint. . . . If we want to defend people against dictators, repri- sals, torture and prison, that principle must be universal and not invoked only when it is convenient, profitable or safe.

Poland was a staunch NATO ally who had sent troops to Iraq and also committed more than 2,300 troops to Afghanistan. The senti- ment that the Libyan intervention was about oil was shared by other members of NATO, so that there were only eight members—Belgium, Canada, Denmark, France, Italy, Norway, Spain, the UK, and the United States—that participated in this operation, called "Operation United Protector." Even those participating in the aggression against the people of Libya could not agree on a command structure, so the United States put up AFRICOM as the front and called their operation "Operation Odyssey Dawn." When the United States understood that the military campaign would be protracted, the Pentagon decided to maintain its key role, but presented to the public the fiction that it was NATO that was carrying out this mission.

Prior to the designation of this opportunistic military campaign, the French had called their action "Operation Harmattan." The British called their involvement "Operation Ellamy," and the Canadians termed theirs "Operation Mobile." Such divisions in the command structures created confusion, and more than once, the bombing of innocent civil- ians. When the United States decided to give up the dominant public role, the Libyan operation was placed in the hands of NATO and called "Operation United Protector." Italy had to be mollified and kept within the alliance with the United States and Britain so that it would not join with Spain and Germany in opposing this illegal action in Libya.

It is worth parsing the statements of the president of Poland, who made direct criticisms of the objectives of France in Libya. The French oil company Total, successor to Elf, hoped to obtain access to a large share of Libya's oil reserves, and in this way edge out the role of others such as the Germans, Turkish, and Spanish oil interests in Libya. Total had been weak against the competition from other European oil companies—Spain's Repsol, Italy's Eni, Germany's Wintershall (a unit of BASF), and Austria's OMV. With the full-throated support from "humanitarians" such as Bernard Kouchner, who had declared that the Libyan crisis had shown how a united Europe can be used as a force for common good, the traditional left in Europe supported this military operation.

French forward planners and strategists had been in touch with opposition elements in Libya (working with Bernard-Henri Lévy) and it was Sarkozy's calculation that a quick application of power from the air would tip the balance; the Libyan "rebels" could then drive trium-phantly into Tripoli. It was the expectation that, with French air power, the "rebels" would finish the Libyan leadership within a week. France was mindful of the fact that Tunisia's Ben Ali had crumbled within one week. It was this calculation that led France's Chief of Defense to declare that military operations would last a matter of "weeks."

But the Libyan regime did not crumble within a week. Despite the bombing, because the "rebels" did not comprise a coherent political formation, there was constant bickering and recriminations between the three leading imperial states as their interlocutors jockeyed with different factions of the National Transitional Council. Britain and the United States had been so close to Gaddafi that they were at a disadvan-tage vis-à-vis the contacts of Bernard-Henri Lévy, but the British did not want to be left out. Italy allowed NATO to use Italian soil to launch bombing campaigns, while at the same time supporting the Gaddafi family with logistics and other forms of support under the radar. When it was reported that the NTC was starting to export oil from terminals in the east at Tobruk, Italian oil interests, not wanting to be left behind, traveled to Benghazi to secure the dominance of the Italian companies in the oil business. Eni chief Paolo Scaroni flew to Benghazi, where he "had contacts with the Libyan National Transitional Council to restart cooperation in the energy sector and get going again the collaboration with Italy in the oil sector." On March 23, 2011, less than a week from the start of the bombing campaign, an interim government was formed by the council, which was at once recognized by France, Qatar, the Maldives, and Italy.

Within the United States, although the U.S. military had launched Tomahawk missiles, the question of the nature and form of the U.S. military intervention was far from finished. Some sectors of the military, especially those in the Africa Command, went on television to voice support and to claim that AFRICOM was coordinating the war in Libya. These claims were meant to shift the balance in the debate because the justification for military intervention was a delicate issue. The mobilization of the international peace forces against NATO was an important consideration for the planning of Operation United Protector. Within the United States, there were deep divisions.

The Divisions within the United States

The Obama administration was caught between three competing interests. The first was represented by the forces of Big Oil that had established the Intercontinental Exchange. Big Oil and the forces involved in the "financialization of energy markets" represent the top 1 percent, to use the language of the Occupy Wall Street movement, in the United States. The loudest call for the ouster of Gaddafi came from the forces who said that Gaddafi had to go, which undermined all efforts by the African Union to organize a negotiated settlement. From the conservative think tanks there was consensus that the United States must fully engage the war in Libya.

The second interest in the U.S. policy-making establishment was the Pentagon. Sectors of the Pentagon, along with the National Security Council, opposed the U.S. involvement. Secretary of Defense Robert Gates's speech to West Point cadets against sending a land army into Asia or into the Middle East or Africa was delivered before the media blitz that called for NATO's intervention and before the Gulf Cooperation Council and the Arab League pushed through their call for a no-fly zone. [173] The secretary of defense testified before Congress that an operation such as that of Libya was below the capabilities of the United States, and that the Pentagon was quite willing to be part of the bombing campaign. With memories of the lack of popular support for the military during the war against the people of Vietnam, the top military planners wanted to walk a tight rope between the rank and file and those generals who understood the dalliance with Goldman Sachs. While sections of the punditry supported the killing of Gaddafi, Robert Gates had opposed this act, stating that this was beyond the UN mandate. Those who disagreed with Gates waited quietly, knowing that in less than three months he would be resigning.

The position of the top brass at the Pentagon had been echoed quite early by James Clapper, the Director of National Intelligence. Clapper told the U.S. Senate that Gaddafi's superior military force would prevail over the long term. He also said that one possible outcome could be the splitting of Libya into three autonomous states. While the Director of National Intelligence was equivocating on the nature of the NATO operation, the CIA was deploying special forces to Libya, to fight beside the so-called rebels. At the same time, this divided U.S. intelligence was sending a signal to its assets in the Gaddafi circles that the CIA would still be keeping in close touch with them. The head of National Intelligence predicted that Gaddafi would prevail even while the head of Obama's NSC, Tom Donilon, was on the phone every day calling on Moussa Koussa (former chief of intelligence and foreign minister) to defect. The anticipation was that this would trigger internal opposition to Gaddafi. Moussa Koussa predicted a Somali-type partitioning if there was no political solution to the uprising. He did defect a few weeks later.

By the end of March, Robert Gates and Admiral Mullen were testifying that the U.S. military would support a scaled-down version. Congressional representatives pressed both leaders on the cost, goal, duration, and legality of the mission, but there was no clear answer as to the extent of U.S. long-term commitment. At that time, March 30, there was the expectation that the operation would be over in a few weeks. Regarding the examination of the internal disputes among the leaders of the United States over Libya it was reported:

> Within the Administration, Robert Gates, the Defense Secretary, was the most strenuous opponent of establishing a no-fly zone,

or any other form of military intervention. Like Scowcroft, Gates objected to intervention because he did not think it was in the United States' vital interest. He also pointed out a fact that many people didn't seem to understand: the first step in creating a no-fly zone would be to bomb the Libyan air defenses. Clinton disagreed with him and argued the case for intervention with Obama. It was the first major issue on which she and Gates had different views.[174]

The third position of the U.S. administration came from the humanitarian hardliners—Samantha Power (Special Assistant to the President and member of the National Security Council), Susan Rice (Permanent Representative of the United States to the United Nations), and Hillary Clinton (Secretary of State).[175] These forces had been trumpeting the call for the exit of Gaddafi even though the United States did not have a mandate for "regime change" under the UN resolution. The Obama administration, in the absence of leadership to oppose the partitioning of Libya, gave publicity to those who argued that all wars, whether humanitarian or not, tend to escalate.

We now know that, throughout this debate on Libya, Barack Obama was in a delicate discussion with his own military about the best way to deal with Osama bin Laden. For six months prior to the storming of the bin Laden compound in Pakistan, Obama had been locked in fierce disagreement with his own military as to the best way to carry out that mission in a Muslim country.[176]

What tipped the balance for the escalation of the war was the lack of unanimity among the peace and justice forces internationally. With French "humanitarians" such as Bernard Kouchner rallying the wavering left in Europe, there was confusion in the ranks of the peace movement about the objectives of NATO.[177] With the endorsement of Kouchner, France was able to play "hawk," while Germany demurred, as the Europeans waged another war with Africa using the diplomatic recognition of the National Transitional Council as the legitimization for the war. The forceful role of France and Britain undermined any legitimacy for the NTC in its representation of itself as a liberation movement fighting to oust Gaddafi. As a fighting force the NTC was disorganized, but it was able to mobilize the early diplomatic recognition of France and Italy as bargaining chips to garner continued military support.

The Italians had traveled early to Benghazi to ensure the flow of oil supplies. Bernard-Henri Lévy, an activist for French interests, and the U.S. oil companies strategized as the NATO bombs were being dropped. The Italians had to move swiftly because the U.S. Treasury had made clear that opposition oil sales would not be subject to the sanctions imposed on Colonel Gaddafi's government. With the full understanding of the potential for France to seek to have oil from the east sold in the euro currency, U.S. Treasury officials cautioned leaders of the NTC that the U.S. dollar should be the currency for the oil trade. The U.S. Treasury was too sophisticated to say this openly, of course, instead using language like "the rebels would have to create a payment mechanism," which was acceptable.

In the final analysis, the combination of the future of the dollar, the outstanding differences between the Libyan Investment Authority, and the future of the U.S. oil companies was too potent. The Obama administration supported the mission in the new foreign policy posture in a way that had *The New Yorker* magazine describing the president's actions in Libya as "leading from behind." Some sections of the U.S. peace movement continued to oppose U.S. involvement, but the corporate media worked to marginalize any opposition in U.S. society to the relentless bombing of Libya.

Under Resolution 1973 of 2011, the UN had widened its economic sanctions against the regime of Muammar Gaddafi—including, for the first time, the oil sector. In addition to the no-fly zone and the threat of air strikes, the resolution also stipulated freezing the assets of the Libyan National Oil Company. Though the state-owned NOC controlled the majority of the country's oil production, international oil companies were crucial for the sustenance output through joint ventures. The NOC was also in full control of at least two of its subsidiaries, its wholly-owned Sirte Oil, a joint venture with U.S.-based Occidental Petroleum, and Waha Oil, a joint venture with American oil companies ConocoPhillips, Marathon, and Hess. Unlike in the 1970s, when U.S. oil companies were dominant internationally, oil companies from Brazil, India, China, Japan, Turkey, and a host of other countries were waiting to move in to sign new deals with Libya's NOC. The presence of these companies meant that the Libyan political leadership had the option of nationalizing oil in the face of the international sanctions. Urgency for the success of the NATO bombing missions in Libya accelerated after the passing of the UN resolution. One day after the *Financial Times* reported that "oil companies fear nationalization in Libya":

> Western oil companies operating in Libya have privately warned that their operations in the country may be nationalised if Colonel Muammer Gaddafi's regime prevails. Executives, speaking on condition of anonymity because of the rapidly moving situation, believe their companies could be targeted, especially if their home countries are taking part in air strikes against Mr. Gaddafi. Allied forces from France, the UK and the U.S. on Saturday unleashed a series of strikes against military targets in Libya. It is certainly a concern. "There are good reserves there," said one executive at a Western oil company with operations in Libya. "We have lost some of our production [because all operations have stopped] but our bigger concern is what will happen to the exploratory work as that gives you a future rather than the immediate impact."[178]

The objectives of the bombings were not only to cripple the Libyan military infrastructure, but also to precipitate the exodus of workers in the Libyan economy whose presence acted as a base of support for normal economic activities. Of the more than 600,000 workers, 280,741 were third-country nationals. The only third-country nationals who were not evacuated were African migrant workers. They suffered in two ways: they were bombed and beaten from the air, and on the ground they were accused of being mercenaries. The African Union called international attention to the plight of these migrants, but it was the desires of oil executives that prevailed.

The private warnings of the executives of the oil companies that the events were moving too rapidly were echoed in loud cries from the U.S. Congress asking President Obama to invoke the War Powers Act in order to receive congressional support for U.S. participation in the war. However, the White House and the Pentagon did not want an open discussion of the role of the U.S. military in this operation. The Pentagon had moved to a new form of warfare, where special forces were linked to private military organizations. According to the *Washington Post,* the United States had deployed special operations forces in seventy-five countries, from South America to Central Asia. In the evolution of this new form of military intervention, small states such as Qatar became important launching pads for the new forms of war. Qatar is not a member of NATO, but its military became central to the operations in Libya.

Divisions beyond NATO and in the Mediterranean Region

Within a week from the start of the bombing campaign, the Secretary-General of the Arab League, Amr Moussa, said that though he supported a no-fly zone, the Arab League was against aerial bombing in principle. This opposition from the main political lifeline of this NATO war induced even more recriminations and panic at the military level. Russian prime minister Vladimir Putin likened the bombing campaign to the "medieval crusades," and Turkey echoed this line. Turkey had been opposed to the French political leadership and was mollified by the British. Hence, although Turkey did not play a frontline role, it became a member of the so-called Libyan Contact Group so that it would not be left behind after the bombs stopped raining on the Libyan people.

Recriminations started between these "partners," with some claiming that others were not pulling their weight. Some NATO members opposed the military engagement, arguing correctly that NATO was exceeding its mandate by the bombing of Libya. Turkish Foreign Minister Ahmet Davutoglu stated that air strikes launched by France had gone beyond what had been sanctioned by the UN Security Council resolution:

There are UN decisions and these decisions clearly have a defined framework. A NATO operation which goes outside this framework cannot be legitimized. It would be impossible for us to share responsibility in an operation that some authorities have described as a "crusade."

This language on a "crusade" from a key ally of NATO reflected the disquiet that emerged after two months of relentless bombing by NATO. In any other war, this kind of bombing would have been termed terrorism. By the beginning of June, as differences among NATO leaders widened, U.S. Secretary of Defense Robert Gates pressured the Germans to give more support. A summit of NATO foreign ministers agreed to continue the ten-week-old bombing campaign "as long as necessary," while Robert Gates and NATO Secretary-General Anders Fogh Rasmussen pushed for other NATO member states, including Germany, Poland, Turkey, and Spain, to join in the bombing of Libya. Before the summit, Tripoli had been subjected to relentless bombardment over a forty-eight-hour period, with warplanes striking the Libyan capital sixty-two times. The daylight air strikes underscored that Libya, its air force, and air defense system, devastated by earlier attacks, remained virtually defenseless in the face of the U.S.-NATO blitzkrieg. Hundreds of innocent citizens perished in these bombing raids.

Professor Michael Clarke, Director-General of the Royal United Services Institute in Britain, was one of the Anglo-Saxon military specialists who made scathing critiques of the NATO quagmire. From the United States, the Atlantic Council (one of the think tanks heavily funded by Big Oil) also provided commentaries. Hence, from their own platforms, there is information on the dysfunctional nature of the campaign. It is not necessary here to revisit the nature of the military campaign and elaborate on the thousands of NATO sorties in Libya over seven months. Military specialists have been able to analyze the strategic blunders and the fact that this massive NATO machine, with an unprecedented level of technology in military weapons and equipment, was held at bay for seven months by a small state. The full day-to-day roster of their military and naval operations to oust Gaddafi is in the public domain on the platforms of military journals. Peace activists and concerned scholars can read the daily strategic operations to learn the full weakness of NATO. Michael Clarke of RUSI argued in an article that the military operation itself created an image of "NATO's limitations rather than its power."[179] From the analysis of Vladimir Socor for the Atlantic Council and the Jamestown Foundation, there was this scathing critique:

> The coalition underestimated the resilience of Colonel Muammar Gaddafi's base of social support in the country's west. It seemed blindsided by the complexity of tribal dynamics among its suddenly acquired protégés in the country's east. In that polarized context, the allies misjudged the level of force necessary for a quick success of their intervention. This proved insufficient for short-term victory over Gaddafi, but only sufficient to shore up the rebels, thus producing a stalemate between the internal forces, and escalation of the civil war. This in turn necessitated escalation of air bombing, with further damage to infrastructure. The coalition did not adequately check the rebels before arming and funding them. Initially it portrayed the rebellion as holding democratic promise for Libya, but has toned down such claims.[180]

These reviews in military journals and websites underscored the operational problems of NATO in an environment where it was internationally agreed that the NATO bombing was illegal. The international peace movement organized protests and African intellectuals and activists called for an end to the bombing and for mediation by the African Union. In August 2011, 200 African intellectuals released a letter opposing the "misuse of the United Nations Security Council to engage in militarized diplomacy to effect regime change in Libya" and the "marginalization of the African Union." These forces of peace called for mediation even after the Qatar ground forces entered Tripoli and claimed they were the NTC forces.

NATO has empowered itself openly to pursue the objective of regime change and therefore the use of force and all other means to overthrow the government of Libya, which objectives are completely at variance with the decisions of the UN Security Council.[181]

These intellectuals were repeating the public position of the AU, but by the time the NATO and so-called NTC forces entered Tripoli, it was clear that the objective was not only regime change but the physical elimination of Muammar Gaddafi. During the bombing campaigns, British military personnel had called for the targeted bombing and killing of Gaddafi. Robert Gates, while he was still the U.S. Defense Secretary, called such a plan "unwise." Gates was not to understand that, for Big Oil and the banks, Gaddafi had to go. Hence, these forces undermined all efforts of the AU to mediate or to have another discussion of Libya in the UN Security Council.

12—THE AFRICAN UNION AND LIBYA

When the African Union was formally inaugurated in Durban, South Africa, on July 8, 2002, the international relations experts were dismissive of this new international organization. They had been taken aback by the speed with which the constitutive act had been drafted, debated, and finally ratified. Gaddafi had been supportive of the process and the Sirte Declaration of 1999 had laid the foundations for the transition from the Organization of African Unity to the AU. The establishment of new organs, including the Peace and Security Council, the Pan-African Parliament, and the Economic, Social and Cultural Council (ECOSOC), had added some optimism in Africa that the AU would evolve beyond the leaders and would represent the aspirations of the people. The vision and mission of the AU continues to be an integrated, prosperous and peaceful Africa, an Africa driven by its own citizens, and a dynamic force in the global arena.

African leaders and scholars such as Kwame Nkrumah and Julius Nyerere had worked for the unity of the peoples of Africa. The AU carried with it the historic traditions of the strengths and weaknesses of the Organization of African Unity's process. The major weakness of that process was that the deliberations were dominated by leaders who were themselves questionable. This weakness notwithstanding, the OAU had worked diligently to achieve the most important task of the last century: ending colonialism and apartheid. Both Julius Nyerere and Nelson Mandela had worked within the context of the negotiating mechanisms to end the genocidal politics and violence in Burundi. It was a long and drawn-out process, one that Western governments sought to undermine every step of the way.[182]

The AU's Diplomatic Efforts

From the start of the uprisings in Libya, the African Union worked hard to lay the basis for negotiations. From February 23, 2011, the Peace and Security Council of the African Union met and discussed in great detail the situation in Libya. The AU was faced with an unprecedented situation, where two heads of state had been removed in the space of one month. Libya was one of the five countries that had been the anchor of the African Union, along with Algeria, Egypt, Nigeria, and South Africa. Between them, these five states provided around 75 percent of the AU's budget. Libya's Muammar Gaddafi was the most energetic of the leaders supporting the African Union and many referred to him as "brother leader."

Very early, Gaddafi showed that he was out of step with the new realities in Tunisia and Egypt.[183] Following the threats he and his son made against the citizens of Benghazi, the Peace and Security Council of the AU worked harder to intervene to ensure that civilians were protected. By March 10, the Peace and Security Council adopted an important resolution that detailed the road map to address the Libyan conflict, consistent with the obligations of the AU under Chapter VIII of the UN Charter. The road map included the following elements:

- Immediate cessation of all hostilities;
- Cooperation of the concerned Libyan authorities to facilitate the timely delivery of humanitarian assistance to needy populations;
- Protection of foreign nationals, including the African migrant workers living in Libya;

- Dialogue between the Libyan parties and establishment of a consensual and inclusive transitional government.

To follow up on the implementation of the AU road map, a high-level ad hoc committee was also established.

However, the principal media outlets of the NATO countries and Qatar went into overdrive to savage, dismiss, and marginalize the AU. When the Peace and Security Council of the AU refused to endorse the need for a no-fly zone over Libya, the Al Jazeera network was willing and able to broadcast information on the "imminent killings of hundreds of civilians." The BBC and CNN repeated the information on massacres in Libya, while downplaying actual killing in the streets of Bahrain.

French media and the government of France had always been uncomfortable with the existence of an independent African Union. Nicolas Sarkozy called the AU to a March meeting in Paris to give its blessing to the NTC, but the leaders of the AU maintained that the matter of the rebellion in Libya had to be solved by Libyans and Africans. Western European and U.S. media downplayed the importance of the African Union, and Western policy makers argued that, as Gaddafi's brainchild, the AU could not be a neutral force. But when the NATO bombing campaign began and the African Union dispatched mediators to Libya, the peoples of Africa understood that the mandate of "responsibility to protect" had been overtaken by the objective of physically eliminating Gaddafi.

On April 10–11, 2011, the ad hoc Committee of the AU, chaired by President Jacob Zuma of South Africa, undertook a visit to Libya. The mission also included the presidents of Congo-Brazzaville, Mali, and Mauritania, and Uganda's foreign minister. The delegation landed at Tripoli's Mitiga Airport after NATO gave permission for their aircraft to enter Libyan airspace—the planes were the first to land in Tripoli since the UN had imposed a no-fly zone over the country—and the NATO forces temporarily slowed the bombing while the AU team was in the capital.

In Tripoli, Gaddafi and the government of Libya confirmed to the AU delegation their acceptance of the AU road map. In Benghazi, the discussions with the NTC leadership focused on the need for an urgent cease-fire. The objective was to ensure the effective protection of the civilian population and to create conducive conditions for the fulfill-ment of the legitimate demands of the Libyan people.

Meanwhile, France worked hard in its former colonies for these states to recognize the NTC. Senegal was the first to break the AU's united front by recognizing the government of the NTC in Benghazi, more than a month before the group was recognized by the United States.

The African Union understood the gravity of the war in Libya, and on April 26, 2011, the Peace and Security Council, meeting at minis-terial level, restated the position of the African Union that the issues in Libya were political and could not be resolved by NATO bombs. In May 2011, the Assembly of the Union convened an extraordinary session. It reiterated the need for a political solution and called for an immediate end to all attacks against civilians and a cease-fire that would lead to the establishment of a consensual transitional period, culminating in elections that would enable the Libyans to freely choose their leaders. The assembly stressed the imperative for all con-cerned to comply with both the letter and spirit of resolution 1973. By this time, it was clear that "black Africans" were being targeted and executed as "mercenaries" and thus the AU called on the UN Security Council to protect these Africans. In a report to the Security Council in June, Foreign Minister Hamady Ould Hamady of Mauritania, speaking on behalf of the AU High-Level ad hoc Committee on the Crisis in Libya, stated:

> We are here to make a plea for an immediate humanitarian pause [in fighting] in order that the pressing needs of the populations affected can be met, a pause that should be followed by a cease-fire linked to the political process, in particular by starting with an inclusive and consensual transition.

The diplomatic efforts of the African Union were dismissed.

There had been over 600,000 foreign workers employed in the Libyan economy. By far the largest numbers of migrant workers were Africans from neighboring countries. When the NATO bombing campaign began, most states evacuated their citizens, but the poorer states in Africa did not have the resources to evacuate their own. Many of these migrant workers were caught in the crossfire and lost their lives and livelihoods.

The AU's diplomatic efforts brought out a number of realities. The most significant was that other states, when evacuating their nationals, were leaving Africans behind. More than 900 Africans drowned in the Mediterranean Sea, trying to escape the fighting in Libya. In one spectacular incident, two survivors reported the tragic story of a boat carrying 72 African immigrants that ran into difficulty trying to reach the Italian port of Lampedusa. The Africans on board, including women and children, were left to drift in the Mediterranean for sixteen days after a number of European military units apparently ignored their cries for help. Two of the nine survivors claimed this included a NATO ship. Despite alarms being raised with the Italian coast guard and the boat making contact with a military helicopter and a warship, no rescue effort was attempted. In fact, facing the prospect of hundreds of African migrants leaving Libya, France and Italy sought to work with other members of the EU to block their departures. As Africans drowned by the hundreds, these NATO states showed both their disregard for the International Maritime Law regarding Safety of Life at Sea (SOLAS) and their lack of respect for African lives.

Neither NATO nor the NTC was interested in the humanity of Africans. These forces were interested in removing Gaddafi from power, and having to negotiate with the African Union was seen as a minor irritation. With the clear intention of undermining the AU negotiations, on June 27, 2011, the Chief Prosecutor of the International Criminal Court issued an arrest warrant for Muammar Gaddafi, Saif al-Islam Gaddafi, and Abdullah al-Senussi, "for alleged criminal responsibility for the commission of murder and persecution as crimes against humanity from 15 February 2011 onwards. The charges related to actions of Libyan State apparatus and security forces in Tripoli, Benghazi, Misrata and elsewhere in Libya."

A Statement from African Intellectuals

Some African leaders had called on Gaddafi to step aside so that the negotiations could proceed. Gaddafi accepted this proposal, as Jean Ping, the chairperson of the AU, observed in his recapitulation of the efforts of the African Union to get NATO to stop the bombing and respect the Union's road map.[184] Africans had been opposed to the incessant bombing and called for a cease fire, and now worked for the establishment of an interim government. These proposals were rejected because the NATO forces were not interested in negotiations. Hugh Roberts, formerly of the International Crisis Group, summarized the position of the NATO handlers in this way:

> London, Paris and Washington could not allow a cease-fire because it would have involved negotiations, first about peace lines, peacekeepers and so forth, and then about fundamental political differences. And all this would have subverted the possibility of the kind of regime change that interested the Western powers. The sight of representatives of the rebellion sitting down to talks with representatives of Gaddafi's regime, Libyans talking to Libyans, would have called the demonization of Gaddafi into question. The moment he became once more someone people talked to and negotiated with, he would in effect have been rehabilitated. And that would have ruled out violent—revolutionary?—regime change and so denied the Western powers their chance of a major intervention in North Africa's [Arab] Spring, and the whole interventionist scheme would have flopped. The logic of the demonization of Gaddafi in late February, crowned by the referral of his alleged crimes against humanity to the International Criminal Court by Resolution 1970 and then by France's decision on 10 March to recognize the NTC as the sole legitimate representative of the Libyan people, meant that Gaddafi was banished forever from the realm of international political discourse, never to be negotiated with, not even about the surrender of Tripoli when in August he offered to talk

terms to spare the city further destruction, an offer once more dismissed with contempt.

This dismissal and contempt was promoted by Western media, which had undertaken a massive psychological warfare campaign against citizens of Libya's west in preparation for the execution of Gaddafi. In August 2011, after the NATO-led forces overran Tripoli, more than 200 African intellectuals issued an "Open Letter to the Peoples of Africa and the World from Concerned Africans." The letter started by stating explicitly that "our action to issue this letter is inspired by our desire, not to take sides, but to protect the sovereignty of Libya and the right of the Libyan people to choose their leaders and determine their own destiny. Libya is an African country."[185] The letter ended:

> Those who have brought a deadly rain of bombs to Libya today should not delude themselves to believe that the apparent silence of the millions of Africans means that Africa approves of the campaign of death, destruction and domination which that rain represents. We are confident that tomorrow we will emerge victorious, regardless of the death-seeking power of the most powerful armies in the world. The answer we must provide practically, and as Africans, is—when, and in what ways, will we act resolutely and meaningfully to defend the right of the Africans of Libya to decide their future, and therefore the right and duty of all Africans to determine their destiny! The AU road map remains the only way to peace for the people of Libya.

This statement from African intellectuals was one more manifestation of the residual resistance to external control that remained in Africa after decades of struggling against apartheid. It was not coincidental that the drafters of the letter had come from South Africa. It was the South African struggles that had been at the forefront of the fight against Western domination and the ideas of white supremacy. The U.S. military and foreign policy establishment had supported white minority regimes and Henry Kissinger had famously said, in

1969, that white power was there to stay in Africa, especially southern Africa. Through the integration of the media, financial houses, military, and oil companies, there had been a sustained attack on Africa as the place of "failed states." Gaddafi and his government had been the butt of Western media stereotypes. When the NATO attack began, Western media went into the archive of pictures and stories that demonized Gaddafi in order to carry out psychological warfare against citizens of the West, in a test of military information operation.

13—NATO in Libya as a Military Information Operation

From the start of its campaign in Libya, control over information was crucial to the mission of Global NATO. It was in this war that the differences among Al Jazeera, CNN, the BBC, and French media became less intense, and there was agreement between these news organizations that they would cooperate with those who were poking the fires of war. For the few days when the top sections of the U.S. military hesitated and there was equivocation from the White House, the corporate media vacillated. But Al Jazeera and the political establishment in the Gulf Cooperation Council understood the stakes involved in the Libyan Investment Authority, the Arab Banking Corporation, and the survival of Gaddafi.

Al Jazeera had championed the Arab Spring, but in the case of Libya the leaders of the Emirates were compromised by their relationship with the Intercontinental Exchange. Although Gaddafi had given the liberal reformers room for their dalliance with the energy brokers, the continued fallout of the financial crisis in Europe and America had stimulated the Libyan leadership to be more vigilant in relation to the operations of sovereign wealth funds. It was one thing for the liberals to consort with external bankers, but when it came to political survival, Saif al-Islam was no exception: he had to make a choice between his loyalty to the family and his intellectual and ideological inclinations. Once Saif al-Islam made the choice of sticking to the family, and not breaking to join his fellow "reform-minded" colleagues such as Mahmoud Jibril, he was fair game for the Western media, which dusted off the old propaganda against Gaddafi to be used for the NATO intervention.

From the time of Ronald Reagan, and even before, Gaddafi had been demonized by the Western media. In an effort to escape this demonization, Gaddafi had worked to abandon weapons of mass destruction and prevent Libya from being placed on the list of countries in the "Axis of Evil." Although the Libyan leadership worked hard to get their country off the U.S. State Department's list of terrorist states, and despite the negotiations over the Lockerbie affair and the huge payouts, the Western media never took away the label of terrorism when discussing the regime in Libya. Although Libya had joined the coalition of the "global war on terrorism," Libya remained a place for the mirth and mockery of the Western media. Even after Gaddafi had been dropped from the list of leaders sponsoring terrorism, Western media made great stories of his supposed eccentricities: his female bodyguards, pitching tents in foreign capitals, his voluptuous nurse, his claim to be the king of kings of Africa, etc.

We know from Wikileaks that Western security agencies paid close attention to "the eccentricities of Gadhafi."[186] These eccentricities were retooled for the military information operations once the NATO intervention began. For the Western media, it was a simple change of script from writing about Gaddafi's voluptuous Ukrainian nurse to writing about mass rapes being carried out by the Gaddafi regime. These tools of information warfare proved as potent as the bombs raining down from NATO jets.

The unspoken line by Western commentators was that any information coming out of Libya and Africa was propaganda, while any news coming out of NATO was information. Throughout the war, Western news agencies downplayed the hundreds of innocent civilians who were killed by seven months of incessant bombing. After the execution of Gaddafi and the "installation" of the NTC government, no less a news organization than the *New York Times* carried a lengthy rendition of the numbers of innocent civilians killed by NATO, stating that there were "scores of civilian casualties the alliance has long refused to acknowledge or investigate."[187] The journalists who produced the report on the killing of innocent civilians had this information as far back as June 2011, when the "precision strikes" failed and there were scores of civilian casualties.

This military failure of the air campaign brought back the sobering reality that "a broad spectrum of military capabilities" are required in "modern" warfare. Military specialists understood from the outset that air power and the assumption of air superiority would not be enough for the mission of "regime change." To be able to implement a no-fly zone, air superiority was indeed sufficient, and the NATO forces indeed had air superiority, but the ability to distinguish between friend and foe on the ground required assets that had to be put in place. These ground assets comprised regulars from Qatar and specialized forces from Britain, France, and the United States. In summing up the failures of the Libyan engagement, Michael Clarke concluded: "Few dispute the assertion that NATO jets enabled Libyan rebels to come knocking on Qadhafi's door in Tripoli. But as he falls, it will be difficult to avoid the conclusion that NATO emerges from this successful operation weaker than it went into it."[188]

Such a conclusion has not been part of the narrative in the mainstream media in the West. The Libyan exercise has become a vivid example of the integration of corporate media into the military planning of Western states.

Before the start of the operation, the media were central to the preparation of the public for the planned operation. The "reliable" information outlets, such as the BBC, CNN, Voice of America, Radio France International, and Al Jazeera, carried the line that Gaddafi was a "threat to his own people" as well as to the peace and security of Western interests. This demonization of Gaddafi was reinforced with unflattering images of the Libyan leader as a "crazy dictator." As journalist Lizzie Phelan summed up the interplay between information and war:

The war on Libya has not only been a war that has vindicated NATO's claim to the most powerful military force on earth, capable of imposing its will through sheer aggression wherever it sees fit, but it has also been a war that has reasserted the Western mainstream media's power to not just fabricate events but to create.[189]

The ability to create events came after years of experience of packaging information for warfare in the wars in Afghanistan and Iraq. These forms of marketing war had emerged out of the experiences of the Cold War, when the media worked with the military-industrial complex to sell war and militarism to U.S. citizens. This was achieved through the strategy of "threat inflation" which was employed to scare the Western world into the Cold War. Frank Kofsky, in *Harry S. Truman and the War Scare of 1948*, exposed the arrival of psychological warfare against U.S. citizens, scaring them that their way of life was threatened by communism. President Dwight Eisenhower had sought to damp down this war scare by warning of the dangers of the military-industrial complex, but his warnings were overshadowed by the intensity of the disinformation and psychological warfare against U.S. citizens.

Sophisticated media campaigns to market and propagate warfare did not end with the Cold War. In fact, with the advent of the war on terror they gave way to more sophisticated mechanisms, which Donald Rumsfeld, former U.S. Secretary of Defense, called "military information operations." Under his tenure, the Pentagon rolled out a comprehensive information onslaught that came under the rubric of Total Information Awareness (TIA). Under George W. Bush, Donald Rumsfeld, and Dick Cheney, the U.S. establishment rolled out this TIA program to take disinformation and psychological warfare to an entirely new level. According to the *New York Times,* the TIA program sought to "revolutionize the ability of the United States to detect, classify and identify foreign terrorists" by developing data-mining and profiling technologies that could analyze commercial transactions and private communications.

Total Information Awareness of transnational threats requires keeping track of individuals and understanding how they fit into models. To this end, T.I.A. seeks to develop architectures for integrating existing databases into a "virtual, centralized, grand database." In addition to analyzing financial, educational, travel and medical records, as well as criminal and other governmental records, the T.I.A. program could include the development of technologies to create risk profiles for millions of visitors and American citizens in its quest for suspicious patterns of behavior.[190]

The intrusiveness of this data-mining mechanism was so extensive that there was an outcry from liberals and the Pentagon dropped the label of Total Information Awareness—only to roll out an Information Operations Roadmap in 2003. Under this banner, the Army defined information operations to include psychological operations, deception, protecting vital data, electronic warfare, and computer network defense and attack. The repackaged TIA outlook was written to provide the U.S. Department of Defense with "a plan to advance the goal of information operations as a core military competency."[191] The Information Operations Roadmap elevated information operations to the same level as other military armed fighting capabilities, and one of its stated benefits was "adversary behavior modification."[192] In the document, Donald Rumsfeld notes that "the recommendations in the Information Operations Roadmap begin the process of developing IO into warfighting capability that will enable Combatant Commanders to target adversary decision-making while protecting our own."[193]

What Rumsfeld did not make explicit was that the United States also deployed information or tools of psychological warfare against its own citizens, controlling their decision making with the goal of gaining uninhibited support for the prosecution of wars around the globe. Russ Hoyle's book *Going To War: How Misinformation, Disinformation, and Arrogance Led America into Iraq* gave extensive details on the role of military information in the Iraq War.[194]

To be able to carry out a meaningful psychological warfare campaign in Africa, the intellectual infrastructure had to rise above the mediocrity of the Africanist establishment. This establishment had no credibility because the ideas of white supremacy had led the United States to be on the side of those who assassinated Patrice Lumumba and designated Nelson Mandela a terrorist. Conscious of this historic limitation, the Pentagon embarked on a special information program for Africa called "Operation Objective Voice." This plan was supplemented by a special social science research network to improve the efficiency of the Pentagon and the U.S. armed forces in Africa.

The psychological warfare and baggage of colonial history weakened the U.S. military, and this weakness was compounded by the intellectual impoverishment of the private military contractors who saw war in Africa as a new gravy train. Hence, though the United States could carry out psychological warfare and disinformation against its own citizens, it could only do this on a limited scale in Africa. For example, African workers returning to their respective countries gave a different picture of what was happening from what was being reported in European and U.S. news outlets. Newspapers in Ghana, Kenya, Namibia, Nigeria, Tanzania, Uganda, Zimbabwe, and South Africa carried detailed comments opposing the NATO war in Libya.

The opposition from African opinion makers takes us back to the information manipulation that preceded the U.S. invasion of Iraq and the deployment of top military experts on psychological operations (psy-ops) to employ mind control in manipulating some senators to support increased/sustained congressional funding for the war in Afghanistan.[195] After this psy-ops operation against the Senate, the top members of the Senate Armed Services Committee called for a federal audit of the Pentagon's "military information support operations" in light of concerns about their "growing cost and questionable merit." In February 2012, the newspaper USA Today reported that spending on information operations had peaked at $580 million in 2009, mostly for the wars in Iraq and Afghanistan.

During the year of the war against Libya, the Pentagon spent $355 million on military information operations. We can now assess the role of these operations in the battles for Tripoli.

Disinformation and Operation Dawn Mermaid:
When Is a War Not a War?

We now know from the strategic analyses and press reports that "Operation Dawn Mermaid," the code name for the secret plan to take Tripoli, had been hatched in the Tunisian city of Djerba in late April 2011, when the NATO leaders realized that the bombing alone would not dislodge the Gaddafi regime.[196] The plans for the military take-over of Tripoli had been discussed in Paris with Nicolas Sarkozy while NATO was intensifying the bombings.

From the same reports on Operation Dawn Mermaid we also know that special forces from France, Britain, and Qatar had been deployed after the UN resolution. According to the *New York Times,* "The United States provided intelligence, refueling and more precision bombing than Paris or London want to acknowledge. Inevitably, then, NATO air power and technology, combined with British, French and Qatari 'trainers' working 'secretly' with the rebels on the ground, have defeated the forces of Col. Muammar el-Qaddafi." Reuters, which had written about the plan to take Tripoli, reported that "former soldiers from an elite British commando unit, the Special Air Service, and other private contractors from Western countries were on the ground in the Libyan city of Misrata."[197] In the same report, it indicated that, according to *The Guardian,* private military contractors were "helping NATO identify possible targets in the heavily contested city and passing this information, as well as information about the movements of Gaddafi's forces, to a NATO command center in Naples, Italy. The newspaper reported that a group of six armed Westerners had been filmed by the Al Jazeera TV network talking to rebels in Misrata; the men fled after realizing they were being filmed."

The importance of these special forces was magnified in the wake of the counteroffensive against the ground forces that were being supported from the air. Though this information on the special forces was discussed in military journals and think tanks, for the broader U.S. public this information had to be kept out of the news because the Obama administration had handed over the operation to NATO and claimed before the Houses of Congress that there were "no boots on the ground" in Libya. This idea of boots on the ground referred to U.S. military personnel engaged in direct combat roles in Libya, but it conjured up old images of previous wars in Vietnam and Iraq and did not grasp the realities of the new forms of warfare that depended on drones, special forces, intelligence assets, and private military contractors working with regional militias. In March, President Obama had directed the CIA to deploy "assets" to carry out a "finding" on the nature of the NTC. Western newspapers carried reports of the coordination between the "rebels" and U.S. and British intelligence operatives on the ground: "C.I.A. Agents in Libya Aid Air Strikes and Meet Rebels."[198]

What these news reports sought was to keep out of the news the role of the elements in the NTC that Vijay Prashad called "America's Libyans." These were the "reformers," along with Khalifa Belqasim Hifter, the military commander who returned to Libya from Virginia to take charge of the military wing of the uprisings. One newspaper columnist called Hifter the "CIA person."[199] After spending twenty years in Virginia, waiting for the moment to be recalled by those who had worked inside and outside for the overthrow of Gaddafi, Hifter competed for the leadership of the rebellion's military wing with General Abdel Fatah Younis, who had been Gaddafi's interior minister until the rebellion broke out in Benghazi. Younis had been the former head of Libya's Special Forces and had defected to the Benghazi elements at the beginning of the uprising. In the first weeks of the uprising, when the U.S. Africa Command was claiming leadership of this NATO intervention, there had been intense rivalry between Younis and Hifter, with differing claims as to who led the armed wing.

In the middle of this wrangle, the Gaddafi government was able to recover its nerve sufficiently to launch a counteroffensive. According to a Royal United Services Institute report, "At the end of March, Qadhafi regime forces launched a counteroffensive on the eastern front. The rebels retreated in disarray from Bin Jawwad within a hundred miles of Sirte all the way to Ajdabiya, the same distance from Benghazi."[200] It was after this counteroffensive that the media war intensified.

The retreat of the rebel forces, two weeks after the start of the bombing, was never in the broader public domain because for most of March and April, after their deployment in Libya, the NATO forces depended on the media to disorient the Libyans while providing false information about what was going on. As the rebels "retreated in disarray" before Gaddafi's counteroffensive, William Hague, the British Foreign Secretary, stated that Gaddafi had fled to Venezuela.[201] This was a blatant lie and the best example of the disinformation campaign that was being waged. Other examples abound, such as journalists who were inside Libya bringing to the attention of the world the use of fake footage from a demonstration in India claiming it was in Tripoli's Green Square, as part of their evidence that the city had fallen.[202] These examples are only small snippets of the role of disinformation in diverting attention from the planning of Operation Dawn Mermaid. After the start of the air campaign, at the end of March 2011, NATO air strikes continued to pound Libyan military positions and units, while the ground war between Gaddafi's forces and the rebels took on a seesaw effect.

For citizens in Western Europe and North America, the media claimed that the Gaddafi regime would fall in a matter of weeks. Groups usually associated with European peace movements were particularly susceptible to this disinformation campaign that Europe was fighting for democracy and human rights in Libya. The entire spectrum of what could be called the European left—social democrats, former communists, socialists, and environmentalists—bought into the narrative and gave political support to their governments. In Germany, although the government had withdrawn from the military campaign, the left continued to support this NATO operation.

The disinformation campaign against Western citizens took on greater urgency after the congressional hearings on March 31, 2011. There, the first rumblings were heard from members of the U.S. Congress that if the Libyan intervention were to continue beyond a few weeks, then the president had to obtain permission through the War Powers Act. Speaking on the House floor on March 31, Congressman Dennis Kucinich said that Obama had already violated the War Powers Act with his initial bombings of Libya:

> The Congress through the War Powers Act provided the execu-
> tive with an exception to unilaterally respond only when the
> nation was in actual or imminent danger: to "repel sudden attacks."
> Today we are in a constitutional crisis because our chief executive
> has assumed for himself powers to wage war which are neither
> expressly defined nor implicit in the Constitution, nor permitted
> under the War Powers Act.[203]

The War Powers Resolution (often referred to as the War Powers
Act), passed in 1973 at the height of the Vietnam War, constrains the
Chief Executive from going to war without authorization from the
U.S. Congress. The act states that the powers of the president, as com-
mander in chief, to introduce U.S. forces into hostilities, or imminent
hostilities, can only be exercised pursuant to:

1. A declaration of war;
2. Specific statutory authorization; or
3. A national emergency created by an attack on the United States or
   its forces.

Under the War Powers Resolution, a president can initiate military action but must receive approval from Congress to continue the
operation within sixty days. If approval is not granted and the president
deems it an emergency, then an additional thirty days are granted for
ending operations.

Challenges to the legality of the military campaign against Libya
mounted as the progressive African American community, academics, peace activists, and politicians from both parties participated in an
outcry on whether the war in Libya met the criteria of a national emergency for the people of the United States. A hearing had been called on
the same day by the House Foreign Relations Committee on "Libya:
Defining U.S. National Security Interests." James Steinberg, the Deputy
Secretary of State, testified before the committee, but the statements
from members of the House were overwhelmingly opposed to the
actions of the president without authorization from Congress. It was

the full-throated opposition from representatives from the Congress that forced the administration and NATO to keep the real activities out of the news. Congressman Ron Paul, the notoriously conservative antiwar libertarian, said:

> Once again the American people are being suckered into one more war; illegal, unconstitutional and undeclared. We have been doing this since World War II and they have not been good for this country, and they have not been good for the world. This is said to be a war that is to prevent something. It is a preventative war. They say there is going to be a slaughter, but there has so far not been a slaughter. In checking the records the best I can, I have seen no pictures of any slaughter. But already it is reported now that our bombs have killed more than 40 civilians. So how can you save a country by killing civilians? This is a bad war. We got into it incorrectly. It will not help us. And unfortunately, I do not see that this administration or any administration is going to move back from this until we become totally bankrupt. It is very necessary for us to assess this properly. And the way we go to war is very important. Just not get token permission, we should never go to war without a full declaration and it should be strongly bipartisan.[204]

Whereas Paul's antiwar and anti-militaristic position was known, it was the opposition from Republicans that brought out the unpopularity of the U.S. engagement in Libya. Congressman Mike Pence, a conservative Republican from Indiana, and Congressman Jeff Duncan made scathing statements about the hypocrisy of the Libyan intervention, demanding that the cover of humanitarianism be lifted. When the bombs started raining down on Libya, the Obama administration had claimed that actions in Libya were not subject to the War Powers Resolution because they did not meet the definition of "hostilities."

By the end of May, after the sixty-day period, there was anxiety because the expected victory did not take place. As these debates were going on, Obama was focused on the question of Osama bin Laden and the best way forward. The national security establishment had known for years that bin Laden was in Pakistan and the Obama White House decided to take action. After the physical elimination of bin Laden in Pakistan, the administration could no longer put off Congress on the Libyan question and in June sent a thirty-two-page report to Congress stating: "U.S. military operations are distinct from the kind of hostilities contemplated by the Resolution's sixty-day termination provision." The report continued: "U.S. operations do not involve sustained fighting or active exchanges of fire with hostile forces, nor do they involve the presence of U.S. ground troops, U.S. casualties or a serious threat thereof, or any significant chance of escalation into a conflict characterized by those factors." The report also argued that NATO was leading the efforts in Libya and that U.S. strikes relied on remotely piloted drone planes.

This claim was a major failure on the part of the military/political establishment to legitimize its actions. The peace movement in the United States was opposed to war against Libya. In the African American community, leaders as diverse as Jesse Jackson, Louis Farrakhan, and former congresswoman Cynthia McKinney vociferously opposed this attack on Libya. In response to this mounting opposition in the United States, and as the factional struggles inside the NTC intensified, Nicolas Sarkozy took over the leadership in the coordination of Operation Dawn Mermaid.

Four months after the start of the NATO intervention, the Gaddafi regime had not fallen. As several towns and positions changed hands, strategic commentators saw the war grinding into a stalemate—with Gaddafi's forces controlling most of western Libya and the rebels most of the east. In the midst of this stalemate, the British media began to complain about the need for real-time information on the ground and strengthening intelligence, surveillance, target acquisition and reconnaissance missions (ISTAR). In the last week of April, the United States announced the introduction of its unmanned Predator drones to the war.

On April 30, 2011, the Libyan government announced that a NATO air strike had killed Gaddafi's youngest son, Saif al-Arab Gaddafi, age twenty-nine, and three of Gaddafi's grandchildren. Although there was jubilation in Benghazi, the failure to kill Gaddafi brought the debate about his execution out into the open. This attack on Gaddafi's family backfired and intensified opposition to the NATO intervention across Africa and the Middle East. Then Secretary-General of the Arab League, Amr Moussa, said, "What is happening in Libya differs from the aim of imposing a no-fly zone, and what we want is the protection of civilians and not the bombardment of more civilians." This attempt to assassinate Gaddafi brought out sharp differences between the civilian and military leadership in both Britain and the United States. The British Chief of the Defense Staff, General Sir David Richards, openly contradicted William Hague, the Foreign Secretary, stating that Gaddafi was not a target.[205] (William Hague and Liam Fox, the Defense Secretary had agreed that Gaddafi was a target.) Robert Gates in the United States sided with Sir David Richards, but by October the elements in Western financial circles who wanted Gaddafi dead had gained the ascendancy. Qatar, the base of the link between the oil giants and the financial wizards, was outside the arena where public pressure could constrain the actions of the government.

From the start of the military operations, the NATO alliance had been caught in a quagmire in Libya. States that were supposed to be fighting al Qaeda joined up with forces in Libya that had in the past been incarcerated in Guantánamo. While NATO was carrying out 150 missions per day—bombing and killing innocent civilians—the infighting and intrigues in Benghazi over the lines of authority over the varying militias were undermining the legitimacy of the NTC. In the international media, the question was persistently asked, "What is the NTC?" In the midst of this infighting, General Abdel Fatah Younis, the military leader of the rebellion, was arrested, shot and killed on July 28, 2011. Less than two weeks later, NTC president Mustafa Abdul Jalil ordered the dismissal of the NTC's executive committee. Mahmoud Jibril, the top leader of the NTC—who had been in on the planning of Operation Dawn Mermaid—was kept on to form the next cabinet. In the wake of the killing of Gen. Younis, the NATO forces decided that the planned "uprising" in Tripoli had to go forward.

14—Who Took Tripoli?

The infighting and intrigue among the militias compounded the weaknesses of NATO in Libya. Despite the coordination with special forces, the rivalries between the militias ensured that there could be no effective planning among them. NATO had been bombing Libya for nearly five months and the demands for ending the bombing had been growing louder. Opinion inside Africa for a negotiated settlement intensified, with African writers calling for the AU road map to be the basis for negotiations. The UN mandate for "the responsibility to protect" ran only until the end of September. Russia was calling for the reconvening of the Security Council to discuss the mandate of the no-fly zone. With the cooperation between Russia, China and South Africa in the Security Council, the military planners in NATO had no assurance that the UN Security Council mandate for action in Libya would be extended if the matter were brought up for discussion before the UN Security Council. For the Obama administration, the sixty-day period allowing the president to engage in "hostilities" without authorization from Congress was over. These external and internal factors impelled the orchestrators of Operation Dawn Mermaid to plan the seizure of Tripoli for August 10. However, the work to place the foreign troops and special forces in Tripoli had not been completed.

Since the April meeting held in Tunisia to organize the Tripoli "uprising," NATO had been working with the Gulf States to ferry troops and equipment to Libya. We know from a detailed Reuters report that this process took months, and that the battle for Misrata was a crucial aspect of the ability of Qatar to land equipment and personnel. In an interim report titled "Accidental Heroes," the Royal United Services Institute acknowledged the role of foreign troops in the assault on Tripoli:

> It is notable that, from April, the UAE established a Special Forces presence in the Zawiyah District and started to supply rebel forces in that area with equipment and provisions by air. Qatar also assumed a very large role; it established training facilities in both Benghazi and, particularly, the Nafusa Mountains on May 9 and acted as a supply route and conduit for French weapons and ammunition supplies to the rebels (notably in June), including by establishing an air strip at Zintan.[206]

European newspapers reported later that Qatar had fielded more than 5,000 troops to Libya to remove Gaddafi.[207] The British military commentary on the seizure of Tripoli also argued that this confidence in Qatar had been built up in Afghanistan:

> Western Special Forces could have confidence in the training roles undertaken by Qatar and the UAE, because the Special Forces in those countries have in turn been trained by the UK and France over many years. Furthermore, Jordanian and UAE Special Forces have increased their operational experience through long term deployments in Afghanistan.[208]

What was missing from the Western military analysis of who took Tripoli was the role played by Western media and Al Jazeera in the war propaganda campaign fabricating false studio images of the entry of the "rebels" in Tripoli. Lizzie Phelan, a British journalist on the ground, gave many examples of the confusion wrought by Al Jazeera on what was happening in the Tripoli "uprising." It is from the reports of journalists on the ground, as well as from following the day-by-day accounts, that one can reconstruct the different elements that constituted Operation Dawn Mermaid.

The reconstruction of NATO's triple assault—by air, land, and sea—to capture Tripoli was followed by military experts all over the world.[209] Operation Dawn Mermaid was initially meant to begin on August 10, but the Qatari troops, disguised as rebels, had not yet been in place in Zawiyah, Zintan and Ghanyan. In Washington, new demands for "boots on the ground" were made when the security establishment grasped the fact that the August 10 date for the capture of Tripoli was approaching without the necessary forces and equipment in place. The desperation within the foreign policy establishment was quite explicit as a commentator from the conservative Jamestown Foundation, in Washington, D.C., produced a report on August 9 stating that, to avoid a worst-case scenario, "the coalition can continue the war of attrition for a long time to come, eroding Gaddafi's forces but also the coalition's own reputation at the same time. It can also resort to an abrupt escalation of air strikes."[210]

The intensified bombing in the two-week period before August 19 contributed to hundreds of civilian deaths. Human Rights Watch, in its report *Unacknowledged Deaths: Civilian Casualties in NATO's Air Campaign in Libya,* revealed the number of civilian casualties in this war.[211] The 82-page report, issued after NATO declared victory, reinforced the argument that it was innocent civilians who perished in this regime change operation that had been billed as "responsibility to protect." In this "War of Contradictions," NATO was compounding the failure to protect civilians by killing them. The entire propaganda for the West had been based on the idea of protecting civilians, but after the pitched battles it was clear that the NATO operation was not for a no-fly zone, but for regime change.

The Western fear of a diplomatic breakthrough intensified when the African Union announced that Gaddafi was willing to step aside in order to facilitate negotiations. The indictment of Gaddafi and his son by the International Criminal Court in June was one more act to bar a negotiated settlement.[212] What was kept out of the international news was the contradiction of labeling Gaddafi a criminal before the international community while turning to another indicted leader, Omar Bashir of Sudan, to support the regime change option. Bashir had his own grievance against Gaddafi because Khalil Ibrahim, from the Darfur region of Sudan, had taken refuge in Libya. Contradictions grew as the Sudanese intelligence services cooperated with NATO and the Gulf Cooperation Council in Libya.

From the Human Rights Watch *Unacknowledged Deaths* report, it is possible to grasp the escalation of air strikes and the push for NATO forces to capture Tripoli. In order to prepare for the assault on the capital there had been intensified air strikes—particularly in the period August 16–18—in the zones immediately east of Tripoli. In order to tip the balance on the side of the special forces and private contractors, the Pentagon sent extra Predator drones to Libya. "It was a controversial issue even as to whether it made sense to pull [drones] from other places to boost this up to try to bring this to a quicker conclusion. Those who backed the use of extra drones won, and the last two Predators were taken from a training base in the United States and sent to north Africa, arriving on August 16." By this time, elements in the U.S. foreign policy establishment such as Richard Haass of the Council on Foreign Relations had been won over to the side calling for intensified U.S. military involvement on the ground.

With the intensified air strikes and coordination, NATO deemed August 19 to August 20 to be the right moment to capture Tripoli. The signal for the NATO- supported "rebels" to "rise up" to take Tripoli was given by the chairman of the NTC:

> The signal to attack came soon after sunset on August 20, in a speech by NTC Chairman Mustafa Abdel Jalil. "The noose is tightening," he said. A "veritable bloodbath" was about to occur. Within 10 minutes of his speech, rebel cells in neighborhoods across Tripoli started moving. Some units were directly linked to the operation; many others were not but had learned about the plan.[213]

Western press then took up the most important aspect of the military information operations: disinformation to confuse the citizens of Tripoli. Nicholas Pelham, from the *New York Times,* gave one account of the coordination in the *New York Review of Books:*

> On Saturday, August 20, as dusk descended and the mosques sounded the prayer call for breakfast, Mustafa Abdel Jalil, Qaddafi's meek-seeming former justice minister who now heads the NTC, went on television to deliver an address. Before he had finished, the rebel flag was flying over Suq al-Juma and other Tripoli neighborhoods. Meanwhile, NATO forces intensified their bombardment of loyalist positions on the Western outskirts of Tripoli, stretching to its limits their UN mandate to protect civilians. As the colonel's forces abandoned their bases, they found themselves sandwiched between rebels sweeping in from the mountains and Tripolitans carving out their own enclaves. Challenged on multiple fronts, Qaddafi's forces melted away.[214]

In August 20, the world was told that there was an uprising in Tripoli and that the overthrow of the regime was imminent. However, journalists on the ground gave a different account of the confusion in Tripoli between August 20 and August 24. Journalist Lizzie Phelan reported:

> On the first day after rebels from sleeper cells inside Tripoli emerged and began attacking checkpoints manned by Libyan Special Forces. As is the pattern with their advance into areas on the way to the capital, they faced a swift initial defeat. But with the first images emerging around the world of the rebels inside Tripoli, NATO ensured it would not be short-lived. The organization sanctioned to "protect civilians" rapidly moved to bomb all checkpoints in the densely packed city. The vast majority of these were manned by volunteers—i.e., ordinary citizens that had been armed with Kalashnikovs since the beginning of the crisis—so that the rebels could easily move into the city by sea and by road. This was followed by masses of youth and other residents in the capital

pouring into the streets to defend their city, as they had pledged to do during the mass rallies.[215]

Faced with the spontaneous resistance of urban dwellers who resisted foreign occupation, NATO intensified the bombing of checkpoints held by urban residents. By this time, there were enough special forces on the ground to assist NATO in the precision bombing that the military analysts like to boast about. Given the importance of the control of information, NATO bombed the main broadcasting station in Tripoli. Nationalist sentiment among the urban population was captured by Hala Misrati, the female presenter on the state-run TV, who waved a gun and said that she was ready to die for her country. (It was significant that the presenter did not say she was willing to die for Gaddafi.)

On Sunday, August 21, while the NATO forces were moving to capture the media outlets controlled by the Gaddafi regime, the international media, along with the psychological operations sector, added to the confusion about what was going on in Tripoli by announcing that Gaddafi's sons had been captured and that Gaddafi and other family members had fled the country. Late the following evening, Saif al-Islam turned up at the Rixos, the Tripoli hotel where foreign reporters were staying, to say, "I am here to disperse the rumors."

The appearance of Saif al-Islam and reports that Gaddafi had been driving around the city rallying supporters led NATO to intensify the bombing, which now concentrated on the supporters of the Libyan government at Gaddafi's compound of Bab al-Azizia. From Phelan, we learned that government supporters were bombed 63 times in one day:

> Following relentless bombardment, the masses were pushed back to Gaddafi's compound Bab al-Azizia where they resisted the rebels' advance for a further 24 hours. It was during this time that Saif al-Islam, who until then the media and International Criminal Court had been insisting was captured and arrested, showed up at the Rixos Hotel where we were trapped. Calm and confident, he took out a group of journalists to Bab al-Azizia where upon their

return they confirmed seeing thousands in and around the compound waving the green flag, including as the tribes had pledged,
from their people across the country. But like the peaceful march
in the western mountains on 24 July, which was attacked by NATO
and the rebels, the masses in Bab al-Azizia were broken up by
NATO bombing an entrance for the rebels and attacks by Apache
gunships. The same fate was visited upon gatherings in Green
Square. Bab al-Azizia alone was reported to have been bombed 63
times during that time.[216]

The fighting for Tripoli went on for at least three days following
the intense bombing. When the state-run television station, the Bab
al-Azizia compound, and Green Square were captured, NATO forces
declared victory. Even while fighting was continuing, President Obama
broke his vacation in Martha's Vineyard to declare: "The Gadhafi
regime is coming to an end, and the future of Libya is in the hands of
its people."

Which people he referred to was not clear. Also unclear was the cost
to citizens who had not supported NATO and the Islamist forces that
were active in the capture of Tripoli. By the end of August, Gaddafi's
wife and children crossed the border to Algeria. Between August 20
and October 20 the focus of the war turned to the capture of Gaddafi.
Before we turn to those events, it is important to highlight the atrocities
that were carried out by the "rebels," with particular reference to the
destruction and dispersal of the people of Tawergha.

15—TAWERGHA AND THE MYTH
OF THE AFRICAN MERCENARIES

The fighting in Tripoli went from neighborhood to neighborhood, with NATO planes and Apache helicopters supporting the ground forces that were in the process of seizing the city of Tripoli. Once the Western media focused on the Libyan leadership that led the assault on Green Square and on the Gaddafi compound, the leader who emerged as head of the Tripoli Military Council was Abdelhakim Belhadj (or Abdul Hakim Belhadj). Here was another contradiction for states that had been fighting jihadists.

Belhadj had been a military commander of the Libya Islamic Fighting Group who received his first military training from U.S.-supported elements fighting against the Soviet occupation in Afghanistan. After his service in Afghanistan, Belhadj was arrested in Malaysia and rendered to Libya by the CIA. (He has recently filed a lawsuit against the British for complicity in torture he sustained following his rendition.) Belhadj had long been associated with the opposition to Gaddafi and the Libyan Islamic Fighting Group's abortive armed struggle in the Benghazi region. As Luis Martinez explained in *Libyan Paradox*, "Between 1995 and 1998, the LIFG carried out guerrilla operations against the security forces in the Benghazi region, prompting a military response on the part of the regime in the form of bombing raids on the mountainous regions of Jebel al Akhadar where the militants had their hideouts."[217]

What the LIFG was unable to accomplish on its own against Gaddafi in the 1990s, it did with NATO's assistance in 2011. The "victory" of the forces that made up the Tripoli Military Council came at a very high price for hundreds of thousands of Libyans. This is because the nature of the fighting pitched neighbors against neighbors when the Libyan armed forces of Gaddafi collapsed early in the "rebellion."

The Libyan armed forces had been degraded under Gaddafi because the regime feared a *coup d'état*. This fear intensified after the rebellion broke out and officers such as Younis defected. Western reports on the divisions in the army outline the depth of the infiltration of the Libyan establishment after years of seeking reconciliation with Western states. Saif al-Islam had developed deep relations with the intellectual front-persons for imperialism and Muammar Gaddafi had enabled the imperial intervention by his close collaboration with their intelligence agencies.

During the initial stages of the integrated Qatar/special forces/private military contractors assault on Tripoli, the spokesman for Gaddafi boasted that the regime had 65,000 armed personnel ready to defend Tripoli. Yet when the special forces of NATO and Qatar entered the capital, with Belhadj as the head of the Tripoli Military Council, the 65,000 troops who were supposed to defend Tripoli were nowhere to be seen. It devolved upon the citizens opposed to NATO to defend their communities.

The mythical 65,000 personnel had been superseded by militias under Gaddafi's sons. These "paramilitary" forces were better at internal repression than dealing with foreign threats. The annual studies of the International Institute of Strategic Studies and from the Stockholm International Peace Research Institute presented detailed information on military expenditures under Gaddafi. According to these sources, there were supposed to be over 120,000 armed persons in Libya by January 2011: Army, 45,000; paramilitary, 40,000; Air Force, 8,000; Air Defense, 15,000; and Navy, 8,000.[218] Undoubtedly, the Libyan armed forces were no match for the sophisticated weaponry of Britain, Canada, France, the United States, and other forces of NATO. The Vietnamese had shown that political mobilization and organization of citizens to defend their society could neutralize superior weaponry, but Gaddafi did not learn this elementary lesson.

Although the Libyan armed forces were composed of a number of paramilitary forces and security services, these armed elements acted as a means of controlling the power of the regular military and providing Gaddafi and his family with security. The narrative of "tribal" loyalties ensured that the military units around Sirte, the birthplace of Gaddafi, were the best equipped and the most loyal. Libya had billions of dollars, but Gaddafi did not know how to buy and maintain weapons, or how to spend money in uplifting the technical and intellectual level of the army. Saif al-Islam, in dabbling with Islam and neoliberalism, only served to confuse the soldiers as to where they should stand. Thus, when a real war emerged, Gaddafi, who had been spending about a billion dollars per year on weapons, was full of bluster but had no real army.

Western military analysts that had studied Gaddafi closely told anyone who wanted to know that between 1970 and 2009, the Gaddafi regime had spent more than $30 billion. As Luis Martinez said in *The Libyan Paradox*, "Libya had to keep many of its aircraft and over 1,000 of its tanks in storage. Its other army equipment purchases require far more manpower than its small active army and low-quality reserves can provide. Its overall ration of weapons to manpower is absurd, and Libya has compounded its problems by buying a wide diversity of equipment types that make it all but impossible to create an effective training and support base." The military analysts who were writing on the absurdity of Gaddafi's military planning and arms purchases came from the same countries that were competing to sell him new weapons. When Gaddafi had visited France in 2007, the regime had ordered billions of dollars for military "modernization." The United States had been eager to get in on this sale of weaponry, and when the rebellion broke out the U.S. military had been trying to convince Congress that it should be given permission to sell weapons to Libya.

The military modernization did not protect the Libyan citizens: when the NATO bombings began, ordinary Libyans got caught between the different factions and militias fighting to take power. In this fight, the people who suffered the most were the dark-skinned Libyans and African migrant workers who were dubbed "Gaddafi's African mercenaries." This narrative of African mercenaries became pervasive after the battles for Misrata.

After the NATO forces decimated the ordnance and anti-aircraft assets of the Gaddafi regime, the battles for control of cities took on vicious proportions, with young fighters driving on the back of converted fighting vehicles known as "technicals." Among these battles the fight for the control of Misrata was one of the biggest, and the most decisive in the war. Before the forces of NATO and Qatar seized the airport at Misrata, toward the end of April, the city was the site of one of the most intense struggles. It was in the midst of the struggle for Misrata that the military information structures declared that Misrata was under siege from African mercenaries. Libyan citizens from the surrounding towns that opposed the "rebels" were marked for revenge during the months of siege. Tawergha was one of those towns—during the fighting, the rebels would put black-skinned African residents on international TV, claiming them as examples of the African mercenaries fighting for Gaddafi.

It is estimated that over one million African migrant workers had flocked to Libya to find work, and many of these were now caught in the anti-African hysteria. However, the Libyans who felt the brunt of the retaliation of the militias from Misrata were the residents of neighboring Tawergha, where the majority of residents were dark-skinned Libyans. The African Union intensified its diplomatic actions when the news began to be reported internationally of the racist attacks against black Africans. Jean Ping, chairman of the Commission of the African Union, decried the attacks on black Africans and reiterated the reasons why the AU wanted to see an inclusive government in Libya. "Blacks are being killed," Ping declared. "Blacks are having their throats slit. Blacks are accused of being mercenaries. Do you think it's normal in a country that's a third black that blacks are confused with mercenaries?

There are mercenaries in Libya, many of them are black, but there are not only blacks and not all blacks there are mercenaries. Sometimes, when they are white, they call them 'technical advisors.'"

This reminder that Libya is in Africa and that a third of the country is black was meant for those celebrating the success of a NATO mission to protect Africans that had ended up killing Africans. In a lengthy report for *Monthly Review,* Maximilian Forte provided a detailed assessment of how Al Jazeera engineered this myth of African mercenaries.[219] Forte and Lizzie Phelan grasped the disinformation war that was going on in labeling Africans as mercenaries when the Libyan people resisted NATO. Forte later developed a lengthy analysis of the myths associated with the ouster of Gaddafi. One of these myths was that of the African mercenaries:

> Black prisoners were put on display for the media (which is a violation of the Geneva Convention), but Amnesty International later found that all the prisoners had supposedly been released since none of them were fighters, but rather were undocumented workers from Mali, Chad, and West Africa. The myth was useful for the opposition to insist that this was a war between "Gaddafi and the Libyan people," as if he had no domestic support at all—an absolute and colossal fabrication such that one would think only little children could believe a story so fantastic. The myth is also useful for cementing the intended rupture between "the new Libya" and Pan-Africanism, realigning Libya with Europe and the "modern world" which some of the opposition so explicitly crave.[220]

After NATO installed Belhadj as the head of the Tripoli Military Council, the robbing, killing, and abduction of black residents in Libya reached the point where Tawergha became a ghost town. This council did not have authority beyond the confines of the protected bases in Tripoli, and the Misrata militias took the law into their own hands to wreak revenge upon the citizens of Tawergha for their supposed role in the three-month siege of Misrata. The 35,000 residents of Tawergha were driven out of their homes. In December, a BBC reporter visited the bombed remnants of what had been a town and reported:

> As you enter Tawergha from the main road, the name is erased from the road sign. It is now eerily silent but for the incongruously beautiful birdsong. There were a few cats skulking about, and one skeletal, limping dog. Building after building is burnt and ransacked. The possessions of the people who lived here are scattered about, suggesting desperate flight. In places, the green flags of the former regime still flutter from some of the houses. Buildings show the scars of heavy bombardment, some are burnt-out shells, some are just abandoned. The town is empty of humans, apart from a small number of Misratan militiamen preventing the return of the town's residents.[221]

A Commission of Inquiry appointed by the UN Human Rights Council concluded in March 2012 that Misrata militias had committed crimes against humanity of torture and killings of Tawerghans. "The Misrata *thuwar* [anti-Gaddafi forces] have killed, arbitrarily arrested and tortured Tawerghans across Libya." [222] When Africans attempted to focus attention on the rape and wanton murder of hundreds of black Libyans, the world was not paying attention because the international media was fixated on the search for Gaddafi, who had escaped when the NATO-backed Tripoli Military Council took over the buildings in Tripoli.

After the ethnic cleansing of Tawergha, the NATO bombs turned to the region of Sirte, the home of Gaddafi. Sirte had another importance for Africa—it was the scene of the 1999 declaration that gave birth to the Constitutive Act of the African Union. This historic site was bombed to smithereens after August 20. While NATO bombed, NTC militias and international special forces agents from Qatar, France, and Great Britain moved to control surrounding communities in order to wipe out the last major pocket of resistance to regime change. According to NATO's own figures, the bombing of Sirte resulted in 427 "key hits" from August 25 to September 29. By the end of October, all of the major buildings in Sirte had been destroyed. With bombs dropping from the sky and NTC militias shelling the city with everything they had at their disposal—tanks, artillery, and Grad rockets—thousands were killed in Sirte. But the real target was Gaddafi, who had made his way out of Tripoli to Sirte.

16—THE EXECUTION OF GADDAFI

The details of the escape of Colonel Gaddafi from Tripoli and the bombing of the convoy ferrying him from Sirte have been provided for posterity by Mansour Dhao Ibrahim, an aide to Gaddafi who survived the NATO attack on the convoy. Dhao, who was then the head of the People's Guard, was with Gaddafi during his final days and told Human Rights Watch officials on Saturday, October 23, 2011, how he was wounded and Gaddafi was killed. According to Dhao:

> The decision for Gaddafi to stay in Sirte was based on Muatassim, the colonel's son. . . . Gaddafi's son and the military entourage had reasoned that the city, long known as an important pro-Qaddafi stronghold and under frequent bombardment by NATO air strikes, was the last place anyone would look.

It was further revealed that

> the colonel traveled with about 10 people, including close aides and guards. Muatassim, who commanded the loyalist forces, traveled separately from his father, fearing that his own satellite

phone was being tracked. Apart from a phone, which the colonel used to make frequent statements to a Syrian television station that became his official outlet, Colonel Qaddafi was largely cut off from the world.

It was this satellite phone that was tracked, so that when Sirte was bombed to smithereens, there was only one option left for Gaddafi, and that was to make a run to escape.

After August 21, 2011, British newspapers *The Telegraph* and *The Independent* had been reporting that British SAS forces and U.S. special forces had been scouring the Sirte area for Gaddafi, unable to find him. According to these reports, when the resistance continued for two months, the British and U.S. special forces on the ground, disguised as Libyan NTC fighters, had been coordinating the bombing campaign of Sirte. These forces synchronized the bombing, and one or two weeks before the execution, "NATO had pinpointed Gaddafi's position after an intelligence breakthrough." Once the SAS and the coordinating forces confirmed Gaddafi's position, "an American drone and an array of NATO eavesdropping aircraft had been trained on his Sirte stronghold to ensure he could not escape."

The possibility of escape had been uppermost in the minds of Africans who had followed the Libyan support for Idi Amin of Uganda in the 1978–79 Kagera war. When the Tanzanian army had taken control of most of the cities in Uganda, the Tanzanian military left the road to Jinja open so that Idi Amin and the Libyans who supported him could escape. Amin used this route to leave Uganda and died peacefully in his sleep in Saudi Arabia twenty-four years later. Tanzania was not fighting against Idi Amin personally, but against the reign of terror he had brought on Uganda. Gaddafi had supported Idi Amin, but he did not learn the major lessons of that Libyan intervention and the Kagera war. We know that Gaddafi escaped to Sirte.

Reports in the international media are that some of the security officials around Gaddafi engaged private security firms through a British security outfit in Kenya. These reports stated that a team of South African mercenaries had helped Muammar Gaddafi's family out of the war zone of Tripoli, to hide out in Algeria. After this operation, a second team was supposed to have gone to Libya to assist the escape of Gaddafi. However, newspapers knowledgeable about the historic operations of British intelligence in Africa stated: "Intelligence sources believe there were agents among the mercenaries, or in some of the security companies, who were spying for the transitional government and reporting the mercenaries' movements."

This information on the role of double agents, some of whom were killed in the attack on the convoy on the morning of October 20, will help the reader in understanding the debates within the National Security Council of the Obama administration, on what to do with Gaddafi once he was caught.[223] According to the *New York Times,*

> There were sharp divisions within Libya's Transitional National Council about what to do with Colonel Qaddafi, according to American officials. Some argued that he should be tried in the country; others said it would impose too big a burden on an interim administration dealing with so many other problems. The ambivalence was mirrored on the American side, with some in the administration concerned that Libya did not have the resources to conduct a proper trial, while others worried that pressuring the Libyans to send him to an international tribunal in The Hague would be viewed as encroaching on their sovereignty.[224]

In this article, "Before Qaddafi's Death, U.S. Debated His Future," Mark Landler stated that the White House had considered the killing of Gaddafi as one of three scenarios. The article also said that "putting the colonel on trial, either in Libya or The Hague, was one of a host of situations for which the administration planned."

It devolved on the Secretary of State, Hillary Clinton, to clear up any ambivalence about what to do with Gaddafi if he were captured. Clearly operating on the basis of specific information, Clinton traveled to Tripoli on October 18 to stiffen the nerve of would-be waverers in the NTC. She was reported to have said in Tripoli, "We hope he can be captured or killed soon."[225]

NTC militias and NATO special forces had blocked road exits from Sirte by October 15, and around the same time the debates on execution intensified; the drones were deployed to ensure that Gaddafi did not escape from Sirte. This military operation to block anyone leaving Sirte (essentially a no-drive zone) ensured that hundreds of innocent civilians were killed. For NATO and their surrogates in the NTC, the no-fly zone to protect civilians did not extend to the citizens of Sirte.

U.S. Drones and French Jets: Pinpointing Gaddafi's Location

History has the benefit of the testimony of Mr. Dhao to reconstruct the gory details of the execution of Gaddafi. The *New York Times* carried his full narrative before NATO's military information and psychological warfare sectors could manage the news:

> About two weeks ago, as the former rebels stormed the city center, the colonel and his sons were trapped shuttling between two houses in a residential area called District No. 2. They were surrounded by hundreds of former rebels, firing at the area with heavy machine guns, rockets and mortars. "The only decision was whether to live or to die," Mr. Dhao said. Colonel Qaddafi decided it was time to leave, and planned to flee to one of his houses nearby, where he had been born. On Thursday, a convoy of more than 40 cars was supposed to leave at about around 3 a.m.[226]

With voice-recognition technology picking up any call made by Gaddafi, the drones were called in when the convoy carrying Gaddafi was pinpointed. The *Daily Telegraph* of Britain reported:

> They built up a normal pattern of life picture so that when something unusual happened this morning such as a large group of vehicles gathering together, that came across as highly unusual activity and the decision was taken to follow them and prosecute an attack. Electronic warfare aircraft, either an American Rivet

Joint or a French C160 Gabriel, also picked up Gaddafi's movements as he attempted to escape.[227]

On the day that Gaddafi was executed, British journalists were not shy to report in the newspapers that U.S. and British special forces were coordinating the hunt for Gaddafi, and that he had been given a code name similar to how the U.S. had given the name "Geronimo" to Osama bin Laden. The reporting from Mr Dhao on the last days of Gaddafi were reported in the Western media two days after the execution.

> In a Toyota Land Cruiser, Colonel Qaddafi traveled with his chief of security, a relative, the driver and Mr. Dhao. The colonel did not say much during the drive. NATO warplanes and former rebel fighters found them half an hour after they left. When a missile struck near the car, the airbags deployed, said Mr. Dhao, who was hit by shrapnel in the strike. He said he tried to escape with Colonel Qaddafi and other men, walking first to a farm, then to the main road, toward some drainage pipes. "The shelling was constant," Mr. Dhao said, adding that he was struck by shrapnel again and fell unconscious. When he woke up, he was in the hospital.

Sensitive to the repercussions of this attack on the convoy, the British media declared early on that the Royal Air Force had not been involved in the aerial attack. In contrast to this equivocation by the British media, and with great bravado, the French took credit for firing the missile that stopped the car carrying Colonel Gaddafi. French Defense Minister Gerard Longuet revealed that a French Mirage-2000 fired a warning shot at a column of several dozen vehicles fleeing Sirte.

The military failures of NATO in Libya were now compounded by the violation of the Geneva Conventions in relation to the summary execution of prisoners of war. The bombing of the innocent civilians in Sirte had been a violation of the Geneva Conventions. When the grainy pictures from cell phone cameras appeared on the World Wide Web, it became even clearer that the nature of the killing of Gaddafi was a clear violation of the Geneva Conventions on the humane treatment of prisoners. Hence the continued effort by NATO headquarters to manage the information on the circumstances surrounding Gaddafi's last moments.

Managing the News of the Nature of Gaddafi's Demise

Video footage shows that Gaddafi was wounded and alive after the air strike. Later footage showed a bruised and bloodied dead Gaddafi. There is also video footage of the humiliating sodomization of the wounded Gaddafi. Additionally, there is video footage of Mutassim, Gaddafi's son, alive and then dead. He was smoking a cigarette and drinking water, and in the next video he had a wound on his chest that had clearly not been there before.

In stumbling and clumsy attempts to control the story, the repackaged account from the NTC was that Gaddafi was killed in crossfire. This idea was repeated by the Western news outlets during the first two days after the reports of the death of Gaddafi. But the inconsistencies were so blatant that it was embarrassing for NATO's psychological warfare experts. Was it crossfire, was it a stray bullet, was it an assassination? There were too many cell-phone images of what transpired for the Western intelligence agencies to attempt to cover the clear violation of international law. One British reporter wrote of the killing in this way:

> Frame by jerky frame, through footage from jostling hand-held camera phones, we watched as the Libyan leader was dragged through the dust, wounded and blood-caked, to a soundtrack of shouting and gunfire. And then the sequel: his corpse cleaned up and on display, a macabre tourist attraction laid out for mockery inside a walk-in fridge.

Another report commented that the synchronization of the attack on the convoy had been orchestrated by Western special forces, who called in the Misrata militias to ensure that Gaddafi was executed. After the execution, the Misrata elements of the "uprising" hijacked the bodies of Gaddafi and his son, and kept them in a meat freezer in Misrata. Humiliation was piled upon total disrespect for religious and traditional customs, as the bodies were made a public spectacle. When the bodies started to decompose, they could no longer keep them, and Gaddafi and his son were buried in the desert. It was the view of those who queried this execution that the orchestrators of the NATO intervention and the financiers who had been using the resources of the Libyan Investment Authority leaders figured that as long as Gaddafi was alive and at liberty, the NTC had no chance of establishing its legitimacy and a stable administration, and of calling an end to the war.

One day after the assassination, NATO was so embarrassed by the gruesome sodomization that the press release distanced NATO from the assassination. I quote the press release in full:

Now that NATO has had the opportunity to conduct a post-strike assessment of yesterday's strike, we are able to provide a more comprehensive picture of events. At approximately 08h30 local time (GMT+2) on Thursday 20 October 2011, NATO aircraft struck 11 armed military vehicles which were part of a larger group of approximately 75 vehicles maneuvering in the vicinity of Sirte. These vehicles were leaving Sirte at high speed and were attempting to force their way around the outskirts of the city. The vehicles had a substantial amount of mounted weapons and ammunition, posing a significant threat to the local civilian population.

The convoy was engaged by NATO aircraft to reduce the threat. Initially, only one vehicle was destroyed, which disrupted the convoy and resulted in many vehicles dispersing and changing direction.

After the disruption, a group of approximately 20 vehicles continued at great speed to proceed in a southerly direction, due west of Sirte, and continuing to pose a significant threat. NATO again engaged these vehicles with another air asset. The post-strike assessment revealed that approximately 10 pro-Qadhafi vehicles were destroyed or damaged.

At the time of the strike, NATO did not know that Qadhafi was in the convoy. NATO's intervention was conducted solely to reduce the threat towards the civilian population, as required to do under our UN mandate. As a matter of policy, NATO does not target individuals.

We later learned from open sources and Allied intelligence that Qadhafi was in the convoy and that the strike likely contributed to his capture. NATO does not divulge specific information on national assets involved in operations.[228]

Such statements could not cover up the widespread disgust and condemnation of NATO internationally.

One month after Gaddafi's execution, Saif al-Islam was captured in the south of Libya. He was arrested and flown to Zintan by airplane, where he was detained by militants from this region. These militants refused to hand over Saif al-Islam to the central authorities, who had moved from Benghazi to Tripoli. This refusal was one more manifestation of the disorder and lack of central political control that had erupted in Libya after the NTC declared victory. The strength of the regional militias deepened the destabilization of Libya, with regional militias staking out territory in a manner similar to Somalia. By the time of the capture of Saif al-Islam, the regional militias were stronger than the interim government's forces and had resorted to jockeying for power against each other. Samir Amin asked the question: "Was the target of the intervention the destruction of Libya?" In recognition that the appearance of these militias struck an even heavier blow than the reports of the deaths of hundreds of civilians, NATO went into damage control instead of the euphoria that was being echoed in the Western press.

17—NATO's Libyan Mission:
A Catastrophic Failure

Was there morality to the insurrection? It is important not to be misdirected by this philosophical detour from Bernard-Henri Lévy:

> There is, in the spectacle of Gaddafi's lynching, something revolting. Worse, I fear that it will pollute the essential morality of an insurrection that had been, up to that point, almost exemplary. And anyone who knows something about revolutionary history knows that this could be the tipping point at which a democratic uprising begins to degenerate into its opposite.[229]

This expression of revulsion by one of the architects of the Western "humanitarian" mission to Libya—Bernard-Henri Lévy—was one indication of the scale of hypocrisy of the Western intellectual establishment. Lévy made a self-congratulatory film, *The Oath of Tobruk,* where he celebrated how he changed the course of history with one long-distance phone call to Sarkozy, in which he convinced the French president to meet and recognize the rebel leaders of the NTC. He continues to be caught in the morass of confusion among British and

French intellectuals who want to claim the high ground of preventing genocide and the deposing of the Gaddafi demon. Not only was this NATO intervention a success, but the intervention was a model to prevent Rwanda-style genocide.

One year after the UN Security Council resolution on "responsibility to protect," it is clear that the threat of "genocide" was exaggerated in order to precipitate Western military intervention in North Africa. From the time of the incessant bombing Amr Moussa distanced the Arab League from the bombing campaign. The African Union was explicit in its opposition to the NATO bombings. The United Nations Human Rights Council and independent human rights organizations around the world called for investigations into war crimes committed by NATO. In response to these calls, Luis Moreno-Ocampo, the former Prosecutor of the International Criminal Court, told the United Nations Security Council on November 2, 2011, that NATO troops would be investigated alongside rebel soldiers and regime forces for alleged breaches of the laws of war during the battle to overthrow Col. Muammar Gaddafi.[230] In a briefing to the Security Council, Moreno-Ocampo said, "There are allegations of crimes committed by NATO forces [and] these allegations will be examined impartially and independently."

These statements were made before a Security Council that wanted answers as to the manner of Muammar and Mutassim Gaddafi's killings. In the immediate aftermath of Gaddafi's execution, the discovery of 53 corpses at the Mahari Hotel and another ten dumped in a nearby reservoir revealed the extent of the bloodletting, indiscriminate killings, and blatant disregard for the basic security of persons. After the assassination, international human rights advocates reminded Western citizens that Article 13 of the Third Geneva Convention clearly states: "Prisoners of war must at all times be protected, particularly against acts of violence or intimidation and against insults and public curiosity."

In August 2011, when African intellectuals and the court of African opinion had been mobilized against the killings of black-skinned Libyans, South African Deputy President Khalema Motlanthe raised the question in the South African parliament whether the ICC would have the will to unearth links and coordination between "rebels" and NATO and bring those who are responsible to book, including the NATO commanders on the ground (and, I would add, NATO politicians as well). Moreno-Ocampo's *volte-face* before the Security Council came at a time of deep divisions within NATO. In public, the NATO information department was claiming that "the actions of NATO were in compliance with international law." In private, the NATO information operations experts wanted Western media to focus on Gaddafi's crimes. Nicolas Beger, Director of the Amnesty International European Institutions Office, rebutted that "if there were to be evidence that NATO is also involved in activities illegal under international law, something should be done about that. Nobody should be allowed to commit war crimes, and nobody should be able to get away with it." Beger called for an impartial probe into Gaddafi's death. "If he was captured alive and then killed, that's a war crime. That's clear."[231]

With the tide of the information barrage turning against NATO and the "rebels," the information department of the U.S. Africa Command went silent. When the bombing started and there was euphoria that the regime would fall in a few weeks, the AFRICOM commander was everywhere, giving interviews. By the time of the stalemate, AFRICOM receded and public information on the "progress" of the mission came from NATO briefings. After the negative publicity associated with mass graves, Ivo H. Daalder, U.S. Permanent Representative to NATO, and Adm. James G. Stavridis, Supreme Allied Commander, Europe, wrote in an opinion piece that the NATO mission was "a historic victory for the people of Libya." This was the same statement that had been issued by the British Foreign Secretary, William Hague. Senator John McCain in the United States and French politicians all made similar statements about the historic victory. Anders Fogh Rasmussen, the NATO Secretary General, flew to Tripoli on October 31, 2011, and declared the end of NATO operations in Libya. In his speech, he gloated, "It's great to be in free Libya."

> Libya is finally free. From Benghazi to Brega, from Misrata to the Nafusa mountains and Tripoli. Your courage, determination and

sacrifice have transformed this country and helped change the region. At midnight tonight, a successful chapter in NATO's history is coming to an end. But you have already started writing a new chapter in the history of Libya. A new Libya, based on freedom, democracy, human rights, the rule of law and reconciliation.[232]

But that "successful" chapter did not come to an end. The chapter of democracy, freedom, and human rights that Rasmussen referred to was very different from the reality of hundreds of militias creating the kind of mayhem and insecurity that had not been seen in Libya for over forty years. In most parts of the world, especially in the countries comprising the Group of 77, diplomats and policy makers raised their voices to say that NATO exceeded its mandate to protect Libyan civilians and instead became the air force to install in power jihadists in what was essentially a civil war. From within Britain itself, Seumas Milne wrote in *The Guardian* that "if the purpose of the NATO intervention in Libya was to protect civilians and save lives, it has been a catastrophic failure." Milne argued convincingly, even before the information from the UN Human Rights Council came out, that while the death toll in Libya when NATO intervened was perhaps around 1,000 to 2,000 (judging by UN estimates), eight months later "it is probably more than ten times that figure. Estimates of the numbers of dead over the last eight months—as NATO leaders vetoed cease-fires and negotiations—range from 10,000 up to 50,000."[233]

Milne then went to the core of the reason for the intervention: the effort to regain the ascendancy after the revolutions in Tunisia and Egypt. He wrote that, of the 50,000,

uncounted thousands will be civilians, including those killed by NATO bombing and NATO-backed forces on the ground. These figures dwarf the death tolls in this year's other most bloody Arab uprisings, in Syria and Yemen. NATO has not protected civilians in Libya—it has multiplied the number of their deaths, while losing not a single soldier of its own. For the Western powers, of course, the Libyan war has allowed them to regain ground lost in Tunisia and Egypt, put themselves at the heart of the upheaval sweeping the most strategically sensitive region in the world.[234]

Alan Kuperman, from the Lyndon B. Johnson School of Public Affairs at the University of Texas, Austin, spoke directly to the idea of success in Libya to draw attention to the 8,000 to 30,000 persons who died as a result of the NATO intervention.[235]

Worldwide Opposition

The challenge to the accepted narrative in the West that the NATO intervention was a success was most explicit in Africa. The African Union never relented in the condemnation of the NATO operation. Undoubtedly, the moral ground for the AU in the year 2011 had been diminished by holding its annual summit in Equatorial Guinea and conferring legitimacy to the leadership of Teodoro Obiang Nguema. Many of the leaders who attended the summit did not have the legitimacy to critique Western destruction and bombing. However, the treatment of African migrants, the images of Africans drowning in the Mediterranean Sea, and the cleansing of the town of Tawergha gave the Libyan war greater urgency than the posturing of individual leaders. This grassroots urgency for action was reflected in the deliberations of the Peace and Security Council of the African Union. In their experience of armed conflicts, the statement by Anders Fogh Rasmussen about a new chapter was hollow—if not a continuation of the disinformation that misrepresented what happened in Libya over the eight months of bombing.

From all corners of Africa there was condemnation when the *New York Times* reported on widespread mourning for Gaddafi. What must have surprised Western news agencies was that the demonization of Gaddafi had not succeeded in Africa. Millions of Africans disagreed with and opposed Gaddafi, but they were outraged at the flagrant disregard for African lives. Older Africans remembered the matter of foreign violation of African space vividly when Tanzania opposed the

Entebbe raid by the Israeli commandos. At that moment, Tanzania was in a near state of war with Idi Amin of Uganda, but the Israelis had violated a higher principle than that of the differences between Tanzania and Uganda. Israel had invaded Africa, and Africans opposed foreign invaders. Julius Nyerere invoked the sovereignty of Africa in the face of the Israeli attack. In June 2011, the African Union's High-Level ad hoc Committee on Libya invoked the long traditions of struggles against colonialism:

> An attack on Libya or any other member of the African Union without express agreement by the AU is a dangerous provocation. Sovereignty has been a tool of emancipation of the peoples of Africa, who are beginning to chart transformational paths for most of the African countries after centuries of predation by the slave trade, colonialism, and neocolonialism. Careless assaults on the sovereignty of the African countries are, therefore, tantamount to inflicting fresh wounds on the destiny of the African peoples.[236]

This sentiment from the Ugandan representative ran deep in Africa. In 2010, Gaddafi had called for the partitioning of Nigeria and there was a clear body of opinion in Nigeria that wanted to see the end of the Libyan leadership—but not by foreign invaders. Former Archbishop Desmond Tutu condemned the killing of Gaddafi, saying mob justice and violence should always be deplored:

> The manner of the killing of Muammar Gaddafi on Thursday totally detracts from the noble enterprise of instilling a culture of human rights and democracy in Libya. The people of Libya should have demonstrated better values than those of their erstwhile oppressor.[237]

Tutu went on to condemn Hillary Clinton for celebrating the death of Gaddafi, saying, "Nor is killing a human being something to be celebrated."

The court of African public opinion changed drastically against NATO and the allies who participated in the bombing and remained silent when black-skinned Africans were being killed. More significantly, the African response to the instability in the Sahel after the NATO debacle demonstrated the need for a stronger body to forge African unity. The *coup d'état* in Mali, the heightened rebellions across the Sahel, and the proliferation of weapons demonstrated that the issues of destruction and destabilization could not be confined to Libya. Tons of weapons that had been held in storage by the Gaddafi regime flowed outside of Libya to her neighbors, with the forces of the Tuareg rebellion strengthened with new weaponry. The U.S. deputy representative to the United Nations said, during a Security Council briefing in New York, "We are concerned about the porous nature of the border between Chad, Niger and Libya and the risk of weapons, including MANPADS [shoulder-launched missiles capable of downing a low-flying airliner], moving across those borders. These weapons, in the hands of terrorists, could further destabilize already fragile areas of the Sahel and surrounding regions."[238]

International diplomats listened with eager ears to this talk of "terrorism" from a government that had put jihadists in control of Libya. Was the United States planning to use this rhetoric later for further intervention in North Africa? Samir Amin drew from the experiences of the shifting positions of the U.S. in East Africa to argue that what the West wanted was a Somali-type situation in Libya:

> Intervention has succeeded in the sense that it destroyed the regime of Gaddafi. But what is the result of the success? Is it democratic Libya? Well, one should laugh at that when one knows that the president of the new regime is nobody else than the very judge who condemned to death the Bulgarian nurses. What a curious democracy it is! But it has also led to the dislocation of the country on a Somalian pattern: that is, local powers—all of them in the name of so-called Islam, but local warlords—with the destruction of the country. One can raise the question: Was this the target of the intervention—that is, the destruction of the country?[239]

The Libyan society under Gaddafi had been one of the anchors of the forging of African unity. Gaddafi had supported the speedy creation of the African Central Bank and the building of an African Monetary Union. These initiatives were now receiving urgent discussion in light of the international capitalist crisis. The aftermath of the Libyan intervention and the destruction of that society reinforced the Pan-African adage that no African will be free until all of Africa is free. This desire for freedom beyond colonial borders was being impressed on Africa by the independence declaration of the Tuareg state, Azawad, in the north of Mali. This declaration had far-reaching implications for all of the states of North and West Africa insofar as the Azawad peoples are spread across Mali, Libya, Niger, and Algeria. The potential for the exploration of oil and minerals along with the promise of new solar technologies had made the Sahara prime property in Africa.

18—European Isolation in Africa

The heightened instability in Africa consequent to the destruction of Libya by NATO was strengthened by new calls for accountability. Within Africa, the media reported on the dislocations and the consequences of NATO military actions. New voices emerged from within the left in the United States, energized by the African commitment to the opposition to NATO. Vijay Prashad argued,

> The scandal here is that NATO, a military alliance, refuses any civilian oversight of its actions. It operated under a UN mandate and yet refuses to allow a UN evaluation of its actions. NATO, in other words, operates as a rogue military entity, outside the bounds of the prejudices of democratic society. The various human rights reports simply underline the necessity of a formal and independent evaluation of NATO's actions in Libya.[240]

This characterization of NATO as a rogue military entity by Professor Prashad differed significantly from mainstream European scholars, who continued to parrot the ideas from the "rebels" and from the press information of Nicolas Sarkozy and David Cameron.

In fact, the narrative of the projection of force to combat al-Qaeda in the Maghreb (AQIM) intensified when the Royal African Society in Britain-hosted closed meetings in the Houses of Parliament on "Libya in Transition—Implications and Opportunities for Britain." While repeating the mantra about combating terrorism in the Maghreb, the British were explicit in their objectives:

> Winning the peace in Libya is a core British national interest. A power vacuum in Libya would have deleterious effects on illegal migration to Europe, combating AQIM, European energy security, investment opportunities and thus European economic recovery. The present British government has, therefore, committed itself to facilitating an efficient transition of power from the NTC to a legitimate constitutional government in Libya based on the rule of law, combating dangerous radicalism, honouring existing contracts, nurturing civil society and the private sector, etc.

Very few writings express the ideas about the Libyan war and European economic recovery so clearly. As a corollary to European economic recovery and guaranteeing European energy and investment opportunities, Europeans had to diminish the growing influence of China in Libya and Africa. Of the major construction, housing, and power projects in Libya, Chinese construction and state-owned enterprises were by far the most visible among the external work force in Libya. The Turks were the second-largest investor in the construction sector. European writers were subtle in their claims "to defend national interests," but U.S. commentators such as Paul Craig Roberts argued that the objective of the war in Libya was to evict China from Libya and Africa.[241] This analysis was put to paper on F. William Engdahl, who argued that the war in Libya was actually a challenge to China in Africa.[242] Going back to the statements from U.S. think tanks and military consultants about the need to build AFRICOM to contain China, Engdahl wrote about its formation and that

NATO's Libya campaign was and is all about oil. But not about simply controlling Libyan high-grade crude because the United States is nervous about reliable foreign supplies. It rather is about controlling China's free access to long-term oil imports from Africa and from the Middle East. In other words, it is about controlling China itself.

The Chinese foreign policy establishment did not help itself with its timid response to the NATO intervention. Prior to the changed international economic situation, when the People's Republic of China was relatively weaker commercially, the Chinese political leadership had articulated a principle of noninterference in each other's internal affairs. By 2010, this principle had been overtaken by the aggressive investment patterns of Chinese corporations, both state-owned and private. There were more than one million Chinese workers involved in other countries. Hence, while the Chinese government maintained its non-interventionist position, its commercial activities had overtaken its posture of non-intervention. The Chinese intellectual and foreign policy establishment timidly engaged politically and muted their criticism of NATO's bombings. From the platform of the BRICS (Brazil, Russia, India, China and South Africa) summit in China, there had been a tepid statement in support of the position of the African Union. While the Russians were using their media to challenge the statements coming from NATO and to continuously call for the reconvening of the Security Council to discuss Libya, the Chinese were more cautious.

With thirteen large-scale projects in Libya being undertaken by the Chinese, China was by far the largest investor in the country. This despite the fact that, prior to the 2006 Forum on China-Africa Cooperation (FOCAC) meeting in Beijing, Gaddafi had lobbied African leaders to stay away from China. Gaddafi's antipathy toward China notwithstanding, the Libyan leadership had engaged with Chinese state-owned enterprises to build houses, a coastal railway, and major cement factories. Hence, aside from migrant workers from Africa, the Chinese were the largest contingent of expatriate workers. Right after the war broke out, China sent out navy, army, and air force missions to Libya to evacuate 35,860 Chinese citizens. This was the first time that China had deployed its armed forces together on an evacuation mission, but throughout the operation China demonstrated strong mobilization and delivery ability. This successful evacuation was viewed through different lenses across the world. For Africans, the Chinese evacuation of its citizens and its silence on the propaganda about "African mer-cenaries" was troubling; for Western military analysts, the successful evacuation was another indication of China's ability to project force well beyond its borders.[243]

The French president, who was concerned about the deepening financial crisis in Europe, flew to Beijing (supposedly en route to New Caledonia) to plead for assistance from China and to promise that there would be a role for Chinese firms in the reconstruction of Libya.[244] However, Nicolas Sarkozy could not make promises about Libya because he himself faced an uncertain future. Having taken the lead in the bombing of Libya, his leadership was rejected by the French voters in the elections of April 2012.

The Italian political leadership had been nervous about Sarkozy's activism in Libya. Italian ministers were reminding French politicians about the Italian "prerogative" in Libya. Italian politicians and business leaders stated on Italian radio and television that "Rome must now assert its leadership in economic relations," and complained that its prerogative in Libya "is being strongly challenged by Paris." Libya had renewed its robust relationship with Italy after 2008, when Italian prime minister Silvio Berlusconi invited Gaddafi to Rome and a "friendship and cooperation agreement" was signed between the two countries. Italy had agreed to invest $5 billion in the construction of a Libyan coast road, and in exchange Libya had promised to favor Italy with regard to oil and gas supplies. It was a pure barter transaction and Italy's Eni received extensive production concessions, which were later extended to the year 2047. Because of these relations, Italy only joined the NATO war against Libya after it was clear that France and Britain were going all-out to remove Gaddafi.

Of these former colonial powers the most self-confident were the British, who were aggressively promoting British business interests to the NTC. Mention was already made of the closed door meetings at the Houses of Parliament. Lord Trefgarne, the chairman of the Libyan British Business Council, was emblematic of the British aristocracy, who were salivating over new opportunities for British companies in Libya. David Anderson, of Oxford University, was probably typical of the fixated Western European academics who remained worried about who would be the winner among the Europeans. Writing soon after the NATO control of Tripoli, Anderson wrote about the insensate struggles and discussions about oil: "Europe's oil giants Eni, Total, BP and Repsol YPF are perfectly positioned to take advantage of these commercial opportunities." Nicolas Sarkozy had flown to Libya even before the execution of Gaddafi, but David Cameron could not countenance the French discussing the future without the British. What was not said by European academics writing on Libya was that behind the British, French, and Italian maneuvering was the support for the different families and regional militias jockeying for power in post-Gaddafi Libya.

U.S. companies worked quietly, through their partners in the Gulf, to rearrange control over the Libyan Investment Authority. Qatar was most explicit in its financial support for the Islamists. It was unclear where the interests of Qatar and the U.S. financial houses met. There were press reports that Muhammad Layas was being replaced as head of the LIA. Numerous obstacles were placed in the process of unfreezing Libyan assets. The Western countries dictated that the new Libyan leadership follow a road map—laid by the IMF and the World Bank—for expending their own money.

Western financial institutions benefited from the political fragmentation within Libya to the point where the assets were being returned to Libya in a trickle. Political infighting for dominance over the energy and banking sectors increased among the "reformers" who were rushing back from exile, as an elitist aristocratic and semi-feudal political leadership sought to impose itself on the feuding militias that controlled different cities. In this political maze, Shukri Ghanem, former head of Libya's National Oil Company, died mysteriously in Austria in early 2012. The privatization and liberalization that Ghanem had started under Gaddafi was now to be completed by the NTC, under the guidance of the International Monetary Fund. A new road map for the economy of Libya was spelled out by the IMF, as it wrote of the "challenges and opportunities" in Libya.[245]

19—FAILURE BEGETS FAILURE: THE NATO QUAGMIRE CONSUMES THE U.S. AMBASSADOR TO LIBYA

Before the end of October 2011, the spokespersons for NATO were proclaiming victory and that the intervention had been a resounding success. Ivo H. Daalder, then the U.S. permanent representative to NATO, and Adm. James G. Stavridis, Supreme Allied Commander, Europe, and commander of the United States European Command, joined together to write for *Foreign Affairs* under the title, "NATO's Victory in Libya: The Right Way to Run an Intervention."[246] Earlier, these same authors had written for the *New York Times* on "NATO's Success in Libya," stating that

> Monday, October 31st, seven months after it started, NATO's operation in Libya will come to an end. It is the first time NATO has ended an operation it started. And it comes on the heels of an historic victory for the people of Libya who, with NATO's help, transformed their country from an international pariah into a nation with the potential to become a productive partner with the West.[247]

From the academic experts on Libya such as Dirk Vandewalle, this narrative of success was promulgated through journals with titles such as "After Qaddafi: The Surprising Success of the New Libya."[248] What was intriguing about this success narrative by Vanderwalle was that it continued the view that the Libyan intervention had been a success even after the death of the U.S. ambassador to Libya, Christopher Stevens, had been reported internationally.

Western military journals and specialists also trumpeted the idea of success and sought to draw lessons from this spectacular achievement.[249] This idea of success had been part of the information necessary to present the NATO intervention as a victory for the people of Libya. This view of victory had been loudly proclaimed from inside Libya by the chairman of the National Transitional Council. On October 23, three days after the execution of Gaddafi, the NTC leader declared that the Liberation of Libya was complete. A few days later the Secretary-General of NATO, Anders Fogh Rasmussen, announced the end of the NATO mission, declaring that the NATO mission to Libya had been "one of the most successful in NATO history." Despite these celebratory statements, throughout the period after these announcements, the conditions for the peoples of Libya were deteriorating daily. For the citizens of the United States and for many in Western Europe, the extent of the insecurity only came to life after the killing of the U.S. ambassador to Libya on September 11, 2012. It was in the aftermath of his death when it was revealed to a wider audience that in the year June 2011 to June 2012, there had been 230 security incidents in Libya. These incidents were reported to the House Oversight and Government Reform Committee of the U.S. Congress. It was during one hearing before the panel of this committee that we learned that there had been daily battles all across Libya, with the levels of insecurity unprecedented in the history of Libya with over 1,700 militias operating. It can now be understood that the stories of success had been part of the military disinformation campaign that had been so central for the prosecution of the NATO military intervention. Ostensibly, because there had been no "boots on the ground," the absence of Western casualties had lulled the citizenry of the West; the intervention had depended on intelligence agencies, private military contractors, and armed militias.

The existence and depth of the militias inside the society was revealed when citizens of the United States learned of the levels of insecurity of the people of Libya on September 11, 2012. This was exactly eleven years after the attack on the World Trade Center. Militias that had been mobilized by the West to fight Gaddafi in Benghazi turned on the sponsors of the "successful intervention." The death of Ambassador Stevens brought out facts of U.S. diplomatic and intelligence activities and their relationship to the militias. The differing accounts of the death of the ambassador entered into the presidential campaign as the Republican-controlled Congress mounted hearings to get to the "truth." Prior to these hearings, reports had been coming out in dribs and drabs about the U.S. intelligence presence in Benghazi. When U.S. security personnel were evacuated after the fateful events of September 11, 2012, the Libyan deputy prime minister, Mustafa Abushagour, told the *Wall Street Journal*, "We were surprised by the numbers of Americans who were at the airport, we have no problem with intelligence sharing or gathering, but our sovereignty is also key." Libyans were awakened to the extent of the integration between the large numbers of U.S. intelligence and the competing militias in Benghazi.

The testimony of the officials of the Bureau of Diplomatic Security at the Department of State before the U.S. Congress only created more uncertainty in relation to the objectives of the United States in Libya. This hearing failed to bring out the important role of the intelligence community in Libya in the coordination of the present war in Syria. The full story did not come out even then. It was only after the resignation of General David Petraeus as director of the Central Intelligence Agency, on November 9, 2012, when the role of the CIA was partially revealed. Then, the world found out via the biographer of David Petraeus that Benghazi was the site of the largest CIA operation in North Africa.

The war in Libya had not finished in October 2011, and when the Benghazi incident exploded before the world, the incidents in Benghazi took on international proportions. An inquiry by the Pentagon into the

September 11, 2012, events led to the reported removal of General Carter Ham of the U.S. Africa Command. The fallout of the failure and the blowback will be the subject of the next chapter. In this chapter, it is important to highlight how the NATO failure in Libya compounded the military project of the United States and the legitimacy of NATO. The U.S. legation in Libya, especially the facilities in Benghazi, had been compromised by the U.S. intelligence operations in Syria, which used Libya as a recruiting base for jihadists to fight in Syria. Ultimately, the triggers of war that spun out of the NATO intervention in Libya were having a tragic effect on all of the peoples of the Middle East and North Africa.

Selling the Success of NATO and the So-Called Transition

After the execution of Gaddafi on October 20, 2011, and the capture of Saif al-Islam in November, Western media went into overdrive to present the idea that a new era of peace and reconstruction had arrived in Libya. Scholars descended on Libya to carry out research, with those from Western Europe and the United States tripping over one another to write about the "New Libya" and the opportunities for investment for Western corporations. Business platforms such as the Economist Intelligence Unit spelled out the challenges and business opportunities, while new publications and business councils emerged in European capitals. U.S. business executives were not far behind in the hype about business opportunities. Comments from David Hamond, president and chief executive officer of the National U.S.-Arab Chamber of Commerce, summed up the sentiments of a section of the U.S. corporate elements when he said:

> There is a gold rush of sorts taking place right now, and the Europeans and Asians are way ahead of us. I'm getting calls daily from members of the business community in Libya. They say, "Come back, we don't want the Americans to lose out."[250]

One month earlier, in September, the U.S. ambassador to Libya, Gene A. Cretz, speaking to reporters after the ceremonial flag-raising over the ambassador's residence, said that U.S. companies should return to Libya. Ambassador Cretz had participated in a State Department conference call with about 150 U.S. companies hoping to do business with Libya:

> We know that oil is the jewel in the crown of Libyan natural resources, but even in Qaddafi's time they were starting from A to Z in terms of building infrastructure and other things. . . . If we can get American companies here on a fairly big scale, which we will try to do everything we can to do that, then this will redound to improve the situation in the United States with respect to our own jobs.[251]

Such an invitation to Western business to return to Libya required painting a rosy picture of the possible profitability of Libya. By carefully managing the news coming out of Libya Western citizens were assured that Libya was in a transition phase. This assurance about the "peaceful transition" had also been presented to the United States by the Congressional Research Service.[252] In tandem, USAID rolled out programs to assist this transition to democracy and committed $5 million toward the Libya Transition Initiative. This initiative was aimed at supporting

> critical aspects of the transition process, strengthen reconciliation, and encourage productive linkages between citizens and their government. For example, USAID sponsored the first national workshop on comparative constitutional development processes, attended by 40 representatives from civil society organizations, the transitional government, and political parties.[253]

According to the "transition to democracy" program of USAID, the United States was working to strengthen "emergent media outlets and civil society organizations, build linkages between the government and its citizens, and support civic education and reconciliation. USAID is particularly focused on engaging marginalized populations, youth, and women, and increasing opportunities for their voices to be heard and their interests to be considered in decision making that will shape Libya's future."[254] The engagement of the USAID was reinforced by analytical presentations to lawmakers in the form of a Congressional Research Report that spelled out the six major steps to achieve democracy in Libya:

Step 1   Declaration of Liberation (which was supposed to be completed on October 23, 2011).

Step 2   Formation of an Interim Government (according to the United States and NATO, this was completed on October 31, 2012).

Step 3   Adoption of Electoral Legislation and Appointment of Election Commission (this was supposed to have been completed in February 2012).

Step 4   Election of National Congress and Selection of Cabinet and Constitutional Committee (supposed to have been completed July–August 2012; national elections for Congress held July 7, 2012; results announced).

Step 5   Constitutional Referendum (to be completed autumn 2012—incomplete at time of writing).

Step 6   National Elections, Spring–Summer 2013 (new election laws to be issued within 60 days of constitution approval).[255]

Democracy based on carefully orchestrated constitution-making, the creation of political parties, and the holding of elections had been identified as low-intensity democracy and an important component of the neoliberal conceptions of democracy in Africa.[256] More than thirty years ago progressive scholars identified the characteristics of "elite democracy or low-intensity democracy." They found that in countries where there had been a low-intensity democratic transition under the tutelage of the United States, there was little evidence to support the widespread assumption that formal elections bring about a lasting progressive breakthrough or that they solve fundamental social and economic problems:

> What should more accurately be called "elite democracies" in effect coexist with tacit military dictatorships. Social reform agendas that could have established the basis for broader popular participation and greater social justice have been abandoned. Human rights violations continue virtually unabated. The new regimes are more readily manipulated by external forces such as the International Monetary Fund or via bilateral political and economic pressures, particularly from the USA. Economic policies often mandate austerity for the majority without, in most cases, bringing about significant economic growth. Progressive movements find it virtually impossible to implement an agenda for reform when powerful domestic and international groups opposing such change, not least the military, remain in place.[257]

Noam Chomsky, who has contributed to the understanding of the hijacking of democracy in societies such as the Philippines and Guatemala, notes the essential modus operandi of conservative forces in society today and in times past when he states that the guardians of world order have sought to establish democracy in one sense of the term while blocking it in another.[258] After the revolutionary changes in the world in 2011, including the emergence of the Occupy Wall Street movement, the liberal establishment of Western Europe and North America were eager to demonstrate that the NATO intervention had laid the basis for a "transition to democracy."

The farcical nature of this transition was soon made obvious when in March 2012 NTC officials in the east of Libya, in Benghazi, launched a campaign to reestablish autonomy for the region, further increasing tension with the central NTC in Tripoli. This push for autonomy in the oil-rich region ensured that there was a flurry of activities as the executives of the oil companies and their private contractors fanned out in Benghazi to make certain that their own companies would emerge as strong forces after the redistribution of oil contracts.

A relevant example of low-intensity democracy can be found in Colombia, where the ruling social elements tolerated and supported paramilitary repression in the society while going through the ritual of regular elections.[259] Colombia holds another lesson for the peoples of Libya insofar as the counterinsurgency tactics of the U.S. military and intelligence had been deployed in that country for over three decades. The United States had been at war against drugs and when the war on terror came into vogue, Colombia joined the international forces fighting terrorism and was thus able to access since 2000 over $7 billion in military capital from the United States. One important study, *Cocaine, Death Squads and the War on Terror: U.S. Imperialism and Class Struggle in Colombia,* pointed out that the war on drugs in Colombia was not geared toward the eradication of coca but to assist the allies of the United States—that is, the Colombian state, paramilitaries, and wealthy elite who are favorable to U.S. business interests and to the United States' desire for exploitation of Colombia's vast resources.[260] These allies of the United States were then able to monopolize the drug trade so critical to their survival. If one substitutes oil for drugs, it can be grasped how the United States and Western Europe were seeking to gain a foothold in Libya by identifying reliable allies. This project was compromised by the alliance with Saudi Arabia and Qatar, which had their own project in their alliance with jihadist groups. From the period of the neoconservative ascendancy in the foreign policy establishment of the United States at the start of the twenty-first century, it was accepted that the promotion of the interests of U.S. corporations took precedence over all other considerations.

The Libya of Competing Militias

It was in the midst of squabbling between oil executives and their contractors and militias that elections for the General National Congress were held in Libya in July 7, 2012. Step 4 of the transition to democracy in Libya had taken place with the election of a national congress and the selection of cabinet and a constitutional committee. International news organizations went overboard to highlight the success of the elections and the "fact" that Islamists and jihadists did not come out as winners. The transitional government handed power to the General National Congress. This Congress then elected Mohammed Magarief of the Liberal National Front Party as its chairman, thereby making him interim head of state.

These well-crafted versions of the transition papered over the continued warfare that was going on all over Libya. The British Broadcasting Corporation (BBC) reported on September 18, 2012, that there were over 1,700 militias all over Libya. As we have seen, under the Gaddafi regime, the central military apparatus had been degraded and security had been placed in the hands of militias commanded by relatives of the "dear leader." The militias from the region of Misrata and the competing militias from Benghazi had caught the attention of Human Rights Watch. The energy of these militias had been too extensive to escape notice, and Human Rights Watch was one of the first to pick up where the African Union had been pointing. In their report on the execution of Gaddafi, Human Rights Watch stated:

> The opposition forces fighting against Gaddafi in Libya's 2011 civil war were loosely organized and often did not fall under the centralized control of the NTC, the interim opposition body that was founded on February 27 in Benghazi and that ultimately succeeded the Gaddafi government. Hundreds of individual militias sprung up to fight against Gaddafi, organized around informal networks such as individual towns, companies, schools, former military units (in the case of defectors), or religious institutions to which members of the militia belonged. In almost every city and town across Libya, the primary loyalty of the city or town's militias was to their place of origin: hence, the myriad of militias became mostly identified with their place of origin, and loosely coordinated their activities along those lines.[261]

Academics who studied the militias to gain empirical data for publications did not see the seriousness of these militias. During the first year after the declaration of success, there had been a number of academic writings on the new "phenomenon" of the Libyan militias.[262] In the enunciation of the typology and roles of the militias in Libya, there had been silence about the fact that these militias had been a central feature of the strategy of the NATO intervention. In their report on the 1,700 militias, the BBC listed the most important groups according to region and linked these groups to differing religious factions. Of these militia groups, the most renowned were from the East Benghazi region: Martyrs of 17 February Brigade, Martyrs of Abu Salim Brigade, theMartyr Rafallah Shahati Battalions, and the Libya Shield Force. In the West there were Al-Zintan Revolutionaries' Military Council (the military council of the Zintan area), Sadun al-Suwayli Brigade (comprising militias from Misrata), Al-Sawaiq Brigade, and the al-Qaqa Brigade. [263]

The competition and rivalry between these hundreds of militias had been so fierce that the NTC had no authority over them. After seeking legitimacy through the July elections, there had been an effort to bring cohesion by seeking to rationalize the relationships between the Ministry of Defense and the Ministry of the Interior. Benghazi and Misrata boasted the two strongest armed groups, and no central authority could bring these groups under control. Reports such as "Militia Integration and Security Sector Reform" sought to pay off hundreds of young persons to give up weapons. One study on the efforts of the NTC to co-opt some of the youths carrying guns noted that the effort to demobilize the militias had been organized through the Warriors Affairs Commission:

> At the forefront of this task is an initiative from the prime minister's office called the Warriors Affairs Commission (WAC), which has conducted an exhaustive registration and data collection of nearly 215,000 revolutionary fighters. It also functions as a sort of placement service, moving these young men into the police and the army, sending them on scholarships abroad, furthering their education at home, or giving them vocational training. After being vetted and screened, roughly 150,000 men are now eligible for placement; what happens to the other 65,000 remains to be seen.[264]

What this writer failed to factor in was the manner in which U.S. relations with the militias had followed the Petraeus strategy in Iraq of buying off the leaders of the Awakening movement. "The Sunni Awakening movement had begun in 2006 before Petraeus arrived in Iraq, but he and his top commanders deftly managed it. The tribal fighters of the Awakening movement ended up on the American payroll in the Sons of Iraq program, which by the spring of 2009 had grown to around 100,000 men. Many of those men had once been shooting at Americans; now they were shooting at al Qaeda." In this celebratory article, the writer had noted Petraeus's success in Iraq: "Iraq today remains a dangerous place, but it is not in the grip of a civil war, and political differences are more likely to be decided by parliamentary maneuvers than by violence."[265]

Iraq had been a far more secular society than Libya, so the application of the counterinsurgency strategy in Libya had failed despite the allocation of resources for the training of new security personnel by the U.S. Congress. In each neighborhood of the country, one militia faction dominated and went into the business of using their weapons to gain access to these new resources. After the death of Ambassador Stevens, U.S. citizens were alerted to the existence of what the State Department called "security incidents." But the 230 security incidents over the previous year were the tip of the iceberg. Navi Pillay, the UN Commissioner for Human Rights, had noted as far back as January 2012 that "the lack of oversight by the central authority creates an environment conducive to torture and ill-treatment." Amnesty International had been carrying reports such as "Militias Threaten New Hope for Libya." [266]

As noted above, there had been major alarm within Africa when certain militias targeted black-skinned Libyans. Black-skinned Libyans from Tawergha had been expelled from their community and more than 30,000 were displaced. Even the usual spokespersons for Western imperial missions had to speak out, and Human Rights Watch joined in the condemnation of the rule of the militias. Amnesty International brought out a report, "Libya: Rule of Law or Rule of Militias," bringing into sharper focus some of the outstanding questions of the role of these armed marauders. In June a militia brigade briefly took over Tripoli's international airport. The fighting between the competing militias ensured that although NATO had declared success, the war was far from over.[267]

Oil and Militias

Despite the 230 security situations in Libya, international oil companies were back in business; by the end of September 2012 Libya was producing 90 percent of its pre-NATO intervention output. In September 2012, the head of the National Oil Company of Libya, Nuri Berruien, told reporters that Libya was then producing an average 1.6 million barrels per day and expected to increase output by 30,000 to 40,000 barrels per day by early 2013 once repairs to a pipeline in eastern Libya were completed. Dr. Berruien told reporters at the Chemical Weapons Convention (CWC) in Tripoli that Libya was targeting production of 1.8 million barrels per day next year. "We have held back production from some oil fields in order to preserve wellhead integrity so that we do not cause any damage," adding that a pipeline being built in partnership with Wintershall of Germany would be completed "in record time."[268] This will allow oil production to resume at higher levels from three or four fields in the Sirte basin that as of September 2012 were being held back.

Foreign companies had been trooping back into Libya, with BP the last to arrive in May 2012. Even without the hundreds of thousands of foreign workers, the stability of the exportation of oil had driven foreign companies to focus on who would be in control of Benghazi, especially after the declaration of autonomy by the militia/political leaders in February.

U.S. oil companies did not want to be left behind in this new struggle, hence the U.S. diplomatic efforts were now directed at Benghazi. Christopher Stevens had been appointed ambassador of the United States to Libya in January 2012 to succeed Gene A. Cretz. Stevens was confirmed by the U.S. Senate in March 2012 and arrived in Tripoli in May 2012. When the uprisings began in February 2011, when Bernard-Henri Lévy was going into Benghazi to mobilize support for French interests, Chris Stevens was one of the first U.S. diplomatic personnel on the ground in Benghazi. Friends of Christopher Stevens wrote glowingly how he boarded a Greek freighter to go to Benghazi to coordinate the rebellion against Gaddafi.[269] He had served as a "Special Representative" to the Libyan Transitional National Council from March 2011 to November 2011 during the NATO intervention. Prior to this period he had served as the Deputy Chief of Mission in Libya from 2007 to 2009. Curiously, at that time, Stevens described Gaddafi as an "engaging and charming interlocutor," as well as a "strong partner in the war against terrorism."

It is worth quoting one of the more insightful reports on the career of Christopher Stevens in Libya, by Robert F. Worth, in the *New York Times*:

> Stevens was not naïve. He had three decades of experience in the Middle East and knew Libya as well as any American. He spoke the Libyan dialect of Arabic fluently. He did not relish danger for its own sake. But in some ways, he really was sailing back to an earlier era, when American diplomats were less tied down. In Benghazi, Stevens and his team became de facto participants in a revolution. They moved into the Tibesti Hotel, a 15-story tower overlooking a fetid lagoon, where the lobby was a constant, promiscuous churn of rumors and frenzied meetings among gunmen, journalists and spies. Unlike all his previous posts, there was no embassy to enclose him. His room then was a dilapidated sixth-floor suite full of gaudy gilded furniture and a four-poster bed; he seemed amused to know that Abdullah al-Senussi, Qaddafi's right-hand man, had often stayed there. Stevens reveled in his freedom. He met people in their homes, ate with them on the floor, Arab-style; cell-phone photos were taken and quickly shot around the Internet. He went running every morning and often stopped to chat with people on the street, to the dismay of the security officer who ran alongside him. In August, after a top rebel commander was killed by

Islamists, Stevens drove out to eastern Libya's tribal heartland and spent hours sitting on the beach with five elders of the Harabi tribe. The men ate grilled lamb and talked in Arabic, sipping tea. Stevens did not push them for answers. He was building connections that would pay off someday. "Chris said Benghazi was his favorite posting ever," said his friend Jennifer Larson, who later served as his deputy in Benghazi when Stevens became ambassador this spring. "He was very, very happy."[270]

While inside the United States the focus on the attack on the U.S. facility in Benghazi had been on the safety of U.S. diplomats, few of the commentaries pointed to how diplomats had been integrated into the war-fighting strategy of counterinsurgency that had been developed in Afghanistan and Iraq. In these battle zones, diplomacy had been subordinated to the strategies of the Pentagon. As far back as 1964, David Galula, writing on counterinsurgency, noted: "Essential though it is, the military action is secondary to the political one, its primary purpose being to afford the political power enough freedom to work safely with the population."[271]

The strategic concept of new forms of fighting had been refined in the 2006 counterinsurgency (COIN) manual produced by the Department of Defense of the United States. This manual was explicit in the description that a counterinsurgency campaign is a mix of offensive, defensive, and stability operations, conducted along multiple lines of operation. It requires:

> Soldiers and Marines to employ a mix of both familiar combat tasks and skills more often associated with nonmilitary agencies, with the balance between them varying depending on the local situation. This is not easy. Leaders at all levels must adjust their approach constantly, ensuring that their elements are ready each day to be greeted with a handshake or a hand grenade, to take on missions only infrequently practiced until recent years at our combat training centers, to be nation builders as well as warriors, to help re-establish institutions and local security forces, to assist in

the rebuilding of infrastructure and basic services, and to facilitate the establishment of local governance and the rule of law. The list of such tasks is a long one and involves extensive coordination and cooperation with a myriad of intergovernmental, indigenous, and international agencies. Indeed, the responsibilities of leaders in a counterinsurgency campaign are daunting—and the discussions in this manual endeavor to alert them to the challenges of such campaigns and to suggest general approaches for grappling with those challenges.[272]

In the manual's chapters on unity of command and unity of effort the military stressed the need for the integration between civilian and military activities and listed the hierarchy of this integration:

1. U.S. government agencies other than the Department of Defense (DOD).
2. International organizations (such as the United Nations and its many sub-organizations).
3. Non-governmental organizations (NGOs).
4. Private corporations.
5. Other organizations that wield diplomatic, informational, and economic power.[273]

The manual stated explicitly that

these civilian organizations bring expertise and capabilities that complement those of military forces engaged in COIN operations. At the same time, civilian capabilities cannot be brought to bear without the security provided by military forces. The interdependent relationship of all these groups must be understood and orchestrated to achieve harmony of action and coherent results.[274]

The COIN manual went on to outline how after the Department of Defense, the Department of State would be the coordinator of on-the-ground COIN fighting capabilities. Within the U.S. government, key organizations include: Department of State, U.S. Agency for International Development (USAID), Central Intelligence Agency, Department of Justice, Department of the Treasury, Department of Homeland Security, and the Department of Agriculture.

Within the U.S. Foreign policy establishment there had been minor turf warfare between the Department of Defense and the Department of State about whether the work of "development" should be subject to the needs of the military. This rift was settled by DOD appropriations because development funds were routed through the interagency coordination dominated by the DoD so that USAID and other "development" agencies had to cooperate with the Pentagon. In the midst of war against the people of Libya, there had been hearings before the House Foreign Affairs Committee Subcommittee on Africa, Global Health, and Human Rights that had been called by Congress to settle whether the work of the USAID should be subservient to the U.S. Africa Command. [275] On the same day, Don Yamamoto, Principal Deputy Assistant Secretary, Bureau of African Affairs, testified on how the State Department was assisting the efforts of the Pentagon, "AFRICOM: Promoting Partnership for Global Security in Africa." Both Don Yamamoto from the State Department and Sharon Cromer from USAID had assured Congress that there was clear inter-agency cooperation for "shared US goals."

Christopher Stevens had been an expert in inter-agency cooperation, so that when AFRICOM had been given the command of U.S. participation in Libya, he had been the senior U.S. representative of the military on the ground in Benghazi. Stevens belonged to the division of the U.S. Department of State that was very knowledgeable about the movements of militia members between Benghazi and the war against the Assad regime in Syria. Libyan Islamists from the eastern region composed the largest single component of the "foreign fighters" that were playing an ever more dominant role in the war being waged in Syria with the aim of toppling the government of President Bashar al-Assad. According to some estimates, between 1,200 and 1,500 jihadists were part of approximately 3,500 fighters that have been infiltrated into Syria from as far away as Chechnya and Pakistan. The relationship

between these jihadists and the NATO intervention became more
public after four Americans, including Ambassador Stevens, were
killed in a six-hour, commando-style attack on the U.S. mission on
September 11, 2012.

Death of an Ambassador

Throughout North Africa, the fallout of the NATO war was being felt,
with the citizens of Libya bearing the brunt of the lawlessness that
had been unleashed. Such lawlessness suited the short-term interests
of the capital equity forces of Wall Street, the oil executives, and the
Emirates. The proliferation of military weaponry from unsecured
Libyan stockpiles—including small arms, explosives, and shoulder-
fired anti-aircraft missiles (MANPADs)—expanded the availability
of weapons, with the border regions suffering directly. The present
destruction in Mali is directly related to these forms of plunder by
Western interests. In April 2012, Tuareg fighters and their Islamist
allies took control of northern Mali, in West Africa. The Tuareg fighters of the National Movement for the Liberation of Azawad (MNLA),
a Libyan-backed rebel group, had been fighting several West African
nations for decades. After the explosion of new weapons in northern
Mali, groups that were purportedly allied with al Qaeda expelled the
Tuaregs and turned northern Mali into an austere Islamist state. The
U.S. Africa Command then started to sound the drumbeat that al
Qaeda elements in northern Mali were turning the region into a terrorist haven. While the U.S. Africa Command was using the instability
in Mali as a basis for its legitimation, Malian women and civil society
activists were calling for support for local cultural and political sources
to resolve the question of instability in Mali.

General Carter Ham, head of the U.S. Africa Command, traveled
the region of West Africa to seek new alliances with states and societies that had been vigorously opposed to AFRICOM. NATO powers
and Western nations remained smug because the instability in Mali
and West Africa temporarily postponed the questions of African

integration. However, some sections of Africa were sufficiently angry to work for the removal of the chairman of the Commission of the African Union, Jean Ping. In July 2012, the former South African Home Affairs minister, Nkosazana Dlamini-Zuma, was overwhelmingly elected to be the chair of the AU Commission, effectively putting the superintending African efforts at peace and security into the hands of a leader who was not servile to Western European interests. The divisions inside Africa over the NATO intervention had been overshadowed by the active lobbying of European states to keep Jean Ping as the AU Commissioner. In South Africa, there had been a vigorous campaign to bring the AU back into the discussions about the future of Libya. It was in this moment of transition that the failure of NATO in Libya was fully exposed: the U.S. government failed to protect even its ambassador.

Suddenly, U.S. citizens were bombarded with information on the Libyan militias. Members of the Republican leadership took the symbolism of the fact that the death of U.S. personnel took place on September 11 (the anniversary of 9/11) was meant to embarrass the Obama administration. It was in pursuit of the strategy to make the death of the ambassador an issue in the 2012 elections that the Republican-led Congress called a hearing in October.

The purpose of the October 10, 2012, hearing of the Oversight and Government Reform Committee was to examine security lapses that led to the killings in Benghazi. What this hearing confirmed was what many experts knew—that there was no real consulate in Benghazi, but a vast web of intelligence and private contractors, in service to the CIA and the oil companies. The testimony of Charlene Lamb before Congress gave away the fact that the facility in Benghazi was not a diplomatic facility. It was later revealed in November that authorities in the Office of the Director of National Intelligence, in consultation with CIA, decided to remove the terms "attack," "al Qaeda," and "terrorism" from unclassified guidance provided to the Obama administration several days after the militant attack on the U.S. mission in Benghazi.

The events of the death of Ambassador Stevens exposed the U.S. presence in Libya at a number of levels. First, Ambassador Stevens, as noted even by his friends, ensured inter-agency cooperation to support the "Libyan revolutionaries." Second, the ambassador was caught in the midst of the COIN strategy of switching sides to engage the jihadists of the east. Third, the evidence pointed to integration between U.S. intelligence and the militias. In testimony before Congress, Charlene Lamb told lawmakers that the intelligence compound depended on the militia in Benghazi known as the 17th February Brigade. Lamb, Deputy Assistant Secretary of the State Department's Bureau of Diplomatic Security, said that, in terms of armed security personnel, there were five diplomatic security agents in the compound on September 11. "There were also three members of the Libyan 17th February Brigade," a reference to the Libyans hired to guard the American compound.

The unspoken rationale for Stevens's activities in Benghazi was the jockeying between French, British, Italian, and U.S. oil companies over political dominance in Benghazi. Traditionally, the Italians had been a force on the ground in Libya, but during the NATO operations French, British, and U.S. operatives muscled out the Italians as junior partners in the imperial operation. These factors did not come out in the hearings, but what did come out was the inter-agency conflicts between the State Department and the Central Intelligence Agency. The U.S. military has kept quiet as these inter-agency squabbles have played out on C-Span. While the mainstream media carried the line that Ambassador Stevens had been killed in the U.S. consulate in Benghazi, but "the compound where Stevens, Smith and 2 U.S. Marines were killed was a gated-villa in Benghazi leased by the U.S. State Department. Mohammad al-Bishari, landlord to the villa, stated that it was burned down, and that Stevens and Smith died of smoke inhalation while 2 other American officials were gunned down at the gated-villa."[276] Before the full information on what had transpired seeped into the media, Eric Nordstrom, who served about ten months in Libya in charge of security, said he sought to obtain more agents and to extend a mission for the security site team in Libya. Even before the hearings, Nordstrom had engaged in a media battle to place his stamp on the events leading up to the death of the ambassador.

There was, in fact, need for security, but as the diary of Ambassador Stevens showed, he was opposed to the presence of official State

Department personnel because of the integration of the private contractors, the intelligence operatives, and the militias. Earlier in June
there had been an attack on the intelligence facility that was called a
consulate, as well as a June 6 bomb attack on the Benghazi consulate, a
June 11 rocket-propelled grenade attack on a convoy carrying Britain's
ambassador to Libya, and an August 27 State Department travel warning noting the threat of car bombings and assassinations in Tripoli and
Benghazi. However, despite these attacks Stevens argued to the State
Department Bureau of Diplomatic Security that the matter of security
should not be entrusted to the Marines who usually guarded U.S. diplomatic establishments.

Stevens took this position to "show faith in Libya's new leaders,"
according to the *Wall Street Journal*: "Officials say Mr. Stevens personally advised against having Marines posted at the embassy in Tripoli,
apparently to avoid a militarized U.S. presence."[277]

Fallout before the U.S. Public

As the media were hailing Ambassador Stevens as a hero, the first major
hint of the depth of intrigue was revealed in the struggle between CNN
and the State Department over the contents of the diary of Ambassador
Stevens. News organizations had been swamped with differing versions of the events in Libya from the State Department, from the CIA,
and from the Pentagon. The conflicting narratives were trumped when
the diary and the appointment calendar of Ambassador Stevens was
picked up by journalists. Parts of this diary, which exposed the multiple roles of Stevens, were aired on CNN. This same network had been
complicit in spreading disinformation during the war, but in its rat-
ings competition, CNN did not wait for clearance before exposing the
activities of Stevens as documented by the ambassador himself. These
revelations displeased the State Department. While Stevens was given
a public tribute by President Obama and Secretary of State Clinton,
the three other U.S. personnel who succumbed to the attack were
buried quietly so that the local papers from their hometowns would

not raise questions about what they were doing in Benghazi. CIA chief David Petraeus did not attend the funeral of two of the four because the CIA did not want to bring out the reality that the battles had emanated from struggles between the CIA and militia forces. The media had identified the CIA fighters in Benghazi as private military contractors. The full details would emerge after David Petraeus resigned on November 9, 2012, in a lecture by Paula Broadwell in Colorado in October 2012. Even before this resignation mainstream organs such as the *New York Times* and *Los Angeles Times* provided lengthy details of the CIA's role.[278] Before the torrent of information on the levels of cooperation between the CIA and the militias, one piece of disinformation in the media purported that the CIA had been deployed in Benghazi to support the "State Department's program to collect the shoulder-fired anti-aircraft missiles." David Ignatius, writing in the *Washington Post,* stated:

> The CIA had a substantial base in Benghazi, with at least a half-dozen former military Special Forces assigned there as part of the "Global Response Staff." These were the muscle-bound security guys known to flippant earlier generations of CIA case officers as "knuckle-draggers." They were in Benghazi in such numbers in part because the CIA was supporting the State Department's program to collect the shoulder-fired anti-aircraft missiles that had gone loose after the fall of Col. Moammar Gaddafi. Agency officers may also have been working with Libyan militias to help them become effective security forces.[279]

CIA against the State Department

After Ambassador Christopher Stevens was killed, U.S. representative to the United Nations Susan Rice appeared on the Sunday television talk shows and stated that the killings took place in the context of demonstrations over the obnoxious video about the prophet Mohammed. Soon afterward it became clearer that the attack on Benghazi was not related to the demonstrations but to the inter-militia warfare in Benghazi. Inside Washington, think tanks were competing with media on where blame should be laid. From the many publications it was soon clear that both the State Department and the CIA were spinning the facts on the protection of U.S. diplomats overseas.[280] This matter was too sensitive for spin but the conservative media had a field day when there was a hint that President Obama could be vulnerable because the United States had been unable to protect its diplomats from terrorist attacks in Africa. The Republican candidate for president, Mitt Romney, pounced on the contradictory accounts, and the Republican-controlled Congress called hearings to embarrass Obama.

However, no sooner were the hearings in session than Republicans found out they were opening a can of worms by exposing the extent of the CIA operations in Libya. Very early in the hearings, Rep. Jason Chaffetz (R-Utah) was the first to unmask the role of the CIA. "Point of order! Point of order!" he called out as a State Department security official, seated in front of an aerial photo of the U.S. facilities in Benghazi, described the night of the attack. "We're getting into classified issues that deal with sources and methods that would be totally inappropriate in an open forum such as this."

The State Department official then retorted that the information being presented was available on commercial sites and easily retrievable through Google Earth maps. The State Department revealed that the material was unclassified, thus revealing to the U.S. public the differences between the CIA and the State Department. "I totally object to the use of that photo," Chaffetz continued. He went on to say that "I was told specifically while I was in Libya I could not and should not ever talk about what you're showing here today."

After Representative Chaffetz alerted the world that something valuable was in the photo, the chairman, Darrell Issa (R-Calif.), attempted to close the barn door after the horses had bolted. "I would direct that that chart be taken down," he said, although it already had been on C-Span. "In this hearing room, we're not going to point out details of what may still in fact be a facility of the United States government or more facilities."

Dana Milbank of the *Washington Post* poked fun at the CIA and how it was outed in the hearings:

> In their questioning and in the public testimony they invited, the lawmakers managed to disclose, without ever mentioning Langley directly, that there was a seven-member "rapid response force" in the compound the State Department was calling an annex. One of the State Department security officials was forced to acknowledge that "not necessarily all of the security people" at the Benghazi compound "fell under my direct operational control."
>
> And whose control might they have fallen under? Well, presumably it's the "other government agency" or "other government entity" the lawmakers and witnesses referred to; Issa informed the public that this agency was not the FBI.[281]

The operations of the CIA in Libya had backfired. The plan of the Republicans to make political capital out of this incident also backfired, and the entire world was brought closer to the multiple roles of the U.S. military, private contractors, intelligence operatives, and oil companies in Libya.

The number of CIA operatives in Benghazi was also a revelation to the provisional government in Libya. When the United States evacuated its personnel from Benghazi, the Libyans were surprised and wanted greater accountability from the United States about its operations. However, for the U.S. intelligence community, the major question was damage control.

"It's a catastrophic intelligence loss," a U.S. official who had been stationed in Libya told the *New York Times*. "We got our eyes poked out." As a military information operation, the reporting of the death of Ambassador Stevens had been too major for the CIA COIN strategy to be forever hidden from the public. If the NATO intervention in Libya had been guided by lies agreed upon beforehand, there could be no agreement about exactly what happened in Benghazi. Slowly, as the scandals and political maneuvering escalated inside the United States, it was revealed that the strong CIA presence in Benghazi before and after the execution of Gaddafi involved more than just surveillance. The CIA and the U.S. government had become deeply compromised by their relationship with the Libyan Islamists. From their experience with the Libyans in Iraq, the CIA had paid attention to the eastern region of Libya that had been dubbed the "Martyr Factory" by U.S. journalists. The CIA had taken note in Iraq that a large number of jihadists who carried out suicide bombings in Iraq had their home in Libya.[282] In 2008, when the media was presenting disinformation on the success of the "surge" in Iraq, little notice was paid to the linkages between extremists in Libya and the anti-imperial sentiments in certain communities in Libya. After the removal of Gaddafi, the CIA had established a large presence in Benghazi to create a rear base for its covert war in Syria.

The CIA also set up a center on the border between Turkey and Syria to oversee the funneling of arms, matériel, money, and fighters into the Syrian civil war. Given the relationship established between the U.S. military intelligence and diplomatic agencies and the Libyan Islamist militias during the US-NATO war against Gaddafi, and previously, with the military intelligence experimentation of COIN in Iraq, some journalists speculated that the departure of jihadist elements from eastern Libya and their infiltration into Syria was being coordinated by CIA personnel on both ends. The full story had to await the outcome of the U.S. presidential elections in November. It was after the removal of the head of the U.S. Africa Command and the resignation of David Petraeus that some clarity was brought to bear on the real failures of the U.S. mission to Libya.

If You Feed a Scorpion It Will Bite You

Robert Fisk of the *Independent* in the United Kingdom described the linkages between the NATO intervention in Libya and the escalating war in Syria, warning the West of the dangers of its duplicity in the Middle East and North Africa. Writing after the death of Ambassador Stevens, Fisk commented:

The United States supported the opposition against Libya's Colonel Gaddafi, helped Saudi Arabia and Qatar pour cash and weapons to the militias and had now reaped the whirlwind. America's Libyan "friends" had turned against them, murdered U.S. ambassador Stevens and his colleagues in Benghazi and started an al-Qa'ida-led anti-American protest movement that had consumed the Muslim world. The U.S. had fed the al-Qa'ida scorpion and now it had bitten America. And so Washington now supports the opposition against Syrian President Bashar al-Assad, was helping Saudi Arabia and Qatar pour cash and weapons to the militias (including Salafists and al-Qa'ida) and would, inevitably, be bitten by the same "scorpion" if Assad was overthrown.[283]

Fisk quoted a friend in Syria who was warning against the current escalation of the war:

> "You know, we're all sorry about Christopher Stevens. This kind of thing is terrible and he was a good friend to Syria—he understood the Arabs." I let him get away with this, though I knew what was coming. "But we have an expression in Syria: 'If you feed a scorpion, it will bite you.'"

This bite was being felt even in the halls of the U.S. Congress as congressional hearings backfired on the Republicans who had hoped to make political capital out of the events in Benghazi. What was emerging was that the CIA was not merely conducting covert surveillance on the Islamists based in eastern Libya, but providing them with direct aid and coordinating their operations with the current war in Syria.

The War in Libya Is Far from Over

After the death of the four Americans in Benghazi, Libya dominated the news as the U.S. government was forced to juggle lies and disinformation. "Colonel Farag al-Dersi, Benghazi's chief of security, was shot dead by three gunmen in the eastern Libyan city where ambassador Chris Stevens and three fellow diplomats died after the U.S. consulate was overrun on 11 September." Dersi had been the security chief in Benghazi leading the anti-militia crackdown and investigating the exchange of firepower of September 2012 that devoured the U.S. diplomat and intelligence agents. The assassination of Dersi raised pertinent questions about the ability of the "Libyan government" to impose law and order.

Even before the death of Ambassador Stevens the situation in Bani Walid provided the clearest indication of the catastrophic failure of the NATO intervention in Libya. Thousands of militiamen, most of them from the city of Misrata, had laid siege to this town of some 70,000, refusing to allow food, medicine, or other supplies in or its residents out. Militia elements from Misrata bombarded the city with Grad rockets and tank fire and, according to doctors at the local hospital, apparently used shells containing gas against residential neighborhoods. Smaller outlying villages that have fallen to the former "rebels" were looted and burned. The Libyan Minister of Defense, Oussama El Jouili, admitted in a speech in October that the government had no control over the battles in Bani Walid. It was the first time that such a high-ranking official had accepted the failure of the state and its powerlessness in the face of the militias. It was an open admission that the militias had the monopoly on violence in Libya and that the government had no control over them.

Disinformation could not block the story of what was happening in Libya. Academics and journalists from the peace and social justice sectors authored at least seven new books that detailed the quagmire of the NATO intervention. Books celebrating the success of the Libyan intervention were now more measured in tone, so that even the contracted academic consultants were writing on the limitations of the Libyan model.[284] After the death of Stevens, the U.S. Navy sent two destroyers to Libyan waters. Inside Libya, there were cries for the disbanding of the militias. Demonstrators were calling on the Libyan government to disband the forces of terrorism. However, the central government was torn between the competing interests of the French,

British, Italian, United States, Emirates, Saudis, and Turks. The continued warfare in Libya pointed to the need for an intensification of the
calls for the UN Security Council to remove the private contractors
and foreign military personnel from the country. On March 12, 2012,
the UN Security Council extended the mandate of the UN Support
Mission in Libya (UNSMIL) for one year in order to assist the transitional authorities with security and administrative challenges. This
extension of the Security Council mandate was in fact assistance to the
external oil companies. The BRICS nations had been angry over the
manipulation of the "responsibility to protect" resolution. The anger of
Brazil, Russia, India, and China was not turned into concrete support
for the peoples of Africa and Libya as they pressured the United States
and NATO to expel the private contractors and intelligence operatives
who are now using Libya as one of the rear bases for the war in Syria.

The media in the Anglo-American world discussed the passing of
Ambassador Stevens and the three others as if their lives were more
important than the thousands of Libyans who had perished. While the
debate on the future of U.S. diplomacy was being debated, the Petraeus
affair brought out the full complexity of the military, the media, and the
intelligence services in Libya. It is to the fall of General Petraeus and
the scandal relating to the CIA in Libya to which we now turn.

20—"Libya All In": A Culture of Dysfunctionality in the U.S. Military and Its Explosion in the U.S. Political System

It was announced by the Pentagon on October 18, 2012, that U.S. Army General Carter F. Ham was to be replaced as head of AFRICOM. Eight days later, the U.S. Navy reassigned Rear Admiral Charles M. Gaouette as the commander of the USS *John C. Stennis* Strike Group. Two weeks later, on November 9, 2012, David Petraeus, a former four-star general in the United States Army, resigned from the Directorship of the Central Intelligence Agency. Petraeus had been sworn in as head of the CIA on September 6, 2011, when the CIA was the main coordinating force for the NATO intervention in Libya, organizing with AFRICOM and with the intelligence agencies of the principal partners of the NATO intervention, Britain and France. Also in November 2012, Defense Secretary Leon Panetta demoted General William E. Ward, the first commander of AFRICOM, by stripping him of one star; thus Ward retired as a three-star lieutenant general and was ordered to repay the government $82,000 for unauthorized lavish spending. These four changes at the top of the U. S. military establishment are symptomatic of the failed NATO intervention in North Africa and the subsequent war and killings that have been unleashed by militias in Libya, especially in Benghazi. These changes exposed the new autonomy and war-fighting capabilities exercised by the CIA and the military leaders, all of whom were making policy independent of the executive branch and civilian leadership. The culture of rampant deception and distortion within the military establishment in Africa was now in full display for the American public and the world.

This culture of deception and distortion did not come out of a vacuum. This military culture emanated from a sense of excessive pride and arrogance (hubris) that had been molded by neoconservatives who had come to believe that the United States could unilaterally lead pre-emptive wars and that the world would thus be safer with the leadership of the United States. After the fateful events of September 11, 2001, these neoconservative forces dominated the U.S. political and military establishment and advocated robust action to promote "democracy, human rights, and free markets and to maintain U.S. primacy around the world."[285] In September 2002 this posture was summarized in a National Security Strategy of George W. Bush that called for the primacy of U.S. interests, preemptive war, and vigorous action to stop terrorism and remove weapons of mass destruction from rogue states.

The war on terrorism had provided the context for a huge military buildup, in which the military saw itself as the supreme defender of Western "Christian values" and the "American way of life." Very early, this war was called "the new crusade." The resources unleashed to the military ensured that the military faction of the neoconservatives (who were called crusaders) believed that they were untouchable. These militarists also mobilized the media to promote the ideas of fighting a war against terrorism. The religious metaphor associated with the Crusades had been invoked when George Bush had proclaimed that there was an "axis of evil" that must be eliminated. After this list of three evils—Iraq, Iran, and North Korea—there were a number of countries designated as "sponsors of terrorism" that had to be brought in line. Libya had been one of the states on the initial list that had been drawn up by the

State Department in April 2001. Apart from Libya and the three from the axis of evil, the other "state sponsors of terrorism" according to the neocons were Cuba, Sudan, and Syria.[286]

From the writings of the leading theoreticians of the neoconservatives we can grasp how the military had been so elevated to believe that there was a revolution in military affairs. Central to this "revolution" was the use of the Special Operations Command, the integration of private military contractors, and the dominance of airspaces (with drones and satellites) coordinated by the intelligence services. Third-country nationals that are allies of the United States would support the "full spectrum dominance" in a context in which the United States would avoid excessive "boots on the ground." In this revolution there had been disagreement with those who believed in the deployment of massive force. The revolution entailed new concepts of war by which the United States had the resources to go anywhere and impose its will. Although reluctant at the outset of the Libyan intervention, once engaged, the intelligence services of the United States and AFRICOM experimented with all of the techniques that had been advocated by Secretary of Defense Donald Rumsfeld. In Libya, the CIA and AFRICOM kept up the pretense that there had been no boots on the ground, while the local militias and forces from Qatar, along with military intelligence resources from Britain and France, allowed the military brass to present the NATO intervention in Libya as a model of success. One social scientist actually cited "no boots on the ground" as one of the principal lessons to be learned from the NATO intervention in Libya.[287] All of this deception seemed to have taken hold until September 11, 2012, when Ambassador Stevens and three others were killed in a battle in Benghazi.

At the start of the twenty-first century, conservative intellectuals had taken the lead in the definition of the relations between the United State and the international community, along with the relationship between the U.S. military and U.S. citizens. The liberal wing of the corporate elements had ceded political and intellectual leadership to the think tanks and universities dominated by a new cadre of intellectuals who had been linked to the Project for a New American Century

(PNAC). The top news and information outlets fell in line as Fox News became central to the revolution in military affairs. Numerous scholars within and outside North America have written on the role of neoconservative forces in the United States and how Republican academics, politicians, and journalists dominated the administration of George W. Bush.[288] Mention has already been made of the role of Donald Rumsfeld as the core neocon who dominated the Department of Defense. The cabal also included Vice President Dick Cheney; Paul Wolfowitz, Deputy Secretary of Defense; Douglas Feith, Under Secretary of Defense for Policy; Lewis "Scooter" Libby, the vice president's chief of staff; Elliott Abrams, the National Security Council staffer for Near East, Southwest Asian, and North African Affairs; and Richard Perle, a member of the Defense Policy Board. Outside the Pentagon and the White House there was John Bolton at the UN, with support outside the administration from William Kristol, Francis Fukuyama, John Negroponte, *Commentary* editor Norman Podhoretz, and others who dominated the reproduction of ideas to influence the media. Fox News and the corporate media elevated the ideas of the neocons so that their views would become mainstream inside the United States.

The neoconservatives set the agenda for the U. S. military and economic policies, but the boldest aspect of their work was the effort to hijack the language and tactics of the international peace movement. Prior to the invasion of Iraq, George Bush had advocated for that intervention in the name of peace. Sreeram Chaulia in his narration of the takeover of the United States Institute of Peace (USIP) highlighted the ways in which the institute had been hostage to successive American administrations' quest for "hegemony in the realm of ideas from its first day in existence. It is a tragic metaphor of how countless U.S. administrations have paid lip service to peace, while remaining primarily concerned with securing American domination of the world."[289]

This effort to achieve hegemony in the realm of ideas was taken further inside the Department of Defense through the ways in which social scientists were suborned by the military strategy of the Pentagon. General David Petraeus had come up inside the military in the heyday of the neoconservatives and had sought to mobilize their propaganda techniques and strategies to advance his own career and the fortunes of the branch of U.S. capital that was in ascendancy. Under the intellectual and ideological vision of General Petraeus, the convergence of the dark capital of financialization and the dark forces of covert wars had merged when he was elevated to become Commander of U.S. Central Command (CENTCOM) and later left the military to head the CIA. When he left the military, Senator Lindsay Graham discussed with him the great opportunities for military action provided by his elevation to CIA director.

General Petraeus now joined the pantheon of intelligence and military professionals such as William Colby and William Casey who had used the CIA for massive covert wars. Petraeus was running a war in Libya, and his actions as a military and intelligence commander blew up in a scandal where the NATO intervention consumed both him and the commander of the AFRICOM. The arrogance and self-deception of the top military brass had reached the point where they considered themselves untouchable, where they became sloppy and amateurish in their skullduggery. The drama that unfolded around the resignation of David Petraeus was like a soap opera, but the tragedy of this opera was that there were real humans who had lost their lives. NATO had intervened in Libya to save lives but at the end of this "successful" intervention, over 50,000 Libyans had been killed. The U.S. ambassador to Libya lost his life along with four other personnel who were deployed in the new fighting template of the CIA and the Pentagon.

The soap opera about Petraeus's extramarital affair overshadowed the real tragedy of the full results of the neocon global war on terror. Inside Washington, it was an open secret that there was a relationship between the general and his biographer, who had written *All In: The Education of General David Petraeus*. This book was published in January 2012, and when Paula Broadwell appeared on *The Daily Show* with Jon Stewart that month to promote her biography, she was full of innuendo, so that those who could read the subtext of her message could discern what she was attempting to communicate. The corporate media reported that the extramarital affair had been uncovered by the FBI, and that it reflected "poor judgment" on the part of Petraeus.

The title of this chapter, "Libya All In," is appropriate in that it seeks to summarize the results of the NATO intervention and its aftermath. The title takes its cue from the work of Paula Broadwell, who was a cheerleader for the sagacity and genius of David Petraeus. Her book was supposed to bring to light all of the positive qualities that have been groomed out of self-deception. The objective was to bring to the world the details of the life of a great military leader and strategist. "Libya All In," says how the self-deception about success of covert war overtook the military and intelligence leadership until the Benghazi attack, which exposed the harsh reality that Libya was still at war.

The Scandal that Broke the Self-Deception in the U.S. Military

The intimate relationship between finance capital, academia, and the media had been refined in the new war template that had been experimented with since the ascendancy of the neoconservatives. On October 18, 2012, Secretary of Defense Leon Panetta announced that President Obama would nominate General David Rodriguez to succeed General Carter Ham as commander of AFRICOM. One month after the episodic disasters for the U.S. legation the internal investigations into the U.S. military response led to the nomination of General David Rodriguez to become head of AFRICOM. Rodriquez had worked closely with Petraeus in Afghanistan, then went to work with Robert Gates, and then went to work with General McChrystal in Afghanistan.

The Petraeus scandal revealed that General John Allen, commander of the U.S. military in Afghanistan, in the midst of a war, had the time and space to send 20,000 to 30,000 pages of email to Jill Kelley, the woman in Tampa, Florida, who was viewed by General Petraeus's mistress as a rival for his attentions. Media hype about "inappropriate communication" with Jill Kelley did not divert attention from the realities of the current state of warfare in Afghanistan, where young U.S. citizens are sent to die. John Allen belonged to the close-knit circle of Petraeus supporters in the military who have now been brought to light by his biographer.

The incestuous relationship between U.S. journalists and the U.S. military had taken new directions when the wars in Afghanistan and Iraq created the media/military relationship called "embedded journalism." One writer outlined the pitfalls of this relationship in an analysis titled "'The Grunt Truth' of Embedded Journalism: The New Media-Military Relationship," which drew out the sexual connotations of the meaning of "embedded":

> Perhaps unwittingly, the Pentagon's choice of the word "embed" implies a sexual pun that illuminates the transgressive and incestuous nature of the media-military relationship. "This time, we're going to embed reporters," says Marjorie Miller, editor of the *LA Times*. "We didn't want to be in bed with the military, but we certainly wanted to be there. And we didn't know if it was a trick or if ... they, for some reason that we couldn't fathom, had decided to give us access." This incestuous intimacy between the media and military has become an unprecedented exploitation of the concept of freedom of the press. Not only are both parties disregarding the notion of a free and independent press, but both are exploiting one another's resources for their own benefit.[290]

The relationship between Paula Broadwell and David Petraeus was one in which two individuals were "exploiting one another's resources for their own benefit." In the words of Douglas MacGregor, "Broadwell and Petraeus were simply two people with converging agendas."

Embedded journalism provided the perfect alliance between the media and the military for military information operations; in short, for the propaganda that sells the military and its success to the public. Embedded journalists were tools of information warfare and enabled the Pentagon to dominate the information about the war on terror. Embedded journalists signed contracts with the military promising not to report information that could compromise unit position, future missions, and classified weapons. With her book, Broadwell reflected the real results of embedded journalism. Despite its sycophancy the book usefully pointed to the names of the journalists and military officers who were in the inner circle of David Petraeus.

When the information on the extramarital relationship between Petraeus and Broadwell entered the public domain, there had been many stories linking this embedded history to the contemporary military leadership. What was less known was how Thomas Ricks, one of the preeminent U.S. military journalists, had introduced Broadwell to his publisher so that she could obtain a book contract. Tom Ricks, like Michael O' Hanlon, senior fellow and director of research at the Brookings Institution, were mentioned favorably in the book by Broadwell. After the scandal, O'Hanlon wrote, "By any reasonable reckoning, Petraeus is one of the handful of greatest generals of his generation. By my admittedly biased reckoning, he is perhaps one of the nation's 10 best of all time."[291] This fiction that Petraeus was one of the greatest generals of all time had also been peddled by the celebrated military authority Thomas Ricks.

Throughout the wars after 2001, Thomas Ricks wrote three major books on the U.S. military forces: *Fiasco: The American Military Adventure In Iraq*, a follow-up, *The Gamble: General David Petraeus and the American Military Adventure in Iraq, 2006–2008*, full of praise for the leadership of General Petraeus, and his most recent *The Generals: American Military Command from World War II to Today*. These books were very different from the scholarship of Andrew Bacevich, an ex-military officer who had become an academic and who had been writing profusely on the failures of the U.S. military project. Bacevich had been very clear about the concrete limitations of the military power of the United States and as a veteran of the wars in Vietnam wanted a proper analysis of the history of the military.[292]

Whereas Bacevich and other historians sought to study the military enterprise as a whole, Ricks took partisan accounts of the reversals for the United States in Vietnam and laid the blame for the failures on different generals in *The Generals*. Numerous generals were critiqued for their incompetence and lack of vision. Ricks argued that many of these generals should have been fired. Of General Petraeus, Ricks was full of praise, noting that Petraeus showed "real independence of thought . . . he is an adaptive general." Petraeus was the one with good judgment, while others such as Tommy Franks and George Casey were compared to William Westmoreland, the poster general of failure in Vietnam. What was significant was the silence of Ricks about the role of the U.S. military in Libya. In this book, published in 2012, the intervention in Libya did not rank as a major military operation for the armed forces of the United States.

When Tom Ricks wrote *Fiasco*, he had joined a growing list of journalists who were beginning to see the dysfunctionality of the U.S. military operations in Iraq. For the people of Libya, the United Nations, and the peace community, the Petraeus scandal as it unfolded was of particular interest because of the close relationships between the oil companies, Western intelligence/military agencies, and the marauding militias that were coercing Libyan citizens. The failure of the counterinsurgency strategy in Iraq and Afghanistan had exposed the incompetence of the U.S. military, with the United States bogged down in Afghanistan for over ten years. The incompetence and corruption in Afghanistan had been papered over by the corporate media, which understood from polling data that more than 75 percent of the U.S. population wanted the United States to leave Afghanistan. But if the United States withdrew from Afghanistan, there would be pressure for a massive reduction of the military budget, and this was anathema to the U.S. oligarchy.

When the information about the attack on the U.S. facility in Benghazi was first brought to light, there had been confusion because this information had the potential to put the vaunted security establishment in its proper perspective. Was the space that was attacked a consulate, a State Department facility, CIA safe house, or, indeed, a prison for captured militias? This confusion took attention away from the reality that elements in the military-intelligence hierarchy had formulated a policy to align with certain militia groups in eastern Libya and that these militias (sometimes called jihadists) had in the past been linked to groups that the United States called "terrorist organizations." France, the CIA, and AFRICOM had aligned with these jihadists to destabilize Libya, freeze billions of dollars of assets, execute Gaddafi, and keep the alliance going, using Libya as a rear base in the drive for regime change in Syria.

The Republicans sought to benefit from the confusion and disinformation spun by U.S. intelligence and the military concerning the causes of the death of the ambassador in Benghazi. Hearings were called before the Republican-controlled Congress; the State Department issued statements; the CIA issued a timeline of the events in Benghazi on the night of September 11; and the conservative media sought to politicize the events in order to present a picture of incompetence on the part of the Obama administration. With every press release and timeline presented, new questions arose about the rot and web of corruption of U.S. war-fighting capabilities. After Petraeus resigned, the U.S. press reported that he had traveled to Libya at the end of October to carry out his own investigation. No sooner than this information came out, it was revealed that the CIA had been holding Libyan militias as prisoners in the CIA annex in Benghazi. It was also revealed that the "Libya annex" was the largest CIA station in North Africa.[293] This information, delivered by Paula Broadwell in a speech before the University of Denver on October 26, deepened the intrigue about what was going on in Libya. The strident denial from the CIA about the secret prison was itself revealing. In that lecture, Broadwell confirmed the reports on Fox News that the CIA had asked for a special unit, the Commander in Chief's In Extremis Force, to come and assist it in Benghazi. It devolved to an Israeli news outlet to bring out this important information.[294]

Petraeus had been the commander of the U.S. forces in Iraq and Afghanistan at a moment in the history of the United States when military information operations were as important as weapons. According to U.S. military doctrine, in this new kind of warfare there had been the struggle to "control the narrative." The U.S. establishment could never control the narrative on Africa because the history of white supremacy and chauvinism precluded a clear understanding of the dynamics of self-determination. In the ten years of the absolute failures of the U.S. military operations in Iraq and Afghanistan, the effort to control the narrative had involved a massive disinformation campaign aimed at U.S. citizens. This campaign had sought to present scholars such as Noam Chomsky as fringe intellectuals, and new liberal voices emerged that soft-pedaled the torture and criminal activities of the military. Younger commentators such as Rachel Maddow, who had written a quasi-critical book on the U.S. military, titled *Drift: The Unmooring of American Military Power*, retreated in her criticisms of the military when it came to Libya.[295] In the case of Libya, the corporate media had presented the end of the war as a victory for the forces of NATO. The truth was never divulged that there was still fighting going on, with the most recent battles at Bani Walid an explicit statement on the ongoing war.

The "successful" NATO intervention had been sold as a narrative until the levels of instability and fighting exposed the reality that there was no real authority in Libya with legitimate control over violence. Marauding militias made life unbearable for all of those without guns. The full backstory relating to the CIA and Libya was still unfolding, but it was important to grasp how the created structures, such as the U.S. Africa Command, sought to function as if it were a parallel government with its own access to USAID resources, financing, health providers, private military contractors, and access to aircraft carrier strike groups such as the USS *John Stennis*. This was a military and intelligence integration, independent of the executive, that was out of control and establishing policy.

Racism Fuels Hubris and Self-Deception

The concept that the war on terror was being presented as the new crusade came from the progressive sector of U.S. academia. Monthly Review Press published early in 2002 Rahul Mahujan's *The New Crusade: America's War on Terrorism*, which exposed how domestic racism in the United States was brought to bear as a psychological prop for the war on terror.[296] Racism also acted as a prop for the self-deception and arrogance of the top generals who tolerated neo-Nazis in their ranks and provided a sanctuary in the military for racists.[297] The rhetoric of fighting terrorism had appealed to white racist groups, and the Southern Poverty Law Center (SPLC) reported in 2006 that some high-profile members of extremist groups were serving in the U.S. military. Domestic terrorist organizations have flourished during the presidency of Barack Obama, as noted by the SPLC in testimony before the Senate Subcommittee on the Constitution, Civil Rights and Human Rights in 2012.

In testimony before the Senate, the SPLC reported a third year of extraordinary growth that has swelled the ranks of extremist groups to record levels. The SPLC tracked 1,018 hate groups—a 69 percent increase since 2000—in addition to 1,274 antigovernment "patriot" groups, which include armed militias.[298]

From the point of view of the top military and intelligence apparatus, the racism that inspired these new domestic militias posed a major threat to peace (especially to social peace inside the United States), but the white racists were tolerated inside the military. According to the SPLC, the presence of extremists in the military increased with the need to bolster ranks for the wars in Iraq and Afghanistan. After the shootings at a Sikh temple in Wisconsin in 2012, U.S. citizens and the world were exposed to the high level of organization among racists in the U.S. military. One writer, who had interviewed the shooter, Michael Page, reported that Page had asserted that it was in the military where he embraced the white power movement.[299] "In the military, he saw and experienced things that really angered him, frustrated him and convinced him that whites were really victimized and the deck was really stacked against whites," criminologist Peter Simi wrote. "What he told me at one point was that if you don't join the military as a racist, then you're certainly going to leave as a racist."[300]

The intensification of racism in the military merged with the expansion of political formations such as the Tea Party that went around with slogans such as "We want our country back." This slogan reflected a wish to return to the era of Jim Crow before the dismantling of the worst forms of segregation and white supremacy. It was not by accident that U.S. military centers, such as the four counties of North Carolina where Fort Bragg is located, and Tampa, Florida, were spaces for very conservative forces. David Petraeus and John Allen were social leaders in the conservative milieu of Tampa. As the head of CENTCOM in Tampa, David Petraeus had been identified as one of the core leaders of a group in the U.S. military called the Crusaders.

The Rocks and Crusaders Revisited

When the U.S. Africa Command was launched in October 2007, William E. "Kip" Ward, a U.S. Army four-star general, served as commander from October 1, 2007, to March 8, 2011. In the same period that the scandal of David Petraeus and John Allen was revealed, General Ward, an African American, was demoted to a three-star lieutenant general, and is now scheduled for retirement. Ward had been quickly removed from AFRICOM after the passing of Resolution 1970 in February 2011, when NATO top brass and the U.S. intelligence agencies knew of the plot against the people of Libya, which was to be routed through AFRICOM. As an African American, Ward had fostered close relationships with African generals and politicians, even those who had publicly opposed AFRICOM. Ward was removed and demoted on the charge that he had spent excessive amounts of money allowing his family members to fly on government planes. A Pentagon report in January 2011 showed that General Ward took an eleven-day trip to Washington, D.C., and Atlanta with an entourage of military and civilian personnel, costing taxpayers $129,000. More relevant, and more damaging, a seventeen-month army investigation alleged that General Ward had "spent several hundred thousand dollars allowing unauthorized people, including family members, to fly on government planes, and spent excessive amounts of money on hotel rooms, transportation and other expenses when he traveled as head of AFRICOM."[301] The saga of General Ward demonstrated that even black officers inside the military had internalized the culture of unaccountability that had prevailed within the Pentagon. Black officers such as Ward who could not be called Crusaders but nonetheless were similar to non-white officials such as Barack Obama, Colin Powell, Condoleezza Rice, and Susan Rice who were willing and able to place their knowledge at the service of empire. As African Americans these officers faced racism inside the U.S. political apparatus.

General Carter Ham had been confirmed by the U.S. Senate in November 2010 to become the next commander of AFRICOM, but the revolutionary upsurge in Tunisia and Egypt hastened his deployment and he assumed the post on March 8, 2011. At that time, the

U.S. military was divided between those I term the "Rocks" and the "Crusaders."[302] The term Crusaders was popularized by the Pulitzer Prize–winning journalist Seymour Hersh to describe the faction of the U.S. military that had taken over the U.S. Army. Hersh asserted that the Crusaders were bent on intensifying a war against Islam, and viewed themselves as protectors of Christianity. According to Hersh, these neoconservative elements dominate the top echelons of the U.S. military, including figures such as former commander of U.S. forces in Afghanistan General Stanley McChrystal and Vice Admiral William McRaven, commander of the U.S. Special Operations Command. Hersh said, "What I'm really talking about is how eight or nine neocon- servatives, radicals if you will, overthrew the American government. Took it over."[303] The Rocks, although primarily non-white senior offi- cers in the military, such as retired four-star general Colin Powell, also comprised the rank-and-file service personnel who believed that the military should not be used for the interest of private capital. Some indication of the differences between the Rocks and the Crusaders arose over the questions of the form of force and the deployment of Special Operations teams and secret wars. Douglas J. Feith, one of the core neocons, had written about the divisions in the Bush administra- tion in his book, *War and Decision: Inside the Pentagon at the Dawn of the War on Terrorism.*

In May 2009, four months after the inauguration of President Barack Obama, *Harper's* magazine carried a lengthy report that placed General David Petraeus at the heart of the Crusaders. The magazine carried a detailed article on the role of the Crusaders in the military, titled "Evangelical Proselytization Still Rampant in U.S. Military," which alerted us to the numerous fronts of the Crusaders. The author discusses a book published in 2005 by Lt. Colonel William McCoy, *Under Orders: A Spiritual Handbook for Military Personnel.* This book outlined an "anti-Christian bias" in the United States and sought to counter it by making the case for the "necessity of Christianity for a properly functioning military." McCoy's book was endorsed by David Petraeus, who said, "*Under Orders* should be in every rucksack for those moments when soldiers need spiritual energy."

Military scholars who wrote on the need for AFRICOM displayed a "moral superiority" that was bound to elicit opposition from Africans. This arrogance espoused the moral superiority of the war on terrorism, but in reality the closest allies in this war on terror had been the Christian extremists and the Islamic extremists. There are decent citizens in opposing societies where the political space exists for moderate and progressive forms of thought. These social forces are sidelined by U.S. policy framers because such engagement would naturally oppose both neoliberal imperialism and religious extremism.

Although the top echelons of the Pentagon and the Obama administration originally recoiled at the push for a French-led military intervention in Libya, once the battles had been engaged, the Obama administration supported the war as long as it could keep the attention of the public unaware that the country was now involved in a new war. For this reason, the Obama administration had resisted the implementation of the War Powers Act to give legitimacy to the U.S. participation in the military activities in Libya. John Barry, who wrote on "America's Secret War in Libya," noted in August 2011: "The U.S. military has spent about $1 billion so far and played a far larger role in Libya than it has acknowledged, quietly implementing an emerging 'covert intervention' strategy that the Obama administration hopes will let America fight small wars with a barely detectable footprint."[304] By the time Petraeus shed his uniform to become director of the CIA in September 2011, the secret war provided the perfect opportunity for the Crusaders to work from positions of power at the top of both the Pentagon and the intelligence apparatus. The Libyan war gave the Crusaders the opportunity to destroy a stable society in North Africa and unleash 1,700 militias in the society. Not only did the Libyan invasion enable the Crusaders an opportunity to create havoc, but it placed great strains within Africa with the fallout from Libya unleashing instability all across northwest Africa. Paula Broadwell revealed that under Petraeus the CIA had built up Benghazi as the largest CIA operation in North Africa. General Carter Ham, who had been handed the responsibility to be the commander for AFRICOM after Gen. Stanley McChrystal was sacked, worked closely with the CIA. The COIN strategy that was being experimented with in Libya demanded the kind of interagency cooperation that placed greater authority in the hands of the commander of AFRICOM.

AFRICOM deepened the strategic concepts of General Petraeus to mobilize "dark" forces to fight wars. This was based on the mobilization of financial resources and personnel outside the formal structures of the U.S. military, with the heavy use of the Central Intelligence Agency and private military contractors. Nick Turse has chronicled this new direction in fighting plan of the military establishment in *The Changing Face of Empire: Special Ops, Drones, Spies, Proxy Fighters, Secret Bases, and Cyberwarfare*.[305] In the case of Africa, Turse wrote online on "Obama's Scramble for Africa," outlining in detail the way in which AFRICOM has, in recent years, spread its influence across that continent, establishing bases and outposts, sending in special operations forces and drones, funding proxy forces on the continent, expanding the U.S. military presence from Djibouti to Libya, and increasing cooperation with the CIA.

> The U.S. is now involved, directly and by proxy, in military and surveillance operations against an expanding list of regional enemies. They include al-Qaeda in the Islamic Maghreb in North Africa; the Islamist movement Boko Haram in Nigeria; possible al-Qaeda-linked militants in post-Qaddafi Libya; Joseph Kony's murderous Lord's Resistance Army (LRA) in the Central African Republic, Congo, and South Sudan; Mali's Islamist Rebels of the Ansar Dine, al-Shabaab in Somalia; and guerrillas from al-Qaeda in the Arabian Peninsula across the Gulf of Aden in Yemen.[306]

Following the publication of this article in July 2012, Turse was involved in a debate with Colonel Tom Davis of AFRICOM over whether the U.S. military presence was growing very fast in Africa.[307] Turse was not an authority on Africa and drew from journalists who had written articles about the growth of AFRICOM.[308] Davis, director of the AFRICOM Office of Public Affairs, disputed in some detail a number of Turse's points, which illustrated just how sensitive the

AFRICOM bureaucracy had become about the new forms of warfare with proxy fighters, special ops, and drones.

General Petraeus found the perfect space to set up an alternative military/intelligence policy-making unit when he requested that he be placed as head of the Central Intelligence Agency after he sought to flee the web of narcotics trafficking and corruption in Afghanistan in 2011. According to the *New York Times*:

> The appointments of General Petraeus and Mr. Panetta were the latest evidence of a significant shift over the past decade in how the United States fights its battles—the blurring of lines between soldiers and spies in secret American missions abroad. . . . General Petraeus aggressively pushed the military deeper into the C.I.A.'s turf, using Special Operations troops and private security contractors to conduct secret intelligence missions. As commander of the United States Central Command in September 2009, he also signed a classified order authorizing American Special Operations troops to collect intelligence in Saudi Arabia, Jordan, Iran and other places outside of traditional war zones.[309]

In *All In: The Education of David Petraeus* the reader is told that Senator Graham of South Carolina "discussed with Petraeus that as head of the CIA he could actually have more impact on the war against terrorism. He could direct the work of covert operations around the world."[310] The unspoken agreement among the neoconservatives was that David Petraeus would still be the dominant force in the military establishment.

Shake-up and Cover-up in the Military Establishment
after the Benghazi Debacle

The alliance with the Crusaders ensnared the State Department and the U.S. diplomatic forces in the war in Libya. Ambassador Stevens had become a cheerleader for cooperation between Special Operations and private military contractors. Christopher Stevens had left his position in the embassy in Tripoli in February 2011 to coordinate this kind of warfare in Benghazi. In this way he was working directly with the AFRICOM forces and the CIA's maintenance of the largest operation in North Africa. When NATO declared victory in October 2011, Stevens was selected as ambassador to Libya, and by May 2012 he was back in Libya as ambassador. However, the principal base for Special Ops and private security intrigue was in Benghazi, where the CIA was recruiting extremists to fight in Syria. Stevens was caught in a battle between militias and the CIA. Ambassador Stevens, information management officer Sean Smith, and CIA agents Tyrone Woods and Glen Doherty were killed in the Benghazi attack. When the news was first reported, Woods and Doherty had been identified as private security contractors in order to divert attention away from the CIA in the Benghazi battle. By the time of the Petraeus scandal, the State Department and the Pentagon wanted to distance themselves from the massive operation in Libya, but as we've seen, in the midst of the NATO intervention, the State Department had ceded authority of "matters of development and democracy" to the Pentagon.

War Is Not a Game

Sean Smith, the information manager of the State Department, was a "geek" who had been mobilized for the new kind of military posture of the United States. After his passing, there was mourning in the cyber community. According to the *New York Times*, "Mr. Smith was an avid player of an online multiplayer game called Eve Online, in which hundreds of thousands of participants across the globe took on roles like pirates or diplomats in a science fiction setting. Mr. Smith's online name was 'vile rat.' " The experience of "vile rat" was indicative of how the U.S. military had mobilized computer specialists in both real and virtual worlds. Coded messages were shared in this virtual world to serve the interests of the military intelligence forces that were operating outside of the policy framework of the government

Smith has been called a maven by his fellow gamers, who mourn his passing. Drawing from Malcolm Gladwell's *The Tipping Point*, Smith was compared to those mavens or connectors who are "information specialists," or "people we rely upon to connect us with new information."[311] These connectors had become crucial for the new forms of warfare where the lines between virtual and real wars are blurred. Increasingly, the gamers draw extensively from real situations so that many of the video games are actual simulations of possible battle scenarios. The conservative militarists who conceive the masculinist forms of entertainment only recently brought out "Call of Duty: Black Ops II," which featured a computer-animated David Petraeus as Secretary of Defense. Sean Smith found out tragically that real war is not a game.

From the point of view of this book, the relationship of Sean Smith to a generation of U.S. citizens had been nurtured to hide the reality of what gamers such as Smith were involved in. These gamers were supporting the hubris and self-deception of the U.S. military establishment.

From the books of Bob Woodward such as *Obama's Wars*, we now know that former general Jack Keane (now on the board of the Institute for the Study of War) is one of the most energetic forces aligned with the Petraeus wing of the military-intelligence establishment. Paula Broadwell described Jack Keane as the mentor of Petraeus. The fact that Jack Keane came forward as the chief explainer for National Public Radio, about the CIA timeline of the events in Benghazi where Sean Smith and Christopher Stevens died gave away the fact that Petraeus was heavily involved in the events of September 11–12, 2012.[312]

In the NPR interview on November 2 Jack Keane told the world of the decision of General Carter Ham to ask for the National Mission Response Force (NMRF) to be deployed to Benghazi. The NMRF is a classified force based on the East Coast of the United States, on alert 24/7, the shortest alert string we have to go anyplace in the world. In this interview Keane told the U.S. public:

> Now, those were ground forces and there were no other forces that were available and that's why he had to request forces from outside of AFRICOM's command and control. General Ham also requested

a similar force that is part of the European command that—this is a classified force, special operations again. They were in central Europe training. They moved them to a base, got them equipped for combat and moved them to Sigonella. And when they arrived there, they also were told that the CIA annex had been evacuated. The problem we have is AFRICOM has no assigned forces stationed anywhere near Libya. So we had to depend—he had to depend on alerting forces to come from the continent of Europe and the continent of North America to participate in a firefight.

This information on the deployment of forces by the commander of AFRICOM was veiled, but there is enough in the interview to grasp the fact that Carter Ham was drawn into a battle for which AFRICOM was not equipped. When the Pentagon carried out its investigation about what happened in Benghazi, Carter Ham was relieved of his post as commander of AFRICOM. He had not served the usual three years. General Petraeus journeyed to Libya after Ham was relieved of his post hoping to save his reputation and the forms of warfare and destruction that he had refined. Douglas Feith's *War and Decision* places the revelations of Jack Keane in proper perspective:

> As a legal matter, the chain of command for military operations is straightforward. The President and the Secretary of Defense are the two civilians—the only two—who can issue an order to U.S military forces. For operations (as opposed to training) the chain runs from the two of them directly to the four-star general or admiral at the top of each combatant command—for example CENTCOM, Pacific Command or Special Operations command. These combatant commanders are responsible for planning and fighting wars—indeed, for planning and executing all military operations, including humanitarian relief and reconstruction. [313]

This chain of command had been in place early in the war on terrorism, before the experimentation in Iraq gave new forms of decision making to the COIN implementers.

Rise and Fall of Petraeus: Making Benghazi an Election Issue

General David Petraeus, an ambitious officer from the U.S. military, had achieved international notoriety based on how he harnessed the resources of the media to burnish his image. In numerous books and articles on Petraeus we have learned how he harnessed the resources for self-aggrandizement. We learned of the comparison to Napoleon when Petraeus mobilized teams of directed telescopes: "The directed telescope concept, once employed by Napoleon, is a process by which a senior commander uses aides or trusted advisors, often junior officers, to focus on issues beyond his sights, thus helping the commander expand his knowledge of the battlefield."[314]

We have learned that there were three layers of the teams of directed telescopes. First were the members of the Counterinsurgency Advisory and Assistance Team (CAAT). This was the team of career and former military officers, heavy on Special Operations experience and PhDs. The second layer of the team of directed telescopes were the Commander's Initiative Group (CIG)—a team of trusted officers all with advanced degrees. The third layer comprised academic experts, outside mentors, and think tankers who were usually brought in by Petraeus to provide another set of eyes. When one adds the role of the fawning embedded journalists, it was possible to see how General Petraeus had been packaged and created for the American people.

Petraeus was known as an ambitious officer from the time he was at West Point when he grasped that marrying the daughter of the superintendent would enhance his career. Holly Knowlton was from a historical military family; her father, General William A. Knowlton, served as head of West Point when Petraeus was a cadet. Petraeus graduated in 1974 from the U.S. Military Academy at West Point, and two months before his graduation he married Holly Knowlton. Petraeus fancied himself as a soldier scholar, so he pursued advanced degrees at Princeton, writing a doctoral dissertation on "The American Military and the Lessons of Vietnam."

Petraeus became adept at mobilizing academics, especially social scientists, to abet his ambitious maneuvering. Such maneuvering could account for the close relationship between Petraeus and Michael O'Hanlon of the Brookings Institution, who was all over the media calling for ways to rehabilitate Petraeus after the scandal broke. The self-deception referred to above was running so wild that O'Hanlon stated: "By any reasonable reckoning, Petraeus is one of the handful of greatest generals of his generation." This point of view was not shared by the thousands of officers who had opposed financing the "Sunni Awakening" and were critical of how Petraeus had turned the top military into an institution to serve the neoconservatives, especially after Donald Rumsfeld was forced out in 2006.

Inside the U.S. military Petraeus had been known by the traditional officers as one who would do anything to advance his career. His close relationship with George W. Bush and the "success" of the surge in Iraq had been chronicled by embedded journalists who wanted the U.S. population to forget Abu Ghraib, Fallujah, and fatal shootings of civilians by Blackwater contractors at Nisoor Square in Baghdad. Petraeus was a figure of disunity within the military, especially because of his close relationship to the neoconservatives. One retired officer posed the question in this way, "Was General David Petraeus the heroic figure his press releases suggested or a piece of fiction created, packaged and presented to the American people by the Bush Administration and its Neocon allies in the media and academia as the poster boy for counterinsurgency?"[315]

The complete history of General Petraeus is now on full display, but what was not widely known is how he was really a work of fiction, created, packaged, and promoted to the American people. Most citizens in the United States are not aware of the immense suffering imposed on the peoples during the "surge" engineered by Petraeus. Inside the military there had been great differences among the officer corps, and efforts to understand the experiences in Afghanistan and Iraq had led to the publication by the Joint Staff of the major study, *Decade of War.* This was written (outside the orbit of the directed telescopes) in order to understand why the U.S. military had failed, caught in the quagmire of corruption and drug wars in Iraq and Afghanistan.

Beyond the military itself, there has been no shortage of texts that explore in great detail how the United States has further corrupted

Afghanistan. Walter Pincus, in the *Washington Post,* was explicit in an article titled "Afghan Corruption, and How the U.S. Facilitates It":

> It is time that we as Americans—in government, in the media, and as analysts and academics—took a hard look at the causes of corruption in Afghanistan. The fact is that we are at least as much to blame for what has happened as the Afghans, and we have been grindingly slow to either admit our efforts or correct them.[316]

Other established military specialists such as Anthony Cordesman wrote extensively on theft and waste in Afghanistan. It was left to the peace writers such as Alfred McCoy to write "Can Anyone Pacify the World's Number One Narco-State? The Opium Wars in Afghanistan."[317]

Though the name of Petraeus did not surface in these reports on drugs and corruption, his high profile as the top commander in Afghanistan and as head of the U.S. Central Command (CENTCOM) brought a focus on him. As an adept manipulator of the media in the refinement of Military Information Operations, Petraeus nurtured the press, and one of the clearest expressions can be found in the book, by Thomas Ricks, *The Generals: American Military Command from World War II to Today.* In this book, generals such as Tommy Franks were assailed in the same vein as Petraeus was venerated. Petraeus was mobilizing the same fawning relationship with Paula Broadwell. Petraeus had met Broadwell in 2006, while she was operating between U.S. military intelligence and Harvard, but this relationship could not be deepened until after the passing of Gen. William A. Knowlton in 2008.

General Petraeus and His Disrespect for Barack Obama

Petraeus had endeared himself to neocons and the Christian fundamentalists as a good example of the West Point cadet Honor Code: "A cadet will not lie, cheat, steal, or tolerate those who do."

Because of his endorsement of Lt.-Colonel William McCoy's *Under Orders: A Spiritual Handbook for Military Personnel,* Petraeus was on the radar of the right. It is not by accident that among the top politicians calling Petraeus at that time was George W. Bush.

It is important for readers to grasp the deep arrogance of Petraeus in relation to Obama. Much of this has come out in the formulation that Petraeus attempted to "box in" the president over the deployment of troops to Afghanistan. Bob Woodward in his book *Obama's Wars* documented the disrespect exhibited from a section of the military (Crusaders) toward Obama. Woodward recounted for history the back-and-forth between Obama and Petraeus and General Stanley A. McChrystal. Stanley McChrystal engineered his exit from the corruption of Afghanistan by making explicit comments about Obama, which he knew would get him out of the opium war in Afghanistan.

Barack Obama immediately appointed General Petraeus as commander to replace McChrystal in Afghanistan. Petraeus understood the stakes of the legacy of generals, and it was based on his sense of history that he supported Paula Broadwell's project to write his biography. Between the biography and Thomas Ricks's book, Petraeus felt that his historical legacy was secure. Inside the military there had been a major debate among the officer corps on whether officers such as Petraeus should be held accountable. Lt.-Colonel Paul Yingling had written a widely discussed article in the *Armed Forces Journal*, "A Failure in Generalship." But with the Crusaders taking over the military, officers who followed the Petraeus line were looked upon favorably.

According to a profile of Petraeus in the *New York Times*:

> Mr. Petraeus had been the most prominent American military commander over the past decade, the architect of the 2007 troop surge in Iraq. He stepped into Gen. Colin L. Powell's shoes as the face of the military, and became a figure extolled on both sides of Washington's partisan divide.

The *New York Times* was fully aware of the divide between the Rocks and the Crusaders and how Obama had relied on Colin Powell to rally the Rocks to checkmate the Crusaders. And we now know that the Obama team was not complacent, since the activities of General

Petraeus were being monitored. Top operatives in the administration had kept an eye on the presidential ambitions of Petraeus, and Petraeus had assured Rahm Emanuel that he was not planning to run for president in 2012.[318] In December 2012 it was finally revealed that Roger Ailes of Fox News had approached Petraeus to recruit him as the presidential candidate for the 2012 elections. Ailes promised Petraeus that he would resign from the news organization to run the campaign and that Rupert Murdoch would offer financial support for his presidential bid.

In the supportive profile of General Petraeus provided by the *New York Times* we are further told:

> Ms. Broadwell became a fixture around the Kabul headquarters of the American-led coalition in Afghanistan soon after General Petraeus assumed command in June 2010. She was seen as ambitious and as a striver who aimed to join Washington's national security elite, and she drew resentment from officers for playing up her connection to their boss.

Six months after General Petraeus assumed command in Kabul and began mentoring his biographer, the administration appointed Holly Knowlton Petraeus as an assistant director of the U.S. Consumer Financial Protection Bureau, charged with advocating on behalf of service members and their families. History will later reveal the extent of the contacts between Michelle Obama and Holly Knowlton and that they among other Washington insiders understood fully the innuendos of Paula Broadwell when she appeared on *The Daily Show*.

Benghazi and Libya Become an Election Issue

Weeks after the battles between the competing militias in Benghazi that claimed the lives of the CIA operatives and the U.S. ambassador, U.S. media sympathetic to the Crusaders "seized on a series of reports by conservative media outlets to make the incendiary charge shortly

before the election that four Americans had died because of the administration's negligence."[319]

General Petraeus said nothing publicly, but from the reports in
the media and from his quick trip to Libya, it was manifest that a big
project of damage control was under way. Conservative media had
been so secure that the narrative of the adminstration's negligence had
taken hold that William Kristol, the editor of the conservative *Weekly
Standard*, concluded that the agency was pointing its finger at the White
House, which he suggested must have refused the requested intervention. "Petraeus Throws Obama Under the Bus" was the headline on the
Weekly Standard's blog.

With the timeline of the Benghazi incident presented by the CIA,
the blog of William Kristol, and the spin presented to National Public
Radio by Jack Keane, there was only one more event that would protect
General Petraeus from being exposed completely: the national election
on November 6, 2012.

Benghazi Does Not Become an Election Issue

Benghazi and Libya did not become an issue in the election in the way
that the conservatives and Crusaders had hoped. Barack Obama was
reelected on November 6. Two days later, Petraeus resigned as head of
the CIA. One writer commented on the way in which the conservative
media had to retreat from the euphoria of the William Kristol blog:

> Given that the CIA was holding prisoners in Benghazi, the goal of
> the Sept. 11 action at the consulate may have been an effort to free
> them, or payback for their detention. And everybody involved in
> that detention, including CIA Director David Petraeus, was com-
> mitting a crime. Unfortunately for Jennifer Griffin of Fox News,
> the right-wing politicians who are looking for ammunition against
> Obama can't make use of her Benghazi reporting because it exposes
> their 4-star hero (who never saw combat or commanded a divi-
> sion) as a perjurer, and the CIA as a rogue agency. After initial calls

for an investigation —even a special commission, a la Watergate—
they realize they mustn't "go there."[320]

The same Tom Ricks who had written about Petraeus as a great
general opined that Fox News had sought to politicize the Benghazi
affair before the election. Ricks had stated clearly and unequivocally
that the channel operates as "a wing of the Republican Party," and that
Fox had spent weeks politicizing and hyping the terrorist attack on the
U.S. consulate in Libya.[321]

We are told by the media that the first time the president learned
of the investigation of the relationship between Paula Broadwell and
David Petraeus was on Thursday, November 8, when Petraeus offered
his resignation. The media had reported that the FBI agent who broke
the news about the relationship between Broadwell and Petraeus had
gone to Eric Cantor of the Republican Party when he felt that the top
leaders of the Justice Department and the FBI were dragging their feet
on investigating Petraeus.

How would Eric Cantor know the full details of the Broadwell-
Petraeus saga and the President not know? Press reports are that the
Attorney General, Eric Holder, had been notified as far back as the
summer.

It defied credulity to read that Barack Obama did not know of the
FBI probe of General David Petraeus:

> White House officials said they were informed on Wednesday
> night that Mr. Petraeus was considering resigning because of
> an extramarital affair. On Thursday morning, just before a staff
> meeting at the White House, President Obama was told. That
> afternoon, Mr. Petraeus went to see him and informed him that he
> strongly believed he had to resign. Mr. Obama did not accept his
> resignation right away, but on Friday, he called Mr. Petraeus and
> accepted it.[322]

Military historians will, however, understand why the President of
the United States had to sleep on the decision to accept the resignation

of the most renowned general in the United States. After all, the influence of Petraeus among journalists and the Crusaders was well known.

Petraeus had served as Commanding General of Fort Leavenworth, Kansas, and the U.S. Army Combined Arms Center (CAC) located there. As commander of CAC, Petraeus had been responsible for oversight of the Command and General Staff College and seventeen other schools, centers, and training programs as well as for developing the Army's doctrinal manuals, training the Army's center for the collection and dissemination of lessons learned.

During his time at CAC, Petraeus and Marine Lt. Gen. James N. Mattis jointly oversaw the publication of Field Manual 3-24, Counterinsurgency, the body of which was written by an extraordinarily diverse group of military officers, academics, human rights advocates, and journalists who had been assembled by Petraeus and Mattis.[323]

I maintain the healthy skepticism that Obama's decision to withhold the acceptance of the resignation of Petraeus was based on the calculated step-by-step approach with the military that had been adopted since 2009. I will also withhold judgment on the effusive praise of Obama for Petraeus at his press conference on November 14, 2012.

Future historians will ponder whether Obama's decision to withhold the acceptance of the resignation of Petraeus was based on the calculated step-by-step approach with the military that had been adopted since 2009 and had been reported by Woodward among others. More importantly, the White House would have been aware of the elaborate plans hatched by Roger Ailes of Fox News to recruit General Petraeus to compete as a candidate in the 2012 Presidential elections. It was the same Bob Woodward of the *Washington Post* who exposed the audio conversation between Petraeus and Kathleen T. McFarland, a Fox News national security analyst and former national security and Pentagon aide in three Republican administrations. It was reported that Roger Ailes would have left his post at Fox News to run the campaign and that this effort would be bankrolled by Rupert Murdoch.

The Libyan War and the Need to Disband Private Military Contractors

With the orientation of the U.S. media toward scandals and celebration of individuals, few in the mainstream media picked up on the information that the CIA had been holding prisoners in Benghazi. The media focused on the salacious details of the extramarital affair of Petraeus, overlooking the more fundamental question of the forms of military destruction that have been unleashed on Iraq, Afghanistan, and then Libya. Within the U.S. military establishment there had been a raging debate on whether generals should be accountable to civilian leadership. The resignation of General Petraeus, the removal of Carter Ham from Africa Command, and the redeployment of Rear Adm. Charles M. Gaouette have brought back the question of civilian control over the military. Despite the book by Tom Ricks crafted to save the reputation of Petraeus and the biography of Broadwell, which was supposed to place Petraeus on the same platform as historic U.S. generals, the new forms of unchecked warfare brought down the top officers of the COIN strategy.

Within a democratic society, the military is supposed to provide advice to military leaders, and military officers are not supposed to deploy troops to engage with militias without the authorization of the civilian leadership. The NATO intervention in Libya and the subsequent CIA operations in Benghazi had been an expensive experiment in new forms of warfare that brought about destruction and the deaths of thousands. After the information on CIA detention centers during the war in Iraq, there had been an outcry about CIA private prisons. Paula Broadwell, who demonstrated that she had access to classified information, told an audience in Denver, Colorado, on October 26, 2012, that "I don't know if a lot of you have heard this, but the CIA annex had actually taken a couple of Libyan militia members prisoner. And they think that the attack on the consulate was an effort to try to get these prisoners back." This information was later confirmed by Jennifer Griffen at Fox News.[324]

U.S. foreign policy makers had resisted the call by sectors of the UN Security Council for a review of the NATO military operations in

Libya. Through the UN Human Rights Council there has been a major effort by peace activists from the Global South to bring private military contractors under international oversight. The Human Rights Council has established an "open-ended intergovernmental working group to consider the possibility of elaborating an international regulatory framework on the regulation, monitoring and oversight of the activities of private military and security companies."[325]

The United States and Britain took the lead in opposing oversight of private military contractors.

Commanders of CENTCOM and AFRICOM have operated over the past five years as if they were running parallel governments. The war on terror had inspired the intellectual climate on counterterror and the rationale for the bureaucratic structure of the unified command that enabled the military to also be a source of "independent" policy creation. This operation had been carried out in a dysfunctional bureaucracy that believed it was untouchable because the media was on its side.

There was no oversight when the military budget placed unlimited resources under the control of military commanders. Why would AFRICOM dig wells in East Africa or hand out schoolbooks? These activities were all part of the public relations exercise to plant the idea that U.S. Africa Command was doing humanitarian work. The confirmation hearings for General Rodriguez will provide another opportunity to expose the CIA/AFRICOM failure in Libya. It is well publicized by African scholars that AFRICOM has been deployed as an auxiliary force to protect U.S. oil companies. In this protection game, some members of the top military apparatus ventured to state explicitly that the role of AFRICOM was to check Chinese influence in Africa. General Petraeus had aggressively pushed the military deeper into the CIA's turf, using Special Operations troops and private security contractors to conduct secret intelligence missions and for fighting. As commander of CENTCOM, Petraeus had refined the scam of fighting with one group and then turning against them later. This double-cross game was taking hold in Libya in order to set back peace and reconstruction for decades, so that Libya would morph into

another Somalia. This is a situation of relentless warfare where competing militias compete for power while external accumulators of capital
such as oil companies can extract resources under the protection of
private military contractors.

With millions of dollars available for suborning journalists and
academics and with a complicit media, the narrative about the success
of AFRICOM has been widely sold within the United States. It is this
attempt to control the narrative that led to the widespread view that
the NATO operation in Libya was a success. The death of Ambassador
Stevens shattered this myth. The firing of Carter Ham uncovered the
ways in which the CIA and sections of the military were making decisions and running policy independent of the civilian leadership.

When one connects the financial dots between CIA front companies such as In-Q-Tel, oil companies, and oil producers, one can see
that global capital is also a partner with the military-industrial complex
and the need for perpetual war on terrorism. That is the circle that must
be broken by those who seek peace.

Petraeus and his supporters had been confident that the circle of war
and destruction would continue for generations. With the support
of the media, Petraeus had been confident that the full details of the
destruction in Libya and alliance with the militias could be kept out
of the public domain. The full story is unfolding. The launch of the
war on terror in September 2001 and the attacks on the U.S. facility
in Benghazi bookended an era of a military strategy in which the military was deceiving U. S. citizens and ended up deceiving itself. The
untimely death of the U. S. ambassador in Libya shattered the smug
press statements and writings that Libya was a success story for a new
kind of warfare in which the United States would lead from behind.
The catastrophic failure in Libya consumed the head of the U.S. Africa
Command and the venerated David Petraeus.

During the period of the Great Depression, militarism and racism
were fused to demobilize the working peoples of Europe to divert
attention from the exploiters. The United States had escaped the worst
aspect of fascist ideas because the anti-racist movement linked racism

to exploitation at home and imperialism abroad. W. E. B. Du Bois, Paul Robeson, and the Council on African Affairs had campaigned against militarism in Africa and against fascism. These forces supported peace and a new mode of economic organization. After the Second World War, the conservatives sought to isolate peace activists such as Du Bois and Robeson by labeling them communist sympathizers. Then, during the Reagan years, a new strata of neoconservatives flourished. One of their main tasks was to achieve hegemony in the realm of ideas inside the United States. Hence, for the past twenty years we have witnessed the distortions of the meaning of peace within the policies and program of the United States Institute of Peace.

For a short moment when the world had been mobilized to oppose the war against Iraq, the peace movement brought out millions in the streets of the world in February 2003. The *New York Times* called this massive organization one of the new superpowers.[326] Faced with this power of public opinion, U.S. warmakers moved aggressively to disperse and disorganize the traditional forms of protests, demonstrations, and petitions of the peace movement. Militarist fronts such as the U.S. Institute of Peace went into full-time operation to turn their centers into arenas for the study of counterterrorism. The interconnecting military lobbies composed of dictators in Saudi Arabia and the Israeli lobby, along with the neoconservative forces of the Project for a New American Century, joined hands with the corporate media to drive fear into the hearts and minds of citizens over terror. Citizens were supposed to forget the real day-to-day terror of unemployment, foreclosure of homes, and environmental degradation. In the specific case of Africa the media and the military teamed up to focus on calls for the deployment of U.S. military in Africa. This was aptly demonstrated in 2012 when the video *Kony 2012* was promoted and over 100 million young persons signed on to the story that the U.S. military should be called in to assist the government of Uganda.[327]

The U.S. military had entered the NATO intervention in Libya always fearing that it would be dragged into a quagmire and exposed for its incompetence. The Petraeus strategy of covert operations and use of third-country nationals, along with the mobilization of militias,

had been undertaken to ensure that the peace movement did not remo-
bilize to the point where millions were once again brought out on the
streets of the world. Nearly thirty years ago the noted peace activist
Johan Galtung posed the question: "Will the peace movement become
a liberation movement?" His answer was simply that it has to.

Peace and justice forces must intensify the call for the disbandment
of the U.S. Africa Command. Africa needs cooperation and support
for reconstruction. Libya needs the support of the entire international
community to rein in the militias and to rebuild the society. It is time
for the peace movement to refocus on the real activities of Petraeus, not
on his extramarital affair.

In fact, European commentators have stated that in Europe some
generals place such information on the gossip circuit to enhance their
reputation. The peace and justice forces need to focus on the interconnections between the departure of Petraeus and Carter Ham, and Rear
Admiral Charles M. Gaouette.

21 — CONCLUSION:
NATO AND THE PROCESSES OF FAILURE
AND DESTRUCTION IN LIBYA

The NATO intervention in Libya, under the mantle of "responsibility to protect," came at a crucial turning point in the history of the world. Multiple crises—economic, ecological, political, military, and social—were demanding new modes of social and economic management. Exploitation, alienation, and dehumanization had deepened in Africa after years of structural adjustment and IMF economic principles. Libya escaped the worst aspects of this market system by seeking to organize a distributive economy. Under the Gaddafi leadership, all students had access to higher education and Libya had the lowest infant mortality rate in Africa. A lower percentage of people lived below the poverty line in Libya than in the Netherlands. Libya had the highest Human Development Index of any country on the continent of Africa.

Yet these material advantages were not sufficient for a generation of Libyans who had lived for forty-two years under one leader. This generation knew that Libya was sitting on billions of dollars of oil, gas, and the largest underground water resources in Africa. Proper management of these resources by the Libyan people continues to be a threat to European domination of Africa as a whole, and North Africa in particular. The revolts against neoliberalism in Tunisia and Egypt exposed the frailty of the governing structures across North Africa. Youths in Libya were inspired by the Tunisian and Egyptian experiences, but their narrow political experience weakened their ability to prevent the hijacking of their protests in Libya. Thus a small group of Libyans with deep intellectual and ideological affinity to the West set themselves up as leaders of this uprising. Some of them had been called reformers and had been closely associated with Saif al-Islam.

From the evidence on the recent history of Libya, these reformers had internalized neoliberal economic thinking and wanted Libya to become like Kuwait or the Gulf States—basically client states of Western capital. State capitalism under Gaddafi had stifled the capabilities and autonomy of "liberal reformers." This small group of capitalists was confronted by another faction inside Libya that promoted Libyan resources nationalism. These nationalists promoted policies designed to increase Libyan government control over and share of revenue from hydrocarbon resources. Western leaders were anxious when reparations from Italy were implemented by the return of cultural artifacts, along with the signing of a treaty under which Italy was to pay $200 million per year for twenty-five years as compensation for colonial wrongdoing.

The Bretton Woods institutions were the chief architects of policies that extended exploitation and capital flight from Africa. In Libya after the sanctions, however, instead of money leaving the control of Libyans, the leadership had renegotiated the EPSA IV agreements whereby major Western oil companies were made to pay $5.4 billion in up-front "bonus" payments. With careful management of the oil revenues, Libya built up substantial reserves, to the point that it held close to $200 billion in overseas financial institutions. As demonstrated in this study, Libyan economic nationalists were poised to play a more dominant role within the Bahrain-based Arab Banking Corporation. The Gulf States had become the epicenter of the financialization of energy resources through the activities of the Intercontinental Exchange (ICE), the brainchild of Morgan Stanley, Goldman Sachs,

British Petroleum, Deutsche Bank, Dean Witter, Royal Dutch Shell, SG Investment Bank, and Totalfina. The financial and energy institutions under ICE had failed to halt the growth of non-Western International Oil Companies (IOC), particularly from India, Japan, Russia, and China. That PetroChina had overtaken ExxonMobil as the largest oil company in the world did not bode well for the future dominance of the dollar, the IMF, and U.S. capitalism. This ascendancy of Chinese petroleum companies, along with the rapid rise of the Brazilian firm Petrobras, created a new international political economy. By 2011, China had overtaken Japan and Brazil had overtaken Britain in the league of economic powerhouses.

Neither Brazil nor China fell under the complete control of the Western energy and financial institutions. Through energetic and skillful negotiations, the political leaders of Brazil, Russia, and China had made great strides in negotiating new agreements with the Libyan leadership. Slowly, China had become a significant trading partner of Libya, with over 35,000 Chinese nationals working in Libyan construction and telecommunications. In April 2008, Russian president Vladimir Putin reportedly traveled to Libya, accompanied by 400 assistants, journalists, and executives, to secure an "agreement to swap Libya's $4.5 billion Soviet-era debt to Russia" for "a large railroad contract and several future contracts in housing construction and electricity development." Several memoranda of understanding were signed with Russian energy giant Gazprom. During that visit, Gaddafi had expressed opposition to NATO's expansion to Ukraine and Georgia—in short, to Global NATO.

From the point of view of Western corporations, the increasing presence of Russia, Brazil, and China in Libya challenged the old world order. Since 1945, scholars and writers from differing sides of the ideological divide have written on the centrality of the oil companies in shaping the foreign and military policies of the United States. There is no shortage of books on the "Seven Sisters of Oil" that underscore the dominance of U.S. and British companies in the international petroleum business and the military/financial imperatives that flow from this dominance.

For a short period, the emergence of the euro suggested that the European Union wanted to challenge the U.S. dollar, but the world capitalist crisis placed the challenge from a different source. State-owned oil companies from seven major states—China's CNPC, Russia's Gazprom, Iran's NIOC, Venezuela's PDVSA, Brazil's Petrobras, Malaysia's Petronas, and Saudi Arabia's Aramco—had shaken the international financial complex, where new barter arrangements were being made to shelter these states against the vagaries of the U.S. dollar. Among these seven countries there was only one firm ally of the West and the dollar, namely Saudi Arabia. This was a state where the political leadership, itself very insecure, expended billions financing conservative jihadists around the world in an effort to divert attention from calls for social and economic restructuring in Saudi Arabia.

Libya's Resource Nationalism and Gaddafi's Support
of a Strong African Union

Both Iraq and Libya were societies with large reserves of oil and natural gas that could further tip the balance of forces against the energy trade indexed in the U.S. dollar. After the end of the war in Iraq, its leaders developed close ties with Iran and began making statements bordering on resource nationalism. Energy consultants who had studied Iraq predicted that, by 2020, this state would be a major global source of oil production growth.[328] In 2009, the Iraqi government awarded the redevelopment of eleven of the country's oil fields to several international oil companies.

Libyan nationalism was driving the Libyan leadership to seek closer relations with Brazil, Russia, India, and China. This nationalism was accompanied by a renewed drive by the Libyan leadership for the creation of the African Union and moving with speed toward a Union government. Libya's leadership had set aside resources to realize the dreams of the three major Pan-African institutions—the African Monetary Fund, the African Investment Bank, and the African Central Bank. The seat of the Libyan Investment Bank was in Libya, and the nationalist leadership in Libya had planned to be as aggressive with investments in Africa as they had been assertive in the meetings of the AU calling for a Union government. Such an African Union government would place Africa in a central position in the world economic league.

Six of the ten fastest-growing economies in the world were in Africa, and every day there were reports of new sources of oil and gas in Africa. Apart from the traditional exporters of oil and natural gas in Africa—such as Algeria, Angola, Cameroon, Chad, Republic of the Congo, Egypt, Equatorial Guinea, Gabon, Libya, Nigeria, Sudan, and Tunisia—there have been new explorations and production in countries such as Ghana, Liberia, Mozambique, Namibia, Tanzania, and Uganda. An African Union that harmonized energy production with a monetary union and a common currency represented new hopes for Africans while sending tremors for the Western companies that dominated the continent in the past. The IMF and the World Bank have been responsible for implementing policies that deepened inequalities and exploitation, and the extension of the impoverishment of Africans. African states were developing novel agreements with the "emerging" nations in order to escape the total dominance of the IMF.

Libya had escaped the worst strictures of the IMF medicine of liberalization and privatization during the period of sanctions. For close to a decade, liberal reformers inside the government, led by Saif al-Islam, attempted to expand engagement with Western financial institutions after the establishment of the Libyan Investment Authority. The LIA was playing in the terrain of the financial oligarchy and did not fully understand the relationship between finance and global political and military power. Gaddafi had proven unpredictable, and promotion of the African Union as well as the ideas of resources nationalism was disquieting for the Western powers, even when they were fawning over him.

Wikileaks has enlightened the world as to the attitude of the West to resource nationalism. As the Wikileaks cables exposed, there had been disquiet in the West over the terms of the fourth exploration and production sharing agreement, which was designed to increase the Libyan government's "control over and share of revenue from hydrocarbon resources." Libyan reformers had warned the U.S. embassy that this threat of resource nationalism and support for the African Union would persist as long as Gaddafi was the leader.[329] Neither Shukri Ghanem nor Muammar Gaddafi survived the NATO intervention.

Although Gaddafi and Ghanem have fallen, there is no guarantee that the IMF and Western financial power will survive this current depression. Not one day goes by without fresh news of its depth. If the intent of Nicolas Sarkozy was to save the euro by launching the NATO war, then every day it is becoming clearer that the Western dominance of Africa is coming to an end. Sarkozy did not achieve the political capital that he expected from the war against Africa, and the eurozone crisis has weakened the position of European capital. Moreover, along with the economic crisis, every day Western banks are being exposed for their criminal behavior. Perhaps the most egregious has been the manipulation by a number of Western banks of the benchmark for international interest rates—the Libor (London Interbank Offered Rate). Africans who remember the days of the debt crisis have not forgotten that, with every percentage point change in the Libor rate, billions of dollars were added to their debt. The daily Libor rate is supposed to measure the average cost of short-term loans between major banks. The rate determines the interest rates for loans and investments that affect hundreds of millions of people around the world. The Libor was supposed to be established by market mechanisms, but the banks were rigging the rates to maintain their profitability after the fall of Lehman Brothers and the Wall Street meltdown.

The amount of money affected by the most recent exposure of manipulation and phony rates was at least $500 trillion. This scandal, which involved Barclays Bank, provided a clear outline of the mechanisms by which a handful of giant banks rig the so-called free market to boost their profits and the fortunes of their executives and big investors. Libor influences trillions of dollars of loans and credit default swaps, and the fact that the banks were manipulating this rate goes to the heart of the global financial system and further exposes the international capitalist system. Fixing the rates exposed one more spoke in the wheel of economic plunder and predation whose result is mass unemployment, poverty, and ever-increasing social inequality.

The book *Predator Nation* makes an explicit link between the Monitor Group of Boston and the unfolding military actions in Libya. Charles Ferguson excoriated the academics who had been making journeys to Libya:

> As its wealth and power grew, [the Monitor Group] subverted America's political system (including both political parties), government and academic institutions in order to free itself from regulation. As deregulation progressed, the industry became even more unethical and dangerous producing ever larger financial crises and more blatant criminality. Since the 1990s, its power has been sufficient to insulate bankers not only from effective regulation but even from criminal law enforcement. The financial sector is now a parasitic and destabilizing industry that constitutes a major drag on America's economic growth.[330]

In the process of outlining the criminal linkages between all sectors of U.S. society, the author excluded how the level of criminality in the financial sector affected the military.

The book started by considering the expansion of NATO, and how the new and enlarged Global NATO coincided with the expansion of the neoliberal operations of Wall Street and the new forms of finance capital. The book was very explicit about the relationship between the financial military complex and the competitiveness—or lack thereof—of U.S. capitalism. At the end of the Second World War, when the United States was the dominant economic power, it could engage Africa at numerous levels—economic, cultural, religious, military, social, and through what some international relations theorists called "soft power." From the start of this century, the dominant engagement of the United States in the international system has been a military one. The business model of finance capital was global, and the rise of this deregulated financial sector encroached upon all parts of the world. Private military companies have been created by different branches of the financial industry to entrench the U.S. position, even when this position had been overtaken by a changed world economy. Libya was caught in this new maze of the financialization of energy resources as the "reformers" in Libya established a sovereign wealth fund and aggressively deepened integration into Western financial institutions. This integration of Libyan resources into the global financial system brought Libya into the clutches of Goldman Sachs.

Libya lost close to one billion dollars at Goldman Sachs, and at the time of the start of the rebellion there had been no solution proposed by the firm on how Libya could effectively recoup its losses. Since the end of the Gaddafi regime, there has been very little discussion of Libya recouping its losses. Instead, the new leaders of Libya are being advised to go back to the IMF. The IMF is integrated into the Wall Street–Treasury nexus, which will deepen the Western choke-hold on Libya. Matt Taibi described the global reach of Goldman Sachs by noting, "The first thing you need to know about Goldman Sachs is that it's everywhere. The world's most powerful investment bank is a great vampire squid wrapped around the face of humanity, relentlessly jamming its blood funnel into anything that smells like money. In fact, the history of the recent financial crisis, which doubles as a history of the rapid decline and fall of the suddenly swindled dry American empire, reads like a Who's Who of Goldman Sachs graduates."[331]

The failure of the Western financial model has brought the world to the most serious depression since 1930. Sir Mervyn King, Governor of the Bank of England, has been warning that this crisis may be deeper and more costly than the Great Depression. Africans remember that it was in the midst of the last depression that the Italians launched the invasion and occupation of Abyssinia.

Africans warned that this attempt to solve the European economic crisis by militarily occupying Africa would lead to a global conflagration. Humanity did not heed the warnings of Africa, and the military techniques of bombing civilians and creating pogroms were taken to a new level of industrial warfare by Adolf Hitler. The League of Nations shattered in that depression, and out of the ashes of that war emerged the United Nations and the Bretton Woods system.

NATO was the third rail of Western capitalist dominance after 1945.

Deft international management of this current depression will be required to ensure that the UN does not suffer the same fate as the League of Nations. In the present international conjuncture, the calls for the democratization of the United Nations need to be intensified to ensure that the same consequences of the Great Depression do not consume humanity during this one. This book was written as part of the struggle for global demilitarization and the democratization of the Security Council of the United Nations.

NATO's Mission in Africa Backfires

The tasks of global demilitarization have been sharpened by the fall-out in Africa over the Libyan intervention, including the interventions by the French in Mali in early 2013. Far from showing the successful engagement of the Western military alliance, the intervention added to the failures of Global NATO. Throughout this book, we have marshaled evidence to demonstrate that, far from saving lives, the NATO intervention caused thousands of civilian deaths and took sides in a war that destroyed Libya. The colossal failure of the Bretton Woods institutions in Africa has now been reinforced by the catastrophic failure of NATO. Even staunch allies of NATO have declared that NATO emerged from Libya weaker than when it went into it: "The military operation itself created an image of NATO's limitations rather than its power."[332]

Military strategists have been willing to explore the failures by using code words such as "limitations," to divert attention from the calls for criminal investigation into the actions of NATO in Libya. Western social scientists have been less willing or able to retreat from the ideas of the Hobbesian state of violence in Africa, with the attendant divisions, dislocations, and bloodletting that has given rise to the literature about "failed states in Africa." The argument of this book is that one cannot separate the work of the Western intellectual establishment from the demonization and misinformation that was mobilized to generate the UN resolution on protecting civilians. Though there has been a blossoming of writings on the "tribal" allegiances of Libyans to explain the rampant lawlessness of regional militias, this mode of thinking has been rejected by the top scholars in Africa. From the moment the killings and ethnic cleansing in Tawergha became evident, Africans spoke out with one voice against the NATO intervention.

Regardless of ideological orientation, Africans felt revulsion ar the blatant racism and dehumanization of black-skinned Libyans. The letter by 200 African intellectuals created a united front among African intellectuals and cultural leaders. The execution and sodomization of the Libyan leader alerted many African allies of the West that their current alliance does not protect them.

As Vladimir Shubin quoted one African diplomat as saying, "No African country is safe now, after Libya."

Today, there are new information networks of African youths who are championing the call for the unity of Africa. Scholars and activists are writing that events in Libya are a clear wake-up call for Africa to unite. Charles Abugre is one such scholar, who has followed the footsteps of Tajudeen Abdul Raheem and calls for a faster pace for African unity. Abugre quoted Kwame Nkrumah:

> If Africa was united, no major power bloc would attempt to subdue it by limited war because, from the very nature of limited war, what can be achieved by it is itself limited. It is only where small states exist that it is possible, by landing a few thousand marines or by financing a mercenary force, to secure a decisive result.

Experience throughout Africa has alerted the new generation to the fact that the same NATO forces that provided the conditions for the execution of Gaddafi will change sides. That the Ambassador of the United States died in the middle of a battle between competing militias in Libya was one manifestation of the tenuous alliances that set in motion the NATO intervention in March 2011. Despite the hollow support for a democratic transition. the rival militias have not shown any commitment to the formal processes of elections and the establishment of a 200-seat national assembly. Individual states of the NATO war continue to support factional leadership, and the war situation in

Libya is far from over. Samir Amin rightly argued that, with the divisions in Libya, the West wants a Somalia-type situation where there is nominal partitioning of the country.

Yet the international situation has changed significantly since the destruction and division of Somalia. In the introduction to this book, I posed the question whether the continued use of proxy states such as Qatar can be maintained within a region where the oppression and occupation of Palestine is challenged. Since the launch of the war on terror in 2001, Saudi Arabia and Qatar became front-line bases for the financial barons and the military supporters. Both of these states were heavily involved in the support for the NATO intervention. At the time of writing at the end of 2012, the Western media attempted to focus the gaze of Western citizens on military operations against Syria and Iran. The Libyan intervention pointed to the new changes, and there can be no guarantee that the well-laid plans of Western military planners, along with Israel, will end up favorably for Western Europe and North America. Just when the West thought that the "transition" within Egypt had settled the alliance between the new leaders of Egypt and Western capitalism, new interventions by the mobilized people who, through their demonstrations, exposed the reality that there are no timetables for revolution.

Fifty years after Patrice Lumumba was assassinated in the Democratic Republic of the Congo, in 1961, Western Europe is in a crisis that will weaken the European domination of African societies and African peoples. Calls for reparative justice in Africa and calls for unity from below came from the World Conference against Racism, and the same constituency in Africa is calling for NATO to be held accountable for civilian deaths in Libya. Today, international law can only be enforced by a new international alliance of societies that want to avoid total destruction. The spillover of the instability into other parts of Africa and the destruction of important historical sites in Timbuktu are creating a new sense of urgency in Africa for united military responses.

Decent human beings all over the world were outraged, and it is now clearer that the decision to execute Muammar Gaddafi was made to silence one voice for anti-imperialism. Far from humiliating and silencing Africans, there is now a realization that the work for the freedom and unity of Africa must be engaged with even more clarity. The execution had the opposite effect, and the work of expelling foreign military forces from Africa will now be more intense.

AFTERWORD:
FROM THE LOCKERBIE AIR CRASH
TO THE LIBYAN REVOLUTION

by Ali A. Mazrui

In the Libyan war of 2011 was NATO an ally of the "Arab Spring"? Or was it a rogue policeman engaged in war crimes? This book by Horace Campbell strips the Atlantic Alliance of some of its moral pretensions when it intervened in an African civil war. It was not an intervention without precedent in North Africa. There had been a similar intervention in the Suez war of 1956 when France and Britain invaded Egypt in defiance of the United States. In 2011 France and Britain invaded Libya with the involvement of the United States. This book addresses this second case of Northern aggression against the South. If the Libyan war was part of the Arab Spring, it was the only one that ended with the lynching of the fallen head of state. It was also the only one that was followed by the assassination of the supportive American ambassador. Blood was spilled at the highest level, and tragically reciprocated.

Despite this tragedy for all there have been numerous foreign policy experts who have called this intervention in Libya a success. What is the measurement of success? Did the Libyan revolution become racist when it turned against any black person encountered in a Libyan street? Most of those blacks encountered were ordinary civilians rather than "mercenaries" fighting for Gaddafi. Many such civilians were murdered by revolutionaries, some of them Libyan citizens from the south. These racist incidents and the reaction of the mainstream Western media brings to the fore the issues of race in international relations theory. More than thirty years ago I had written of the importance of of race in *Africa's International Relations: The Diplomacy of Dependency and Change.* Since the appearance of that book numerous scholars inside and outside of Africa have been writing on the impact that Africa will have on IR and IR theory. Realist conceptions of power informed the hubris that had germinated from the ideas of scholars such as Samuel P. Huntington.

In the summer of 1993 Professor Samuel P. Huntington of Harvard University unleashed a debate about the nature of conflict in the post–Cold War era. In an article in the influential U.S. journal *Foreign Affairs*, Huntington argued that now that the Cold War was over, future conflicts would not be primarily between states or ideological blocs, but would be between civilizations and cultural coalitions.[333] To use Huntington's own words: The fault lines between civilizations will be the battle lines of the future. Conflict between civilizations will be the latest phase in the evolution of conflict in the modern world.[334]

The late Samuel Huntington was at his best when he discussed how the West masquerades as "the world community," and uses the United Nations to give universalist credentials to Western interests. In Huntington's words:

> Global political and security issues are effectively settled by a directorate of the United States, Britain and France; world economic issues by a directorate of the United States, Germany and Japan, all of which maintain extraordinary close relations with each other, to the exclusion of lesser and largely non-Western countries. Decisions made at the U.N. Security Council or in the International Monetary Fund that reflect the interests of the West are presented to the world as the desires of the world community.

The very phrase " world community" has become the euphemistic collective noun (replacing " Free World") to give global legitimacy to actions reflecting the interests of the United States and other Western powers.[335]

We have here a situation where the universalism of the United Nations is far less than it seems. The United Nations has become the collective fig-leaf for rapacious Western actions.

On becoming a member of the *ummah,* a Muslim convert must recite the Shahadah, saying, "There is no god but Allah." It seems that to remain a member of the United Nations in good standing, all countries must acknowledge that "there is no political god but the West." Only the West has the right to determine when and how force should be used in world politics.

Samuel Huntington goes on to show how the West had used the U.N. Security Council to impose sanctions against Muslim countries or invoke the use of force. After Iraq occupied Kuwait, the West was faced with a choice between saving time and saving lives. The West chose to save time. In Huntington's words:

Western domination of the U.N. Security Council and its decisions, tempered only by occasional abstention by China, produced U.N. legitimation of the West's use of force to drive Iraq out of Kuwait and its elimination of Iraq's sophisticated weapons. It also produced the quite unprecedented action by the United States, Britain and France in getting the Security Council to demand that Libya hand over the Pan Am 103 bombing suspects and then impose sanctions when Libya refused.[336]

There now seems to be evidence that Libya might not have been the culprit in the Pan American 103 air crash of 1988 at Lockerbie, Scotland, after all. Some other Middle Eastern country might have been implicated, and not Libya. Unfortunately Muammar al-Gaddafi handed over two "suspects" as sacrificial lambs more than a decade later. Washington, London and Paris remained reluctant to eat their own words even if there was evidence of a miscarriage of justice. The arrogance of power remains stubborn.

While the fallout from the from the destructiveness of the NATO intervention is still unfolding, it is pertinent that readers have a historical understanding of the relationships between the West and Libya, especially the recent history from the Lockerbie crash to the intervention that had been justified in the name of "responsibility to protect." When I wrote on Africa's international relations, I concluded:

> Africa is not a continent in either splendid or squalid isolation. It is a region operating in a global context. We have attempted to outline both the internationality of Africa's past and the globalism of Africa's future. We have seen ancestral Africa's contacts with regions which range from India to the Iberian Peninsula, from China to the Middle East. The issue at stake in turn ranged from technology to religion, from problems of population to the tensions of cultural dependency. At the center of it all is a race of people which was once relegated to the outer periphery of world events, and condemned to the imperial roles in diplomatic history. These people are now reaching out for a new definition of their place in the global scheme of things. This is what black diplomacy is all about—a new resolve by black nations to decide the destiny of the human race and the fate of the planet they share.[337]

One can see the impact of the NATO intervention in all parts of the world, but especially in Africa where there is a new resolve for the African Union to be more vigorous in the resolution of matters relating to social peace.

Here it is pertinent to pose a number of questions:

- Was Muammar al-Gaddafi a martyr to his African identity? It was in the 1990s that Gaddafi decided that he was "*an African first and an Arab second.*" He supported and helped to finance more African ventures than Arab ones. The Arab League had its revenge when they threw him under the bus of the Security Council and the tank of NATO.

- In the Libyan revolution of 2011 the African Union was the only institution that tried to find a peaceful solution between Gaddafi in Tripoli and his opponents in Benghazi. NATO purposefully marginalized and humiliated the African Union. Efforts by African Heads of State to reconcile Libyans were thwarted by the Atlantic Alliance. Was the intervention by France and NATO part of a continuum to diminish African initiatives?

- Did the Libyan revolution become *racist* when it turned against any black person encountered in a Libyan street? Most of those blacks encountered were ordinary civilians rather than "mercenaries" fighting for Gaddafi. Many such civilians were murdered by revolutionaries, some of the victims were Libyan citizens from the south.

- Relations between Africa and the Arab world have been damaged by six factors—half of them connected with Libya. The Libyan war of 2011 alienated the League of Arab States from the African Union; the death of Gaddafi deprived Pan-Africanism of its most committed Arab leader; the secession of Northern Mali was triggered by the chaos of postwar Libya and the flow of weapons in the region as a whole. Damage to Afro-Arab relations was also caused by the partition of Sudan in 2011; the collapse of Somalia into a failed state thus neutralizing Somalia's role as Africa's link with the Arab world; and finally, the militarization of Islam among the Hausa. Boku Haram is turning other Nigerians against Muslim influence and Arab Africa as a whole.

- Did the death of Gaddafi deprive Africa of a political leader with truly original ideas? His *Green Book* outlined an egalitarian society that distrusted such titles as "President" or "Prime Minister." He also experimented with gender equality by creating a regiment of women to defend his residential tent.

- Gaddafi will also be remembered for his proposed tripartite policy for post-colonial Africa. He recommended three official languages for each African country—the main indigenous tongue of the country, the relevant Euro-imperial language, and the Arabic language. Arabic would thus be recognized as a language with more native speakers in Africa than any indigenous or European language.

•. Did not the U.S. Marine anthem or hymn consist of the patriotic song *"From the Halls of Montezuma to the Shores of Tripoli"*? In 2011 American power was once again at work. However, this time the heroism was not along "the shores of Tripoli" but "over the skies of Tripoli." The question nevertheless remains whether the 2011 American performance was indeed "heroic." Was American might violating African rights?

These questions will dominate the discussions on Pan-Africanism and Pan-Arabism for decades. This book is one more effort to raise the consciousness of students of international relations on the paths of a people who "are now reaching out for a new definition of their place in the global scheme of things." This book by Horace Campbell chronicles the failure of the imperial powers to turn back Africa to the period of colonial overrule.

APPENDIX 1

LIBYA, AFRICA, AND THE NEW WORLD ORDER

An Open Letter to the Peoples of Africa and the World
from Concerned Africans

We, the undersigned, are ordinary citizens of Africa who are immensely pained and angered that fellow Africans are and have been subjected to the fury of war by foreign powers which have clearly repudiated the noble and very relevant vision enshrined in the Charter of the United Nations.

Our action to issue this letter is inspired by our desire, not to take sides, but to protect the sovereignty of Libya and the right of the Libyan people to choose their leaders and determine their own destiny.

Libya is an African country.

On March 10, the African Union Peace and Security Council adopted an important Resolution (3) which spelled out the road map to address the Libyan conflict, consistent with the obligations of the AU under Chapter VIII of the UN Charter.

When the UN Security Council adopted its Resolution 1973, it was aware of the AU decision which had been announced seven days earlier.

By deciding to ignore this fact, the Security Council further and consciously contributed to the subversion of international law as well as undermining the legitimacy of the UN in the eyes of the African people.

In other ways since then, it has helped to promote and entrench the immensely pernicious process of the international marginalisation of

Africa even with regard to the resolution of the problems of the Continent.

Contrary to the provisions of the UN Charter, the UN Security Council declared its own war on Libya on March 17, 2011.

The Security Council allowed itself to be informed by what the International Crisis Group (ICG) in its June 6, 2011, Report on Libya characterizes as the "more sensational reports that the regime was using its air force to slaughter demonstrators."

On this basis it adopted Resolution 1973 which mandated the imposition of a "no-fly zone" over Libya, and resolved "to take all necessary measures . . . to protect civilians and civilian populated areas under threat of attack in the Libyan Arab Jamahiriya . . ."

Thus, first of all, the Security Council used the still unresolved issue in international law of "the right to protect," the so-called R2P, to justify the Chapter VII military intervention in Libya.

In this context the UN Security Council has committed a litany of offenses which have underlined, the further transformation of the Council into a willing instrument of the most powerful among its Member States.

Thus the Security Council produced no evidence to prove that its authorization of the use of force under Chapter VII of the UN Charter was a proportionate and appropriate response to what had, in reality, in Libya, developed into a civil war.

It then proceeded to "outsource" or "sub-contract" the implementation of its resolutions to NATO, mandating this military alliance to act as a "coalition of the willing."

It did not put in place any mechanism and process to supervise the "subcontractor," to ensure that it faithfully honors the provisions of its Resolutions.

It has made no effort otherwise to monitor and analyse the actions of NATO in this regard.

It has allowed the establishment of a legally unauthorized "Contact Group," yet another "coalition of the willing," which has displaced it as the authority which has the effective responsibility to help determine the future of Libya.

To confirm this unacceptable reality, the July 15, 2011, meeting of the "Contact Group" in Istanbul "reaffirmed that the Contact Group remains the appropriate platform for the international community to be a focal point of contact with the Libyan people, to coordinate international policy and to be a forum for discussion of humanitarian and post-conflict support."

Duly permitted by the Security Council, the two "coalitions of the willing," NATO and the "Contact Group," have effectively and practically rewritten Resolution 1973.

Thus they have empowered themselves openly to pursue the objective of "regime change" and therefore the use of force and all other means to overthrow the government of Libya, which objectives are completely at variance with the decisions of the UN Security Council.

Because of this, with no regard to UNSC Resolutions 1970 and 1973, they have made bold to declare the government of Libya illegitimate and to proclaim the Benghazi-based "Transitional National Council" as "the legitimate governing authority in Libya."

The Security Council has failed to answer the question how the decisions taken by NATO and the "Contact Group" address the vital issue of "facilitating dialogue to lead to the political reforms necessary to find a peaceful and sustainable solution."

The actions of its "sub-contractors," NATO and the "Contact Group," have positioned the UN as a partisan belligerent in the Libyan conflict, rather than a committed but neutral peacemaker standing equidistant from the Libyan armed factions.

The Security Council has further willfully decided to repudiate the rule of international law by consciously ignoring the provisions of Chapter VIII of the UN Charter relating to the role of legitimate regional institutions.

The George W. Bush war against Iraq began on March 20, 2003.

The following day, March 21, the UK newspaper, *The Guardian,* published an abbreviated article by the prominent U.S. neoconservative, Richard Perle, entitled "Thank God for the death of the UN."

But the post–Second World War global architecture for the maintenance of international peace and security centred on respect for the UN Charter.

The UN Security Council must therefore know that at least with regard to Libya, it has acted in a manner which will result in and has led to the loss of its moral authority effectively to preside over the critical processes of achieving global peace and the realization of the objective of peaceful coexistence among the diverse peoples of the world.

Contrary to the provisions of the UN Charter, the UN Security Council authorized and has permitted the destruction and anarchy which has descended on the Libyan people.

At the end of it all:

- many Libyans will have died and have been maimed;
- much infrastructure will have been destroyed, further impoverishing the Libyan people;
- the bitterness and mutual animosity among the Libyan people will have been further entrenched;
- the possibility to arrive at a negotiated, inclusive and stable settlement will have become that much more difficult;
- instability will have been reinforced among the countries neighbouring Libya, especially the countries of the African Sahel, such as Sudan, Chad, Niger, Mali and Mauritania;
- Africa will inherit a much more difficult challenge successfully to address issues of peace and stability, and therefore the task of sustained development; and,
- those who have intervened to perpetuate violence and war in Libya will have the possibility to set the parameters within which the Libyans will have the possibility to determine their destiny, and thus further constrain the space for the Africans to exercise their right to self-determination.

As Africans we have predicated our future as relevant players in an equitable system of international relations on the expectation that the United Nations would indeed serve "as the foundation of a new world order." The ICG Report to which we have referred says:

"The prospect for Libya, but also North Africa as a whole, is increasingly ominous, unless some way can be found to induce the two sides in the armed conflict to negotiate a compromise allowing for an orderly transition to a post-Qaddafi, post-Jamahiriya state that has legitimacy in the eyes of the Libyan people. A political breakthrough is by far the best way out of the costly situation created by the military impasse."

When Richard Perle wrote in 2003 about the "abject failure of the United Nations," he was bemoaning the refusal of the UN to submit to dictation by the world's sole superpower, the United States.

The UN took this position because it was conscious of, and was inspired by its obligation to act as a true representative of all peoples of the world, consistent with the opening words of the UN Charter—"We the peoples of the United Nations."

However, and tragically, eight years later, in 2011, the UN Security Council abandoned its commitment to this perspective.

Chastened by the humiliating experience of 2003, when the U.S. demonstrated that might is right, it decided that it was more expedient to submit to the demands of the powerful rather than honor its obligation to respect the imperative to uphold the will of the peoples, including the African nations.

Thus it has communicated the message that it has become no more than an instrument in the hands and service of the most powerful within the system of international relations and therefore the vital process of the peaceful ordering of human affairs.

As Africans we have no choice but to stand up and reassert our right and duty to determine our destiny in Libya and everywhere else on our Continent.

We demand that all governments, everywhere in the world, including Africa, which expect genuine respect by the governed, such as us, should act immediately to assert "that law by which all nations may live in dignity."

We demand that:

- the NATO war of aggression in Libya should end immediately;
- the AU should be supported to implement its Plan to help the Libyan people to achieve peace, democracy, shared prosperity and national reconciliation in a united Libya; and,
- the UN Security Council must act immediately to discharge its responsibilities as defined in the UN Charter.

Those who have brought a deadly rain of bombs to Libya today should not delude themselves to believe that the apparent silence of the millions of Africans means that Africa approves of the campaign of death, destruction and domination which that rain represents.

We are confident that tomorrow we will emerge victorious, regardless of the death-seeking power of the most powerful armies in the world.

The answer we must provide practically, and as Africans, is—when, and in what ways, will we act resolutely and meaningfully to defend the right of the Africans of Libya to decide their future, and therefore the right and duty of all Africans to determine their destiny.

The AU Road Map remains the only way to peace for the people of Libya.

APPENDIX 2

Communiqué of the 265th Meeting of the Peace and Security Council of the African Union

Addis Ababa, Ethiopia, 10 March 2011, PSC/PR/Comm.2 (CCLXV)

The Peace and Security Council of the African Union (AU), at its 265th meeting held at the level of Heads of State and Government, on 10 March 2011, adopted the following decision on the situation in Libya.

Council:

1. Takes note of the statements made by the Chairperson of the Commission, as well as by the representative of the Great Socialist People's Libyan Arab Jamahiriya;

2. Recalls communiqué PSC/PR/COMM(CCLXI) adopted at its 261st meeting, held on 23 February 2011, and the statement issued, the same day, by the Chairperson of the Commission;

3. Expresses AU's deep concern at the prevailing situation in Libya, which poses a serious threat to peace and security in that country and in the region as a whole, as well as to the safety and dignity of Libyans and of the migrant workers, notably the African ones, living in Libya. Council is equally deeply concerned with the resulting humanitarian situation;

4. Expresses AU's solidarity with Libya, and underscores the legitimacy of the aspirations of the Libyan people for democracy, political reform,

justice, peace and security, as well as for socioeconomic development, and the need to ensure that these aspirations are fulfilled in a peaceful and democratic manner; in this context, Council takes note of the stated commitment of the Libyan authorities to embark upon the path of reforms;

5. Reiterates AU's strong and unequivocal condemnation of the indiscriminate use of force and lethal weapons, whoever it comes from, resulting in the loss of life, both civilian and military, and the transformation of pacific demonstrations into an armed rebellion; Council deeply deplores the loss of human life, conveys its condolences to the families of the victims and wishes early recovery to those who have been injured;

6. Reaffirms its strong commitment to the respect of the unity and territorial integrity of Libya, as well as its rejection of any foreign military intervention, whatever its form;

7. Expresses its conviction that the current situation in Libya calls for an urgent African action for: (i) the immediate cessation of all hostilities, (ii) the cooperation of the competent Libyan authorities to facilitate the timely delivery of humanitarian assistance to the needy populations, (iii) the protection of foreign nationals, including the African migrants living in Libya, and (iv) the adoption and implementation of the political reforms necessary for the elimination of the causes of the current crisis;

8. Decides to establish an AU ad hoc High-Level Committee on Libya comprising five Heads of State and Government, as well as the Chairperson of the Commission; Council requests the Chairperson of the Commission to finalize the consultations undertaken in this respect and to announce the composition of the Committee as soon as possible. Council further decides that the Committee is mandated to:

   (i) engage with all parties in Libya and continuously assess the evolution of the situation on the ground,

   (ii) facilitate an inclusive dialogue among the Libyan parties on the appropriate reforms,

   (iii) engage AU's partners, in particular the League of Arab States, the Organization of the Islamic Conference, the European Union and the United Nations, to facilitate coordination of efforts and seek their support for the early resolution of the crisis;

9. Further decides that the AU ad hoc High-Level Committee on Libya be supported by a team comprising the Ministers of Foreign Affairs/

External Relations and/or other relevant Ministers of the countries concerned, as well as the AU Commissioner for Peace and Security;

10. Requests all AU Member States to provide logistical and humanitarian support to all African migrant workers wishing to leave Libya, as well as to those neighboring countries forced to bear a disproportionate burden and to the countries of origin to facilitate the socioeconomic reinsertion of these migrant workers. In this respect, Council requests the Chairperson of the Commission to take the necessary steps to coordinate such an effort, including the convening of a conference to facilitate the mobilization of the required resources and other related measures;

11. Recalls the provisions of the OAU Convention on the Elimination of Mercenarism in Africa; Council requests the Commission to gather information on the reported presence of mercenaries in Libya and their actions, to enable it, should these reports be confirmed, to take the required measures in line with the Convention;

12. Requests the Chairperson of the Commission to transmit this decision to the United Nations Security Council, the League of Arab States, the Organization of the Islamic Conference, the European Union and other concerned AU partners, for their action as appropriate;

13. Decides to remain actively seized of the matter.

APPENDIX 3

UNITED NATIONS SECURITY COUNCIL RESOLUTION 1973

Adopted by the Security Council at its 6,498th meeting, 17 March 2011

The Security Council,

Recalling its resolution 1970 (2011) of 26 February 2011,

Deploring the failure of the Libyan authorities to comply with resolution 1970 (2011),

Expressing grave concern at the deteriorating situation, the escalation of violence, and the heavy civilian casualties,

Reiterating the responsibility of the Libyan authorities to protect the Libyan population and *reaffirming* that parties to armed conflicts bear the primary responsibility to take all feasible steps to ensure the protection of civilians,

Condemning the gross and systematic violation of human rights, including arbitrary detentions, enforced disappearances, torture and summary executions,

Further condemning acts of violence and intimidation committed by the Libyan authorities against journalists, media professionals and associated personnel and *urging* these authorities to comply with their obligations under international humanitarian law as outlined in resolution 1738 (2006),

Considering that the widespread and systematic attacks currently taking place in the Libyan Arab Jamahiriya against the civilian population may amount to crimes against humanity,

Recalling paragraph 26 of resolution 1970 (2011) in which the Council expressed its readiness to consider taking additional appropriate measures, as necessary, to facilitate and support the return of humanitarian agencies and make available humanitarian and related assistance in the Libyan Arab Jamahiriya,

Expressing its determination to ensure the protection of civilians and civilian populated areas and the rapid and unimpeded passage of humanitarian assistance and the safety of humanitarian personnel,

Recalling the condemnation by the League of Arab States, the African Union, and the Secretary General of the Organization of the Islamic Conference of the serious violations of human rights and international humanitarian law that have been and are being committed in the Libyan Arab Jamahiriya,

Taking note of the final communiqué of the Organisation of the Islamic Conference of 8 March 2011, and the communiqué of the Peace and Security Council of the African Union of 10 March 2011 which established an ad hoc High Level Committee on Libya,

Taking note also of the decision of the Council of the League of Arab States of 12 March 2011 to call for the imposition of a no-fly zone on Libyan military aviation, and to establish safe areas in places exposed to shelling as a precautionary measure that allows the protection of the Libyan people and foreign nationals residing in the Libyan Arab Jamahiriya,

Taking note further of the Secretary-General's call on 16 March 2011 for an immediate cease-fire,

Recalling its decision to refer the situation in the Libyan Arab Jamahiriya since 15 February 2011 to the Prosecutor of the International Criminal Court, and *stressing* that those responsible for or complicit in attacks targeting the civilian population, including aerial and naval attacks, must be held to account,

Reiterating its concern at the plight of refugees and foreign workers forced to flee the violence in the Libyan Arab Jamahiriya, *welcoming* the response of neighbouring States, in particular Tunisia and Egypt, to address the needs of those refugees and foreign workers, and *calling on* the international community to support those efforts,

Deploring the continuing use of mercenaries by the Libyan authorities,

Considering that the establishment of a ban on all flights in the airspace of the Libyan Arab Jamahiriya constitutes an important element for the protection of civilians as well as the safety of the delivery of humanitarian assistance and a decisive step for the cessation of hostilities in Libya,

Expressing concern also for the safety of foreign nationals and their rights in the Libyan Arab Jamahiriya,

Welcoming the appointment by the Secretary General of his Special Envoy to Libya, Mr. Abdel-Elah Mohamed Al-Khatib, and supporting his efforts to find a sustainable and peaceful solution to the crisis in the Libyan Arab Jamahiriya,

Reaffirming its strong commitment to the sovereignty, independence, territorial integrity and national unity of the Libyan Arab Jamahiriya,

Determining that the situation in the Libyan Arab Jamahiriya continues to constitute a threat to international peace and security,

Acting under Chapter VII of the Charter of the United Nations,

1. *Demands* the immediate establishment of a cease-fire and a complete end to violence and all attacks against, and abuses of, civilians;
2. *Stresses* the need to intensify efforts to find a solution to the crisis which responds to the legitimate demands of the Libyan people and *notes* the decisions of the Secretary-General to send his Special Envoy to Libya and of the Peace and Security Council of the African Union to send its ad hoc High Level Committee to Libya with the aim of facilitating dialogue to lead to the political reforms necessary to find a peaceful and sustainable solution;
3. *Demands* that the Libyan authorities comply with their obligations under international law, including international humanitarian law, human rights and refugee law and take all measures to protect civilians and meet their basic needs, and to ensure the rapid and unimpeded passage of humanitarian assistance;

Protection of civilians

4. *Authorizes* Member States that have notified the Secretary-General, acting nationally or through regional organizations or arrangements, and acting in cooperation with the Secretary-General, to take all necessary measures, notwithstanding paragraph 9 of resolution 1970 (2011), to protect civilians and civilian populated areas under threat of attack in the Libyan Arab Jamahiriya, including Benghazi, while excluding a foreign occupation force of any form on any part of Libyan territory, and *requests* the Member States concerned to inform the

Secretary-General immediately of the measures they take pursuant to the authorization conferred by this paragraph which shall be immediately reported to the Security Council;

5. *Recognizes* the important role of the League of Arab States in matters relating to the maintenance of international peace and security in the region, and bearing in mind Chapter VIII of the Charter of the United Nations, requests the Member States of the League of Arab States to cooperate with other Member States in the implementation of paragraph 4;

No-Fly Zone

6. *Decides* to establish a ban on all flights in the airspace of the Libyan Arab Jamahiriya in order to help protect civilians;

7. *Decides further* that the ban imposed by paragraph 6 shall not apply to flights whose sole purpose is humanitarian, such as delivering or facilitating the delivery of assistance, including medical supplies, food, humanitarian workers and related assistance, or evacuating foreign nationals from the Libyan Arab Jamahiriya, nor shall it apply to flights authorized by paragraphs 4 or 8, nor other flights which are deemed necessary by States acting under the authorization conferred in paragraph 8 to be for the benefit of the Libyan people, and that these flights shall be coordinated with any mechanism established under paragraph 8;

8. *Authorizes* Member States that have notified the Secretary-General and the Secretary-General of the League of Arab States, acting nationally or through regional organizations or arrangements, to take all necessary measures to enforce compliance with the ban on flights imposed by paragraph 6 above, as necessary, and *requests* the States concerned in cooperation with the League of Arab States to coordinate closely with the Secretary-General on the measures they are taking to implement this ban, including by establishing an appropriate mechanism for implementing the provisions of paragraphs 6 and 7 above,

9. *Calls upon* all Member States, acting nationally or through regional organizations or arrangements, to provide assistance, including any necessary overflight approvals, for the purposes of implementing paragraphs 4, 6, 7 and 8 above;

10. *Requests* the Member States concerned to coordinate closely with each other and the Secretary-General on the measures they are taking to implement paragraphs 4, 6, 7 and 8 above, including practical measures for the monitoring and approval of authorized humanitarian or evacuation flights;

11. *Decides* that the Member States concerned shall inform the Secretary-General and the Secretary-General of the League of Arab States immediately of measures taken in exercise of the authority conferred by paragraph 8 above, including to supply a concept of operations;

12. *Requests* the Secretary-General to inform the Council immediately of any actions taken by the Member States concerned in exercise of the authority conferred by paragraph 8 above and to report to the Council within 7 days and every month thereafter on the implementation of this resolution, including information on any violations of the flight ban imposed by paragraph 6 above;

Enforcement of the Arms Embargo

13. *Decides that* paragraph 11 of Resolution 1970 (2011) shall be replaced by the following paragraph : "Calls upon all Member States, in particular States of the region, acting nationally or through regional organisations or arrangements, in order to ensure strict implementation of the arms embargo established by paragraphs 9 and 10 of Resolution 1970 (2011), to inspect in their territory, including seaports and airports, and on the high seas, vessels and aircraft bound to or from the Libyan Arab Jamahiriya, if the State concerned has information that provides reasonable grounds to believe that the cargo contains items the supply, sale, transfer or export of which is prohibited by paragraphs 9 or 10 of Resolution 1970 (2011) as modified by this resolution, including the provision of armed mercenary personnel, *calls upon* all flag States of such vessels and aircraft to cooperate with such inspections and authorizes Member States to use all measures commensurate to the specific circumstances to carry out such inspections";

14. *Requests* Member States which are taking action under paragraph 13 above on the high seas to coordinate closely with each other and the Secretary-General and *further requests* the States concerned to inform the Secretary-General and the Committee established pursuant to paragraph 24 of Resolution 1970 (2011) ("the Committee") immediately of measures taken in the exercise of the authority conferred by paragraph 13 above;

15. *Requires* any Member State whether acting nationally or through regional organizations or arrangements, when it undertakes an inspection pursuant to paragraph 13 above, to submit promptly an initial written report to the Committee containing, in particular, explanation of the grounds for the inspection, the results of such

inspection, and whether or not cooperation was provided, and, if prohibited items for transfer are found, further requires such Member States to submit to the Committee, at a later stage, a subsequent written report containing relevant details on the inspection, seizure, and disposal, and relevant details of the transfer, including a description of the items, their origin and intended destination, if this information is not in the initial report;

16. *Deplores* the continuing flows of mercenaries into the Libyan Arab Jamahiriya and *calls upon* all Member States to comply strictly with their obligations under paragraph 9 of resolution 1970 (2011) to prevent the provision of armed mercenary personnel to the Libyan Arab Jamahiriya;

Ban on Flights

17. *Decides* that all States shall deny permission to any aircraft registered in the Libyan Arab Jamahiriya or owned or operated by Libyan nationals or companies to take off from, land in or overfly their territory unless the particular flight has been approved in advance by the Committee, or in the case of an emergency landing;

18. *Decides that* all States shall deny permission to any aircraft to take off from, land in or overfly their territory, if they have information that provides reasonable grounds to believe that the aircraft contains items the supply, sale, transfer, or export of which is prohibited by paragraphs 9 and 10 of Resolution 1970 (2011) as modified by this resolution, including the provision of armed mercenary personnel, except in the case of an emergency landing;

Asset Freeze

19. *Decides* that the asset freeze imposed by paragraphs 17, 19, 20 and 21 of Resolution 1970 (2011) shall apply to all funds, other financial assets and economic resources which are on their territories, which are owned or controlled, directly or indirectly, by the Libyan authorities, as designated by the Committee, or by individuals or entities acting on their behalf or at their direction, or by entities owned or controlled by them, as designated by the Committee, and *decides further* that all States shall ensure that any funds, financial assets or economic resources are prevented from being made available by their nationals or by any individuals or entities within their territories, to or for the benefit of the Libyan authorities, as designated by the Committee, or individuals or entities acting on their behalf or at their direction, or entities owned or

controlled by them, as designated by the Committee, and directs the Committee to designate such Libyan authorities, individuals or entities within 30 days of the date of the adoption of this resolution and as appropriate thereafter;

20. *Affirms* its determination to ensure that assets frozen pursuant to paragraph 17 of Resolution 1970 (2011) shall, at a later stage, as soon as possible be made available to and for the benefit of the people of the Libyan Arab Jamahiriya;

21. *Decides* that all States shall require their nationals, persons subject to their jurisdiction and firms incorporated in their territory or subject to their jurisdiction to exercise vigilance when doing business with entities incorporated in the Libyan Arab Jamahiriya or subject to its jurisdiction, and any individuals or entities acting on their behalf or at their direction, and entities owned or controlled by them, if the States have information that provides reasonable grounds to believe that such business could contribute to violence and use of force against civilians;

Designations

22. *Decides* that the individuals listed in Annex I shall be subject to the travel restrictions imposed in paragraphs 15 and 16 of Resolution 1970 (2011), and *decides* further that the individuals and entities listed in Annex II shall be subject to the asset freeze imposed in paragraphs 17, 19, 20 and 21 of Resolution 1970 (2011);

23. *Decides* that the measures specified in paragraphs 15, 16, 17, 19, 20 and 21 of Resolution 1970 (2011) shall apply also to individuals and entities determined by the Council or the Committee to have violated the provisions of resolution 1970 (2011), particularly paragraphs 9 and 10 thereof, or to have assisted others in doing so;

Panel of Experts

24. *Requests* the Secretary-General to create for an initial period of one year, in consultation with the Committee, a group of up to eight experts ("Panel of Experts"), under the direction of the Committee to carry out the following tasks:

   a) Assist the Committee in carrying out its mandate as specified in paragraph 24 of Resolution 1970 (2011) and this resolution;

   b) Gather, examine and analyse information from States, relevant United Nations bodies, regional organizations and other interested parties regarding the implementation of the measures decided in Resolution 1970 (2011) and this resolution, in particular incidents of non-compliance;

c)   Make recommendations on actions the Council, or the Committee or State, may consider to improve implementation of the relevant measures;

d)   Provide to the Council an interim report on its work no later than 90 days after the Panel's appointment, and a final report to the Council no later than 30 days prior to the termination of its mandate with its findings and recommendations;

25. *Urges* all States, relevant United Nations bodies and other interested parties, to cooperate fully with the Committee and the Panel of Experts, in particular by supplying any information at their disposal on the implementation of the measures decided in resolution 1970 (2011) and this resolution, in particular incidents of non-compliance;

26. *Decides* that the mandate of the Committee as set out in paragraph 24 of Resolution 1970 (2011) shall also apply to the measures decided in this resolution;

27. *Decides* that all States, including the Libyan Arab Jamahiriya, shall take the necessary measures to ensure that no claim shall lie at the instance of the Libyan authorities, or of any person or body in the Libyan Arab Jamahiriya, or of any person claiming through or for the benefit of any such person or body, in connection with any contract or other transaction where its performance was affected by reason of the measures taken by the Security Council in Resolution 1970 (2011), this resolution and related resolutions;

28. *Reaffirms* its intention to keep the actions of the Libyan authorities under continuous review and underlines its readiness to review at any time the measures imposed by this resolution and resolution 1970 (2011), including by strengthening, suspending or lifting those measures, as appropriate, based on compliance by the Libyan authorities with this resolution and resolution 1970 (2011).

29. *Decides* to remain actively seized of the matter.

APPENDIX 4 / CHINESE BUSINESSES IN LIBYA

COMPANY NAME	PROJECT	INVESTMENT AMOUNT
China Railway Engineering Corp	Coastal Railway and its extension line (Tripoli-Sirte), South-North Railway, Western Railway	US$4.237 billion
China Architecture Engineering Corp.	Government Housing Project, about 20,000 houses	RMB 17.6 bn. (US$2.78 bn.)
China Gezhouba Group	Housing Construction, 7,300 houses	US$5.54 billion
No. 15 Metallurgical Construction Grp.	FWAM cement plant and NALOUT cement plant	unknown
China National Building Materials Group Corp.	Construction and installation of a cement factory producing 4,600 tons of cement every day	US$0.15 billion
No. 1 Metallurgical Construction Group	5,000 apartments and service facilities in East Melita Dictrict, EPC project, construction project of cement production	RMB 5.131 bn. (US$0.81 bn.)
CNPC	Entered Libya in 2002; owned 5 subsidiary companies before the war	unknown
SINOHYDRO Corp.	6 projects under construction	US$1.788 billion
China Communication Construction Co.	unknown	US$4.8 billion
CHINA CAMC Engineering Co.	unknown	US$4 billion
PetroChina Company Ltd.	unknown	US$0.38 billion
Zhong Xing Communication Manufacturing Industry	unknown	US$92.7 million
Hua Wei (Information and communication solution provider)	unknown	US$40 million

About 75 Chinese companies operated in Libya before the start of the NATO intervention. There were about 36,000 staff and 50 projects. Many of those firms were engaged in building roads, buildings. China's top three state oil firms, CNPC, Sinopec Group, and CNOOC, all had engineering projects in Libya, but no oil production at the time of the NATO intervention.

APPENDIX 5

"This Is My Will," by Muammar Gaddafi

This is my will. I, Muammar bin Mohammad bin Abdussalam bi Humayd bin Abu Manyar bin Humayd bin Nayil al Fuhsi Gaddafi, do swear that there is no god but God and that Mohammad is God's Prophet, peace be upon him. I pledge that I will die as Muslim.

Should I be killed, I would like to be buried, according to Muslim rituals, in the clothes I was wearing at the time of my death and my body unwashed, in the cemetery of Sirte, next to my family and relatives.

I would like that my family, especially women and children, be treated well after my death.

The Libyan people should protect its identity, achievements, history, and the honorable image of its ancestors and heroes. The Libyan people should not relinquish the sacrifices of the free and best people.

I call on my supporters to continue the resistance, and fight any foreign aggressor against Libya, today, tomorrow, and always.

Let the free people of the world know that we could have bargained over and sold out our cause in return for a personal secure and stable life. We received many offers to this effect but we chose to be at the vanguard of the confrontation as a badge of duty and honor.

Even if we do not win immediately, we will give a lesson to future generations that choosing to protect the nation is an honor and selling it out is the greatest betrayal that history will remember forever despite the attempts of the others to tell you otherwise.

NOTES

1. Security Council Resolution 1973 established a no-fly zone over Libya, authorized the enforcement of an arms embargo, and authorized "all necessary measures" to protect civilians. UN Security Council Resolution 1973, UN Doc. S/Res/1973, 17 March 2011, para. 6. and para 13.

2. The name of the late President of Libya has been alternately spelt as Moammar/Muammar Gadaffi/Gaddafi/Gathafi/Kadafi/Kaddafi/Khadafy/Qadhafi/Qathafi. For the purposes of this book, the name will be spelled as Muammar Gaddafi, except when quoting the name from other sources.

3. "An Open Letter to the Peoples of Africa and the World from Concerned Africans," *Pambazuka News.* August 9, 2011.

4. Editorial, "A Victory that Lays Bare NATO's Weakness," *Independent,* October 22, 2011; http://www.independent.co.uk/opinion/leading-articles/leading-article-a-victory-that- lays-bare-natos-weakness-2374297.html. See also Thom Shanker and Eric Schmitt, "Seeing Limits to 'New' Kind of War in Libya," *New York Times,* by October 21, 2011.

5. Seumas Milne, "If the Libyan War Was about Saving Lives, It Was a Catastrophic Failure," *The Guardian,* October 26, 2011, www.guardian.co.uk/commentis-free/2011/oct/26/libya-war-saving-lives-catastrophic-failure.

6. Amnesty International, "Militias Threaten Hopes for the New Libya," London, February 2012.

7. See *Report of the Independent Civil Society Fact-Finding Mission to Libya,* January 2012, based upon a fact-finding mission to Libya conducted by the Arab Organization for Human Rights together with the Palestinian Center for Human Rights and the International Legal Assistance Consortium.

8. The question of regular Qatar troops in the war in Libya was resolved when the Chief of Staff of the Qatari armed forces admitted the role of hundreds of Qatar forces in Libya. See Ian Black, "Qatar admits sending hundreds of troops to support Libya rebels," *The Guardian*, October 26, 2011, www.guardian.co.uk/world/2011/oct/26/qatar-troops-libya-rebels-support.

9. See especially the statement after the killing of Gaddafi, http://www.concernedafricans. co.za/index.php/news.

10. Ali A. Mazrui, ed. *UNESCO General History of Africa*, vol. 8, *Africa Since 1935* (Berkeley: University of California Press, 1999). See also S.K.B. Asante, *Pan-African Protest: West Africa and the Italo-Ethiopian crisis, 1934–1941* (London: Longmans, 1977).

11. For an account of the work of the Pan-Africanists during the last depression, see James Hooker, *Black Revolutionary: George Padmore's Path from Communism to Pan-Africanism* (Santa Barbara, CA: Praeger, 1967).

12. David Anderson, "The Fight for Libya's Oil," *Sustainable Security*, September 2011, http://sustainablesecurity.org/article/fight-libya%E2%80%99s-oil.

13. Antonia Juhasz, *The Tyranny of Oil: The World's Most Powerful Industry—And What We Must Do to Stop It* (New York: HarperCollins, 2009).

14. For a fascinating account of the impact of the Libyan diplomatic efforts in the oil sector and its repercussions in the world of the Organization of Petroleum Exporting Countries (OPEC), see "The Libyan Ultimatum," chap. 7, in Anthony Samson, *The Seven Sisters: The Great Oil Companies and the World They Made* (London: Bantam Books, 1991).

15. Anderson, "The Fight for Libya's Oil"; see also Michael Klare, *Rising Powers, Shrinking Planet: The New Geopolitics of Energy* (New York: Metropolitan Books, 2008); and by the same author, *The Race for What's Left: The Global Scramble for the World's Last Resources* (New York: Metropolitan Books, 2012).

16. "Before War in Libya, Professors Advised Gaddafi," *Harvard Crimson*, May 26, 2011, http:// www.thecrimson.com/article/2011/5/26/harvard-libya-monitor-gaddafi/. For the views of Joseph Nye on his meetings with Gaddafi, see "Tripoli Diarist: Big Tent," *The New Republic*, December 10, 2007, http://www.tnr.com/article/tripoli-diarist.

17. See Dirk Vandewalle, *Libya Since Independence: Oil and State Building* (Ithaca, NY: Cornell University Press, 1998); Dirk Vandewalle, ed., *Libya since Independence: Qadahfi's Revolution Revisited* (New York: Palgrave Macmillan, 2008); Anna Baldinetti, *The Origins of the Libyan Nation: Colonial Legacy, Exile and the Emergence of a New Nation-State* (New York: Routledge, 2010); Yehudit Ronen, *Qaddafi's Libya in World Politics* (Boulder, CO: Lynne Reiner, 2008); and Luis Martinez, *The Libyan Paradox* (New York: Columbia University Press, 2007).

18. Ghislaine Lydon, "Writing Trans-Saharan History: Methods, Sources and Interpretations across the African Divide," *Journal of North African Studies* 10/3–4 (September–December 2005): 293–324.

19. In an otherwise excellent book, Vijay Prashad fell prey to this discourse on the Arab Spring to characterize the revolution in Egypt. See his *Arab Spring, Libyan Winter* (New York: AK Press, 2012). For an African revolutionary perspective,

see Firoze Manji and Sokari Ekine, eds., *Africa Awakening: The Emerging Revolutions* (Oxford: Pambazuka Press, 2012). See James Gelvin, *The Arab Uprisings: What Everyone Needs to Know* (Oxford: Oxford University Press, 2012).

20. Samir Amin, "The Arab Nation: Some Conclusions and Problems," *MERIPReports*, 68 (June 1978): 3–14.

21. Paul Krugman, *End This Depression Now* (New York: W.W. Norton, 2012).

22. Simon Johnson, "The Quiet Coup," *The Atlantic*, May 2009. These ideas were elaborated in the book by the same author, *13 Bankers: The Wall Street Takeover and the Next Financial Meltdown* (New York: Vintage Books, 2010).

23. For an elaboration of the forms of coercion deployed in Africa during the capitalist depression, see Walter Rodney, *How Europe Underdeveloped Africa* (Dar es Salaam: Tanzania Publishing House, 1972).

24. Hugh Roberts, "Who Said Gaddafi Had to Go?" *London Review of Books*, 33/22–17 (November 2011), http://www.lrb.co.uk/v33/n22/hugh-roberts/who-said-gaddafi-had-to-go.

25. Yoweri Museveni, "The Qaddafi I Know," *Foreign Policy Magazine*, March 24, 2011, www.foreignpolicy.com/articles/2011/03/24/the_qaddafi_I_know.

26. F. William Engdahl, "NATO's War on Libya Is Directed against China: AFRICOM and the Threat to China's National Energy Security," *Global Research*, September 25, 2011, http://www.globalresearch.ca/index.php?context=va&aid=26763.

27. Samir Amin, "2011: An Arab Springtime?" in *African Awakening: The Emerging Revolutions*, ed. Firoze Manji and Sokari Ekine (Oxford: Pambazuka Press, 2012).

28. Center for Strategic and International Studies (CSIS), "Implications of the Uprising in Egypt," *Schieffer Series*, February 3, 2012, http://csis.org/event/implications-uprising-egypt.

29. Henry Kissinger, *On China* (New York: Penguin, 2011), 213.

30. Hsain Ilahiane, *Historical Dictionary of the Berbers (Imazighen)* (Oxford: Scarecrow Press, 2006).

31. Louis Dupree, "The Non-Arab Ethnic Groups of Libya," *Middle East Journal*, 12/1 (Winter 1958).

32. John L. Wright, *A History of Libya* (New York: Columbia University Press, 2010), 37.

33. Edward Evan Evans-Pritchard was a significant figure in British anthropology, whose work led to the development of social anthropology. He wrote a book on the Sanussi. See E.E. Evans-Pritchard, *The Sanusi of Cyrenaica* (Oxford: Clarendon Press, 1949). For a critique of the negative impact of this brand of scholarship, see Archie Mafeje, *Anthropology in Post-Independence Africa: End of an Era and the Problem of Self-Definition* (Nairobi: Heinrich Boll Foundation, 2001).

34. The Treaty of Brussels, signed on March 17, 1948, by Belgium, the Netherlands, Luxembourg, France, and the United Kingdom, is considered the precursor to the NATO agreement. In April 1949, when NATO was created, it included the five Treaty of Brussels states plus the United States, Canada, Portugal, Italy, Norway, Denmark, and Iceland.

35. There were supposed to be 49 countries who were members of the Coalition of the Willing. Today, it is difficult to reconstruct that history because the Bush administration kept changing and altering the records of those who accepted to collaborate in the occupation of Iraq. See Scott Althaus and Kalev Leetaru, *Airbrushing History, American Style,* Cline Center for Democracy, University of Illinois Urbana-Champaign, November 25, 2008, http://www.clinecenter.illi-nois.edu/research/airbrushing_history/.

36. Congressional Research Service, *NATO: A Brief History of Expansion,* Library of Congress, Washington, D.C., July 1998. See also Mordecai Roshwald, "NATO– Where to?" *International Journal on World Peace,* 15/3 (September 1998).

37. Michael McCgwire, "NATO Expansion: A Policy Error of Historic Importance," *Review of International Studies,* 24/1 (January 1998).

38. Ivo Daalder and James Goldgeier, "Global NATO," *Foreign Affairs,* 85/5 (September–October 2006).

39. Rick Rozoff, "NATO in the Persian Gulf: From Third World War to the Istanbul Cooperation Initiative," *Global Research,* February 7, 2009, http://www.global-research.ca/index.php?context=va&aid=12190.

40. Robert Menotti, "NATO's Mediterranean Dialogue Initiative: Italian Positions, Interests, Perceptions, and the Implications for Italy-U.S. Relations," Final Report, NATO Institutional Fellowship, 1999.

41. *Arab Spring, Libyan Winter,* 181.

42. For one historical account, see Robert D. Schulzinger, *The Wise Men of Foreign Affairs: The History of the Council on Foreign Relations* (New York: Columbia University Press, 1984).

43. Ron Shelp, *Fallen Giant: The Amazing Story of Hank Greenberg and the History of AIG* (New York: Wiley, 2009). When Elliot Spitzer, the Governor of New York State, sought to regulate the financial services industry, he was brought down by his relationship to a prostitution ring. See Peter Elkind, *Rough Justice: The Rise and Fall of Elliot Spitzer* (New York: Portfolio Books, 2010).

44. *Fallen Giant: The Amazing Story of Hank Greenberg and the History of AIG.* He was one of the chief proponents of the WTO position on the Trade in Services. See his seminal book on the topic, *Beyond Industrialization: Ascendancy of the Global Service Economy* (Praeger, 1981).

45. *13 Bankers: The Wall Street Takeover and the Next Financial Meltdown.*

46. Stanley Fischer, "Capital Accounts Liberalization and the Role of the IMF" (lecture presented at the annual meeting of IMF, September 9, 1997) later published as "Capital-Account Liberalization and the Role of the IMF: Should the IMF pursue capital-account convertibility?" in *Essays in International Finance* (Princeton: Princeton University Press, 1998), 207.

47. Leonce Ndikumana and James K. Boyce, *Africa's Odious Debts: How Foreign Loans and Capital Flight Bled a Continent (African Arguments)* (London: Zed Books, 2011). For an account of the impact of structural adjustment policies, see Adebayo O. Olukoshi, "Structural Adjustment and Social Policies in Africa: Some Notes" (paper presented at the Seminar on Global Social Policies and Global Rights, India, November, 2000).

48. Jean Bricmont, *Humanitarian Imperialism: Using Human Rights to Sell War* (New York: Monthly Review Press, 2006).

49. Edgar S. Furniss, Jr., "De Gaulle's France and NATO: An Interpretation," *International Organization*, 15/3 (Summer 1961).

50. Tobias Bunde and Noetzel Timo, "Unavoidable Tensions: The Liberal Path to Global NATO," *Contemporary Security Policy*, 31/2 (August 2010): 295–318. See also Emiliano Alessandri, "Global NATO: Its Place in the Evolving Atlanticist Tradition," *Politics & Policy*, 37/1 (February 2009): 241–7.

51. Tobias Bunde and Noetzel Timo, ibid.

52. The North Atlantic Council expressed this view succinctly in Reykjavik in 2002, "Final Communiqué: Ministerial Meeting of the North Atlantic Council, Held in Reykjavik on 14 May 2002," NATO Press Release M-NAC-1(2002)59, http://www.nato.int/docu/pr/2002/p02-059e.htm.

53. "Admit Defeat and Bring the Soldiers Home," *Scotsman*, March 28, 2012.

54. For an elaboration of the career of Gaddafi see Moussa Koussa, "The Political Leader and His Social Background: Muammar Qaddafi, the Libyan Leader" (M.A. thesis, Michigan State University, 1978). See also, *Libya Since Independence: Oil and State Building*, especially chapter 4, "From Kingdom to Republic."

55. Ruth First, *Libya: The Elusive Revolution* (New York: Penguin, 1974).

56. For a chronology of the actions of the Libyan leadership in this period, see *Libya since Independence: Oil and State Building*.

57. Lillian Craig Harris, *Libya: Quadhafi's Revolution and the Modern State* (Boulder: Westview Press, 1986), 86.

58. Mario J. Azevedo, *Roots of Violence: A History of War in Chad* (New York: Routledge, 1998). This war is also called the Toyota War by some Western journalists.

59. "Charles Taylor Tied to CIA," *Boston Globe*, January 19, 2012. See also "Charles Taylor 'worked' for the CIA in Liberia," BBC News, January 19, 2012, http://www.bbc.co.uk/news/world-africa-16627628.

60. *The Libyan Paradox*.

61. "Who Said Gaddafi Had to Go?" *London Review of Books*.

62. Ibid.

63. Martin Bright, "MI6 'halted bid to arrest bin Laden,' " *The Observer*, November 10, 2002, http://www.guardian.co.uk/politics/2002/nov/10/uk.davidshayler. For further details of the relationships between Western intelligence agencies and the Islamicists in Libya and Saudi Arabia, see Jean-Charles Brisard and Guillaume Dasquie, *Forbidden Truth: U.S. Taliban Secret Oil Diplomacy, Saudi Arabia and the Failed Search for bin Laden* (New York: Nation Books, 2002).

64. The title of the dissertation is "The Role of Civil Society in the Democratisation of Global Governance Institutions."

65. This line of reasoning has been developed by Luis Martinez and Vijay Prashad. See *Arab Spring, Libyan Winter*, 135–7.

66. *Arab Spring, Libyan Winter*, 136–8.

67. Jon Lee Anderson, "King of Kings," *The New Yorker*, November 7, 2011, http://www.newyorker.com/reporting/2011/11/07/111107fa_fact_anderson?currentPage=all.

68. See "BP Agrees Major Exploration and Production Deal with Libya," May 29, 2007, http://www.bp.com/genericarticle.do?categoryId=2012968&contentId=7033600. For comparison, the acreage awarded in the North Ghadames block alone is the size of Kuwait. The acreage in the offshore Sirte basin is the size of Belgium, or nearly three North Sea quadrants. In total, the acreage is more than ten times the size of BP-operated Block 31 in Angola, where BP has announced 14 discoveries so far, or more than 2000 Gulf of Mexico deepwater blocks.

69. "Fees go Unpaid as Gaddafi Crumbles," *Times Higher Educational Supplement*, August 25, 2011, http://www.timeshighereducation.co.uk/story.asp?storycode=417222.

70. Charlotte Allen, "Harvard Professors and the Complication with Libya," *Harvard Crimson*, May 1, 2011. See also "U.S. Firm Monitor Group Admits Mistakes Over $3m Gaddafi Deal," *The Guardian*, March 3, 2011, http://www.guardian.co.uk/world/2011/mar/04/monitor-group-us-libya-gaddafi.

71. Michael Barnett and Raymond Duvall, "Power in International Politics," *International Organization*, 59/1 (Winter 2005).

72. David Corn and Siddharta Mahanta, "From Libya with Love: How a U.S. Consulting Firm Used American Academics to Rehab Muammar Qaddafi's Image," *Mother Jones*, March 3, 2011, http://motherjones.com/politics/2011/03/libya-qaddafi-monitor-group. This public relations work yielded a number of friendly articles in the Western press.

73. Dirk Vandewalle, "Libya in the New Millennium," in *Libya since 1969: Qadhafi's Revolution Revisited*, Dirk Vandewalle, ed. (New York: Palgrave Macmillan, 2008), 223–6 on IMF reforms in Libya.

74. "2011: An Arab Springtime?" *African Awakening: The Emerging Revolutions*, 292.

75. *Arab Spring, Libyan Winter*, 199–204, described what he termed "America's Libyans."

76. For details of the contents of the cables, see *The Telegraph*, http://www.telegraph.co.uk/news/wikileaks-files/libya-wikileaks/8294934/libya-commercial-round-up-for-december-2008-and-january-2009.html.

77. *The Libya Paradox*, 61–80.

78. Center for Defense Information, "In the Spotlight: The Libyan Islamic Fighting Group (LIFG)," January 18, 2005.

79. Rohan Gunaratna, *Inside Al Qaeda: Global Network of Terror* (New York: Columbia University Press, 2002), 142.

80. *The Libya Paradox*, 68

81. Ibid., 81. "In general the 'republican' constituents of the nation were not mobilized in the trial of strength with the Islamists. Quite the contrary, in fact: the regime recruited foreign 'mercenaries' to carry out air attacks, as the only way to maintain a distance between these operations and the 'political community.' "

82. "MI6 'worked with Gaddafi regime,' " *The Guardian*, September 3, 2011, http://www.guardian.co.uk/uk/feedarticle/9829331.

83. Scott Petersen, "How US, British Intelligence Worked to Bring Qaddafi's Libya in from the Cold," *Christian Science Monitor*, September 6, 2011, http://www.cs-

monitor.com/World/Middle-East/2011/0905/How-US-British-intelligence-worked-to-bring-Qaddafi-s-Libya-in-from-the-cold.

84. Arms Control Association, "Chronology of Libya's Disarmament and Relations with the United States," March 1, 2011, http://www.armscontrol.org/fact-sheets/LibyaChronology.

85. Jeremy Keenan, *The Dark Sahara: America's War on Terror in Africa* (London: Pluto Press, 2009).

86. *Arab Spring, Libyan Winter*, 98.

87. News Transcript, DOD News Briefing with Secretary Gates and Adm. Mullen from the Pentagon, U.S. Department of Defense, March 1, 2011, http://www.defense.gov/transcripts/transcript.aspx?transcriptid=4777.

88. UN Security Council Resolution 1970, February 26, 2011, http://daccess-dds-ny.un.org/doc/UNDOC/GEN/N11/245/58/PDF/N1124558.pdf

89. *Arab Spring, Libyan Winter*, 99.

90. Samantha Power, *A Problem from Hell: America and the Age of Genocide* (New York: Harper Perennial, 2007). It is significant that in her chronicling of genocides in the twentieth century Power excluded acts of genocide carried out by the U.S. supported governments in Indonesia, Vietnam, Guatemala and numerous other spaces, such as Iraq and Chile.

91. Jacob Heilbrunn, "Samantha and Her Subjects," *The National Interest*, May–June 2011.

92. Thomas P.M. Barnett, *The Pentagon's New Map: War and Peace in the Twenty-First Century* (New York: Putman Books, 2004). See also by the same author, *Blueprint for Action: A Future Worth Creating* (New York: Berkley Books, 2006).

93. The Old Core was supposed to be anchored by America, Europe, and Japan; and the New Core, whose leading pillars are China, India, Brazil, and Russia.

94. Robert Kaplan, "The Coming Anarchy," *The Atlantic*, February 1994. In this article, Kaplan had warned, "West Africa is becoming the symbol of worldwide demographic, environmental, and societal stress, in which criminal anarchy emerges as the real 'strategic' danger. Disease, overpopulation, unprovoked crime, scarcity of resources, refugee migrations, the increasing erosion of nation-states and international borders, and the empowerment of private armies, security firms, and international drug cartels are now most tellingly demonstrated through a West African prism."

95. Ruben Reike on "Responsibility to Protect: Cultural Perspectives in the Global South." See also the book that was reviewed, Rama Mani and Thomas G. Weiss, *Responsibility to Protect: Cultural Perspectives in the Global South* (New York: Routledge, 2011).

96. Frances Abiew, "Humanitarian Intervention and the Responsibility to Protect: Redefining a Role for 'Kind-Hearted Gunmen,' " *Criminal Justice Ethics*, 29/2 (August 2010). See also Carsten Stahn, "Responsibility to Protect: Political Rhetoric or Emerging Legal Norm?" *The American Journal of International Law*, 101/99 (January 2007); and Alan J. Kuperman, "Rethinking the Responsibility to Protect," *Whitehead Journal of Diplomacy and International Relations* (Winter/Spring 2009).

97. "Responsibility to Protect: Political Rhetoric or Emerging Legal Norm?" *The American Journal of International Law,* 101/99 (January 2007). See also Sreeran Chaulia, *International Organizations and Civilian Protection: Power, Ideas and Humanitarian Aid* (London: Tauris Academic Studies, 2011).

98. "Wikileaks Documents Shed Light on US-backed Intervention in Libya," *African Globe,* July 27, 2011, http://www.africanglobe.net/africa/wikileaks-documents-shed-light-on-us-backed-intervention-in-libya/.

99. For one account of the plans of the British intelligence to execute Gaddafi, see Annie Machon, *Spies, Lies & Whistleblowers: MI5, MI6 and the Shayler Affair* (Lewes, Sussex: Book Guild, 2005).

100. Benjamin Wallace Wells, "European Superhero Quashes Libyan Dictator," *The New Yorker,* December 26, 2011, nymag.com/news/features/bernard-henri-levy-2012-1/.

101. Ibid.

102. Patricia Daley, *Gender and Genocide in Burundi: The Search for Spaces of Peace in the Great Lakes Region* (Oxford: James Currey, 2008).

103. President Nelson Mandela (statement presented at the OAU Meeting of Heads of State and Government, June 13, 1994, Tunis).

104. The Gulf Cooperation Council (GCC) had been established in an agreement concluded on May 25, 1981, in Riyadh, Saudi Arabia, between Bahrain, Kuwait, Oman, Qatar, Saudi Arabia and the United Arab Emirates (UAE).

105. Abdullah Al-Hassan, May Khamis, and Nada Oulidi, "The GCC Banking Sector: Topography and Analysis," IMF Working Paper, Monetary and Capital Markets and Middle East and Central Asia Departments, April 2010.

106. In December, after the execution of Gaddafi, the Arab Banking Corporation (ABC) announced the appointment of Central Bank of Libya governor Saddek El Kaber as chairman of its board.

107. *Qaddafi's Libya in World Politics,* 136.

108. Gaddafi's impromptu speech at the summit was reported by Al Jazeera as follows, "The Libyan leader, Muammar al-Qadhafi, makes a short impromptu speech, in which he congratulates Qatari Emir Shaykh Hamad on assuming the presidency of the summit and then takes the opportunity to address Saudi King Abdallah, amid attempts by the Qatari emir to try to stop him from talking. Al-Qadhafi continues with his remarks and says: 'On this occasion, I tell my brother Abdallah: You have been afraid of, and avoiding, a confrontation for six years. Do not be afraid. After six years, it has been proven that you are the one who has lies behind him and the grave in front of him [reference to a statement made by the Saudi King and addressed to Al-Qadhafi at an earlier Arab summit], and you are the one who was made by Britain and protected by America.' " Then, there was interruption in the audio. When the audio is heard again, Al-Qadhafi is heard saying that he considers that the personal quarrel between them to be over and that he is willing to visit the Saudi king and to receive him in Libya. Al-Qadhafi goes on to say that his "international standing" of being "king of the kings of Africa and the imam of the Muslims" prevents him from stooping to any other level. Throughout Al-Qadhafi's intervention, the Qatari emir tries to interrupt him and asks that his microphone be turned off.

109. The full list of members is as follows: Algeria, Bahrain, Comoros—an island nation near Madagascar in the Indian Ocean—Djibouti, Egypt, Iraq, Jordan, Kuwait, Lebanon, Libya, Mauritania, Morocco, Oman, Palestine, Qatar, Saudi Arabia, Somalia, Sudan, Syria, Tunisia, United Arab Emirates, and Yemen.

110. For an analysis of the members who supported this resolution see Pepe Escobar, "Exposed: the U.S.-Saudi Libya Deal," *Asia Times,* April 2, 2011, http://atimes.com/atimes/Middle_East/MD02Ak01.html.

111. "If the Libyan War Was about Saving Lives, It Was a Catastrophic Failure," *The Guardian.*

112. Garikai Chengu, "Death for Libyans; Billions for the West," *The Citizen* (Dar es Salaam, Tanzania) September 9, 2011.

113. Simon Tisdall, "Psychological Warfare in Libya," *The Guardian,* April 6, 2011.

114. Maximilian Forte, "The Top Ten Myths in the War against Libya," *Counterpunch,* August 31, 2011, http://www.counterpunch.org/2011/08/31/the-top-ten-myths-in-the-war-against-libya/.

115. Simon Tisdall, "To the Victors the Problems: Cameron and Sarkozy in Libya," *The Guardian,* September 15, 2011, http://www.guardian.co.uk/world/2011/sep/15/victors-problems-cameron-sarkozy-libya.

116. Julian Borger and Terry Macalister, "The Race Is on for Libya's Oil, with Britain and France Both Staking a Claim," *The Guardian,* September 1, 2011, http://www.guardian.co.uk/world/2011/sep/01/libya-oil.

117. Anthony Samson, *The Seven Sisters: The Great Oil Companies and the World They Made* (London: Bantam Books, 1991). The seven were comprised of (1) Anglo-Persian Oil Company (now BP); (2) Gulf Oil; (3) Standard Oil of California (Socal); (4) Texaco (now Chevron); (5) Royal Dutch Shell; (6) Standard Oil of New Jersey (Esso); and (7) Standard Oil Company of New York (Socony, now ExxonMobil). By the end of the twentieth century, through mergers and acquisitions, the seven had merged to become four: (1) Exxon Mobil; (2) Chevron Texaco; (3) BP Amoco; and (4) Royal Dutch/Shell.

118. The Oasis Group (originally the Conorada Group) is a consortium composed of three U.S. "independent" oil companies: Amerada (now Amerada Hess), Continental (now ConocoPhillips), and Marathon. Bidding independently, the companies won concessions throughout Libya during the first auction of oil rights in 1955. For details of the oil companies, see *The Libyan Paradox* and *Libya Since Independence: Oil and State Building.*

119. *The Seven Sisters: The Great Oil Companies and the World They Made.*

120. *The Tyranny of Oil: The World's Most Powerful Industry and What We Must Do to Stop It* (New York: William Morrow, 2008), 101.

121. The top three enemies were the Soviet Union, China, and North Korea. Cuba was ranked fifth on this list. See *Qaddafi's Libya in World Politics,* 15.

122. Ibid., 32–34.

123. In the United States, Libya was linked to the 1988 bombing of PanAm flight 103 over Lockerbie, Scotland, and the 1989 downing of UTA flight 772 over Niger. In early 1992, the UN Security Council passed a number of resolutions, including Resolution 748, which called upon Libya to turn over the Lockerbie bombing

suspects and to forswear terrorism, while threatening UN-mandated sanctions if Gaddafi's government were to fail to cooperate. By April 1992, the UN had sanctioned Libya with a ban on all air links and an end to arms sales, though it expressly indicated that sanctions would be lifted once Libya surrendered the Lockerbie suspects and ended its support for terrorism. Gaddafi's refusal to do so prompted the Security Council to pass Resolution 883 in November 1993, which tightened air restrictions, froze Libyan government assets abroad and banned certain oil technology and equipment exports to Libya. For one analysis of the context of the sanctions see Yahya Zoubir, "Libya in U.S. Foreign Policy: From Rogue State to Good Fellow?" *Third World Quarterly,* 23/1 (February 2002).

124. Richard B. Cheney, "Defending Liberty in a Global Economy" (speech presented at the CATO Institute, June 23, 1998) http://www.cato.org/speeches/sp-dc062398.html.

125. Duncan Clarke, *Crude Continent: The Struggle for Africa's Oil Prize* (London: Profile Books, 2008), 225.

126. Energy Information Administration, "Libyan Supply Disruption May Have Both Direct and Indirect Effects," http://www.eia.gov/countries/cab.cfm?fips=LY.

127. Ronald Bruce St. John, "The Libyan Economy in Transition: Opportunities and Challenges," in Dirk Vandewalle, ed., *Libya since 1969: Gaddafi's Revolution Revisited* (New York: Palgrave Macmillan, 2008), 138.

128. Ibid., 141.

129. Ibid., 140.

130. *Crude Continent: The Struggle for Africa's Oil Prize,* 228.

131. A.M. MacDonald et al., "Quantitative Maps of Groundwater Resources in Africa," British Geological Survey, London, April 2012.

132. Ibid., see Table 1: Estimated groundwater storage for African countries.

133. Richard Black, "Water map shows billions at risk of 'water insecurity,' " BBC News, September 29, 2010, http://www.bbc.co.uk/news/science-environment-11435522. See also Dhirendra K. Vajpeyi, *Water Resource Conflicts and International Security: A Global Perspective* (Lanham, MD: Lexington Books, 2011).

134. Ian Black and Kim Willsher, "Sarkozy Election Campaign Was Funded by Libya–Gaddafi Son," *The Guardian,* March 16, 2011, http://www.guardian.co.uk/world/2011/mar/16/sarkozy-election-campaign-libya-claim.

135. Robin Luckham, "French Militarism in Africa," *Review of African Political Economy, The French Connection,* 24 (May–August, 1982), 55–84. For an examination of how Africans were used as a pool of cheap labor for the French military, see Anthony Clayton, *France, Soldiers, and Africa* (London: Brasseys, 1988).

136. Bruno Charbonneau, *France and the New Imperialism: Security Policy in Sub-Saharan Africa* (Vermont: Ashgate Publishing, 2008). For another figure which placed the number of French interventions at 40, see Christopher Griffin, "France, the United Kingdom, and European Union Capacities for Military Action in Africa," and Andrew Hansen, "The French Military in Africa," Council on Foreign Relations, February 8, 2008, http://www.cfr.org/france/french-military-africa/p12578.

137. The Mucyo Commission, led by Jean de Mucyo, outlined the gory details of the role of France in training those who committed genocide. This report indicted 33 members of President Mitterrand's government and military of 1994, which reads like a who's who of luminaries and heavyweights—ex-prime ministers Dominque de Villepin and Edouard Balladur, and Alain Juppé, as well as generals and colonels. There are enough studies on this episode in African history. See Romeo Dallaire, *Shake Hands with the Devil: The Failure of Humanity in Rwanda* (1st ed.) (London: Arrow Books, 2004); and Linda Malvern, *Conspiracy to Murder: The Rwandan Genocide* (New York: Verso Books, 2006). See also Mel McNulty, "French Arms, War and Genocide in Rwanda," *Crime, Law & Social Change*, 33 (2000): 105–29; and the United Nations Organization, "Report of the Independent Inquiry into the Actions of the UN during the 1994 Genocide in Rwanda," http://www.ess.uwe.ac.uk/documents/RwandaReport3.htm.

138. Andrew Wallis, *Silent Accomplice: The Untold Story of France's Role in the Rwandan Genocide* (London: I.B. Taurus, 2007).

139. Gordon D. Cumming and Tony Chafer, "From Rivalry to Partnership? Critical Reflections on Anglo-French Cooperation in Africa," *Review of International Studies*, 37 (2011): 2439–63.

140. "Joint Declaration on European Defense" (joint declaration issued at the British-French Summit, St-Mâlo, December 3–4, 1998). Foreign and Commonwealth Office of the United Kingdom, http://www.fco.gov.uk/en/newsroom/latest-news.

141. Andrew Hansen, "The French Military in Africa," *Foreign Affairs,* February 8, 2008.

142. Niagale Bagayoko, "French Reactions to AFRICOM: An Historic Perspective," *Contemporary Security Policy*, 30 (April 2009): 28–31.

143. NATO Mediterranean Dialogue, www.nato.int/cps/en/SID-EA36E091-5B096A89/natolive/topics_60021.htm.

144. *The Libyan Paradox,* 114.

145. German Institute for Security and International Affairs, Berlin 2005, http://www.swp-berlin.org/fileadmin/contents/products/arbeitspapiere/wp_prt_june_2005_KS.pdf.

146. *The Libyan Paradox,* 10.

147. See George Walden's review of Bernard-Henri Lévy's *La Guerre sans l'Aimer Journal d'un écrivain au coeur du printemps libyen.* George Walden, "How Is Bernard-Henri Lévy Possible?" *Times Literary Supplement,* December 2011, http://www.the-tls.co.uk/tls/public/article848402.ece.

148. "European Superhero Quashes Libyan Dictator," *The New Yorker.*

149. Steven Earlanger, "By his own reckoning, one man made Libya a French cause," *New York Times,* April 1, 2011, www.nytimes.com/2011/04/02/world/africa/02levy.html?pagewanted=all.

150. *13 Bankers: The Wall Street Takeover and the Next Financial Meltdown.* See also Charles Ferguson, *Predator Nation: Corporate Criminals, Political Corruption and the Hijacking of America* (New York: Crown Books, 2012).

151. *The Tyranny of Oil: The World's Most Powerful Industry—And What We Must Do to Stop It,* 161.

152. The ICE is organized into three business lines: (a) ICE Markets—futures, options, and OTC markets (energy futures are traded via ICE Futures Europe; soft commodity futures/ options are handled by ICE Futures U.S.); (b) ICE Services—electronic trade confirmations and education; and (c) ICE Data—electronic delivery of market data, including real-time trades, historical prices and daily indices. For an analysis of the role of the ICE, see Phillip Davis, "The Global Oil Scam: Fifty Times Bigger than Madoff," *Seeking Alpha*, November 11, 2009, http://seekingalpha.com/article/172797-the-global-oil-scam-50-times-bigger-than-madoff.

153. Quoted in *The Tyranny of Oil: The World's Most Powerful Industry—And What We Must Do to Stop It*, 126.

154. www.libyaninvestmentauthority.com/002E

155. Paul Richter, "Kadafi had a 'staggering' $200 billion stashed around the world," *Los Angeles Times*, October 21, 2011, http://latimesblogs.latimes.com/world_now/2011/10/kadafi-bank-account-200-billion-hidden-cash-asset-search.html.

156. Margaret Coker and Liz Rappaport, "Libya's Goldman Dalliance Ends in Losses, Acrimony," *The Wall Street Journal*, May 31, 2011, http://online.wsj.com/article/SB10001424052702304066504576347190532098376.html.

157. *Predator Nation: Corporate Criminals, Political Corruption and the Hijacking of America*, 16.

158. "Libya's Goldman Dalliance Ends in Losses, Acrimony," *The Wall Street Journal*, May 31, 2011, http://online.wsj.com/article/SB1000142405270230406650457634719053209 8376.html.

159. Ibid.

160. Reported in the *New York Times*, February 26, 2011.

161. "Gates Warns of Risks of a No-Flight Zone," *New York Times*, March 2, 2011, http://www.nytimes.com/2011/03/03/world/africa/03military.html?pagewanted=2&ref=robertmgates.

162. "War in Libya: Europe's Confused Response," International Institute of Strategic Studies, June 2011, http://www.iiss.org/publications/strategic-comments/past-issues/volume-17-2011/april/war-in-libya-europes-confused-response/mobile-edition/.

163. "Accidental Heroes: Britain, France and the Libyan operation," Royal United Services Institute (RUSI), Interim Libya Campaign Report, September 2011, http://www.scribd.com/doc/66189909/Accidental-Heroes-Rusi-Interim-Libya-Report.

164. Ibid.

165. "Who's in Charge? Germans Pull Forces out of NATO as Libyan Coalition Falls Apart," *Daily Mail*, March 22, 2011, http://www.dailymail.co.uk/news/article-1368693/Libya-war-Germans-pull-forces-NATO-Libyan-coalition-falls-apart.html.

166. Ibid.

167. Ibid.

168. Ibid.

169. C. J. Chivers and Eric Schmitt, "In Strikes on Libya by NATO: An Unspoken Civilian Toll," *New York Times*, December 17, 2011, http://www.nytimes. com/2011/12/18/world/africa/scores-of-unintended-casualties-in-nato-war-in-libya.html?pagewanted=all. In this report, the number of air strikes was given at 9,700 sorties.

170. "Early Military Lessons from Libya," Survival, IISS Strategic Comments, Volume 17, Comment 34, September 2011.

171. "Who's in Charge? Germans Pull Forces out of NATO as Libyan Coalition Falls Apart," *Daily Mail.*

172. "Early Military Lessons from Libya," IISS.

173. "Warning against Wars like Iraq and Afghanistan," *New York Times*, February 25, 2011, http://www.nytimes.com/2011/02/26/world/26gates.html. See also the testimonies by Gates and the Chairperson of the Joint Chiefs of Staff at this time.

174. Ryan Lizza, "The Consequentialist: How the Arab Spring Remade Obama's Foreign Policy," *The New Yorker*, May 2011, http://www.newyorker.com/ reporting/2011/05/02/110502fa_fact_lizza#ixzz1oNNdTL45.

175. See also Robert Dreyfuss, "Obama's Women Advisors Pushed War against Libya," *The Nation*, March 19, 2011, http://www.thenation.com/print/ blog/159346/obamas-women-pushed-war-against-libya.

176. Nicholas Schmidle, "Getting Bin Laden," *The New Yorker*, August 2011, http:// www.newyorker.com/reporting/2011/08/08/110808fa_fact_schmidle.

177. Bernard Kouchner, "Libya: The Morality of Intervention," *The Guardian*, March 24, 2011, http://www.guardian.co.uk/commentisfree/2011/mar/24/libya-morality-intervention-united-europe. In this article, Kouchner, a co-founder of the NGO Médecins Sans Frontières, argued that "The Libyan crisis has shown how a united Europe can be used as a force for common good."

178. Sylvia Pfeifer and Javier Blas, "Oil Companies Fear Nationalization in Libya," *Financial Times*, March 20, 2011, http://www.ft.com/intl/cms/s/0/67d1d02a-5314-11e0-86e6-00144feab49a.html#axzz1esljkNWX.

179. Michael Clarke, "Curious Victory for NATO in Libya," RU.S.I Analysis, August 23, 2011, http://www.rusi.org/analysis/commentary/ref:C4E53CF030EB3B/

180. Vladimir Socor, "Under NATO's Flag: An Interim Assessment of the Mission in Libya (Part 3)," Atlantic Council, August 12, 2011, http://www.acus.org/ new_atlanticist/under-nato%E2%80%99s-flag-interim-assessment-mission-libya-part-three.

181. For a text of the statement by African intellectuals, see Appendix.

182. *Gender & Genocide in Burundi: The Search for Spaces of Peace in the Great Lakes Region.*

183. It was later revealed in Tunisia that Gaddafi had provided tear gas canisters for the Ben Ali regime, http://www.tunisia-live.net/2011/11/03/former-tunisian-chief-of-presidential-security-reveals-gaddafi-provided-ben-ali-police-with-tear-gas-bomb/.

184. Jean Ping, "African Union Role in the Libyan Crisis," *Pambazuka News*, 563–15 (December 2011).

185. For the full text of this open letter, see Appendix.
186. "U.S. Embassy Cables: The Eccentricities of Gadaffi Revealed," *The Guardian*, December 7, 2010, http://www.guardian.co.uk/world/us-embassy-cables-documents/227491.
187. "In Strikes on Libya by NATO: An Unspoken Civilian Toll," *New York Times*.
188. "Curious Victory for NATO in Libya," RUSI Analysis.
189. Lizzie Phelan, " 'Free Tripoli,' just don't mention the corpses," *Pambazuka News*, September 7, 2011, http://www.pambazuka.org/en/category/features/76085.
190. Jeffrey Rosen, "Total Information Awareness," *New York Times*, December 15, 2002, www.nytimes.com/2002/12/15/magazine/15TOTA.html.
191. Information Operations Roadmap, 1, http://news.bbc.co.uk/2/shared/bsp/hi/pdfs/ 27_01_06_psyops.pdf.
192. Information Operations Roadmap, 7.
193. Information Operations Roadmap, 1.
194. Russ Hoyle, *Going to War: How Misinformation, Disinformation, and Arrogance Led America into Iraq* (New York: Thomas Donne Books, 2008).
195. Michael Hastings, "Another Runaway General: Army Deploys Psy-ops on U.S. Senators," *Rolling Stone*, February 23, 2011, http://www.rollingstone.com/politics/news/another-runaway-general-army-deploys-psy-ops-on-u-s-senators-20110223?page=1.
196. For early media details of the planning, see "The Secret Plan to Take Tripoli," *Reuters*, September 6, 2011, http://www.reuters.com/article/2011/09/06/us-libya-endgame-idU.S.TRE7853C520110906. See also Nicolas Pelham, "Libya: How They Did It," *New York Review of Books*, August 29, 2011, http://www.nybooks.com/articles/archives/2011/sep/29/libya-how-they-did-it/?pagination=false.
197. Mark Hosenball, "Mercenaries Joining Both Sides in Libya Conflict," Reuters, June 2, 2011, http://af.reuters.com/article/libyaNews/idAFN0229488620110602?sp=true.
198. Mark Mazzetti and Eric Schmitt, "C.I.A. Agents in Libya Aid Airstrikes and Meet Rebels," *New York Times*, March 30, 2011, http://www.nytimes.com/2011/03/31/world/africa/31intel.html. See also, "Libya: Barack Obama signed order for CIA to help rebels," *The Telegraph*, March 30, 2011, http://www.telegraph.co.uk/news/worldnews/africaandindianocean/libya/8417399/Libya-Barack-Obama-signed-order-for-CIA-to-help-rebels.html.
199. Russ Baker, "Is General Khalifa Hifter the CIA's Man in Libya?" BusinessInsider, April 22, 2011, http://articles.businessinsider.com/2011-04-22/politics/30085091_1_libyan-leader-moammar-gadhafi-rebel-army-qaddafi#ixzz1z6Xx5xiw.
200. RUSI, "Interim Libya Campaign Report."
201. "Libya: Colonel Gaddafi 'Flees' to Venezuela as Cities Fall to Protesters," *The Telegraph*, February 21, 2011, http://www.telegraph.co.uk/news/worldnews/africaandindianocean/libya/8338948/Libya-Colonel-Gaddafi-flees-to-Venezuela-as-cities-fall-to-protesters.html.
202. " 'Free Tripoli,' Just Don't Mention the Corpses," *Pambazuka News*.

203. Dennis Kucinich, "Congressman Kucinich's Address to Congress on the War in Libya," *The Nation*, April 4, 2011, http://www.thenation.com/article/159674/congressman-kucinichs-address-congress-war-libya.

204. Statement of Congressman Ron Paul in "Hearing before the Committee on Foreign Affairs House of Representatives One Hundred Twelfth Congress First Session, March 31, 2011," http://www.gpo.gov/fdsys/pkg/CHRG-112hhrg65492/html/CHRG-112hhrg65492.htm.

205. Richard Norton-Taylor and Nick Hopkins, "Military Top Brass Question British Strategy over Gaddafi," *The Guardian*, March 21, 2011, http://www.guardian.co.uk/world/2011/mar/21/top-brass-question-libya-strategy.

206. "Accidental Heroes: Britain, France and the Libyan operation," RUSI Analysis.

207. Ian Black, "Qatar Admits Sending Hundreds of Troops to Support Libya Rebels," *The Guardian*, October 26, 2011, http://www.guardian.co.uk/world/2011/oct/26/qatar-troops-libya-rebels-support. The figure of 5,000 Qatari troops was carried by the "5,000 forces spéciales du Qatar avaient été deployées en Libye," by Georges Malbrunot, *Le Figaro*, November 6, 2011, http://blog.lefigaro.fr/malbrunot/2011/11/5-000-forces-speciales-du-qata.html.

208. "Accidental Heroes: Britain, France and the Libyan operation," RUSI Analysis.

209. This author was told that Fidel Castro of Cuba was following the battles and the reports with maps on a daily basis.

210. Vladimir Socor, "Under Nato's Flag: An Interim Assessment of the Mission in Libya," Jamestown Foundation, http://www.jamestown.org/single/?no_cache=1&tx_ttnews%5Btt_news%5D=38295.

211. Human Rights Watch, "Unacknowledged Deaths: Civilian Casualties in NATO's Air Campaign in Libya," www.hrw.org/reports/2012/05/13/unacknowledged-deaths.

212. At the end of June 2011, the International Criminal Court (ICC) announced the arrest warrants for Muammar Gaddafi and one of his sons, Saif al-Islam Gaddafi, on charges of ordering and organizing the arrest, imprisonment, and killing of hundreds of civilians in the initial days of the uprising against the Gaddafi regime. Also indicted was Gaddafi's intelligence chief, Abdullah al-Sanoussi.

213. Samia Nakhoul, "The Secret Plan to Take Tripoli," Reuters, September 6, 2011, www.reuters.com/article/2011/09/06/us-libya-endgame-idUSTRE7853C520110906. Several allied and U.S. officials, as well as a source close to the Libyan rebels, said that around the beginning of May foreign military trainers, including British, French, and Italian operatives as well as representatives from Qatar and the United Arab Emirates, began to organize serious efforts to hone the rebels into a more effective fighting force.

214. "Libya: How They Did It," *New York Review of Books*.

215. " 'Free Tripoli,' just don't mention the corpses," *Pambazuka News*.

216. Ibid.

217. *The Libyan Paradox*, 61.

218. "Libya: How the Opposing Sides are Armed," BBC, August 23, 2011, http://www.bbc.co.uk/news/world-africa-12692068.

219. Maximilian Forte, "The War in Libya: Race, 'Humanitarianism,' and the Media," *MRZine*, April 20, 2011, http://mrzine.monthlyreview.org/2011/forte200411.html.

220. "The Top Ten Myths in the War against Libya," *Counterpunch.*
221. Tarik Kafala, " 'Cleansed' Libyan Town Spills its Terrible Secrets," BBC, December 12, 2011, http://www.bbc.co.uk/news/magazine-16051349. See also Houda Mzioudet, "Libya: Tawergha—The Town Destroyed by Nation's Revolution," *allAfrica,* February 27, 2012, http://allafrica.com/stories/201202280501.html.
222. David Enders, "Empty Village Raises Concerns about Fate of Black Libyans," *McClatchy,* September 13, 2011, http://www.mcclatchydc.com/2011/09/13/123999/empty-village-raises-concerns.html#storylink=cpy.
223. Mark Landler, "Before Qaddafi's Death, U.S. Debated His Future," *New York Times,* October 24, 2011, http://www.nytimes.com/2011/10/25/us/politics/before-qaddafis-death-us-debated-his-future.html.
224. Ibid.
225. Shirin Sadeghi, "Hillary Wants Gaddafi Killed," *Huffington Post,* October 19, 2011, http://www.huffingtonpost.com/shirin-sadeghi/hillary-clinton-wants-gad_b_1020705.html.
226. Kareem Fahim, "In His Last Days, Qaddafi Wearied of Fugitive's Life," *New York Times,* October 22, 2011, www.nytimes.com/2011/10/23/world/africa/in-his-last-days-qaddafi-wearied-of-fugitives-life.html?pagewanted=all.
227. Thomas Harding, "Col. Gaddafi Killed: Convoy Bombed by Drone Flown by Pilot in Las Vegas," *The Telegraph,* October 20, 2011, http://www.telegraph.co.uk/news/worldnews/africaandindianocean/libya/8839964/Col-Gaddafi-killed-convoy-bombed-by-drone-flown-by-pilot-in-Las-Vegas.html.
228. "NATO Strike in Sirte Area 20 October 2011," October 21, 2011, NATO Press Release, NATO and Libya, Operational Media Update.
229. Bernard-Henri Lévy, "A Moral Tipping Point," *The Daily Beast,* October 23, 2011, http://www.bernard-henri-levy.com/a-moral-tipping-point-the-daily-beast-23octobre-2011-23966.html.
230. Damien McElroy, "Libya: Nato to Be Investigated by ICC for War Crimes," *The Telegraph,* November 2, 2011.
231. Mike Corder and Slobodan Lekic, "NATO Fears Libya War Crimes Investigation by World Court," AP Report reproduced on MSNBC, November 11, 2011, http://www.msnbc.msn.com/id/45252513/ns/world_news-europe/t/nato-fears-libya-war-crimes-investigation-world-court/.
232. Anders Fogh Rasmussen, "NATO Secretary General Makes Historic Libya Trip," NATO Press Release, October 31, 2011, http://www.nato.int/cps/en/natolive/news_80100.htm.
233. "If the Libyan War Was about Saving Lives, It Was a Catastrophic Failure," *The Guardian.*
234. Ibid.
235. Alan Kuperman, "Was NATO's Libya Intervention a Humanitarian Success?" Lecture to the International Institute of Social Studies, Erasmus University, Rotterdam, in The Hague, Netherlands, May 29, 2012, http://www.youtube.com/watch?v=d_F_QHeQ4MU&feature=youtu.be.
236. Ruhakana Rugunda, "AU on Libya: Political Solution Needed," *Pambazuka News,* June 29, 2011, http://pambazuka.org/en/category/features/74462.

237. "Libya: Tutu Condemns Leader's Killing," *allAfrica,* October 21, 2011, http://allafrica.com/stories/201110211491.html.

238. Glen Johnson, "Libya Weapons Aid Tuareg Rebellion in Mali," *Los Angeles Times,* June 12, 2012, http://articles.latimes.com/2012/jun/12/world/la-fg-libya-arms-smuggle-20120612. See also "Arms and Men out of Libya Fortify Mali Rebellion," Reuters, February 10, 2012, http://www.reuters.com/article/2012/02/10/us-mali-libya-idU.S.TRE8190UX20120210.

239. "An Imperialist Springtime? Libya, Syria, and Beyond," Samir Amin interviewed by Aijaz Ahmad, *MRZine,* April 28, 2012, http://mrzine.monthlyreview.org/2012/amin280412.html.

240. Vijay Prashad, "The Arteries of Petroleum: A Libyan Diary," *Economic and Political Weekly,* June 16, 2012, www.epw.in/commentary/arteries-petroleum.html.

241. Paul Craig Roberts, speaking on Russian television, "Why is NATO really in Libya?" http://www.youtube.com/watch?v=OPmlUFAXvdU.

242. "NATO's War on Libya Is Directed Against China," *Global Research.* http://www.globalresearch.ca/index.php?context=va&aid=26763. See also the analysis of Moncef Djaziri who had argued that "the West was increasingly becoming nervous in 2010, not so much about the fate of Libyan oil and gas resources as about the degree to which Gaddafi was courting the BRIC countries to invest in Libya and to block Western access to mineral and oil rich countries of Africa." Quoted in Ethan Chorin, *Exit the Colonel: The Hidden History of the Libyan Revolution* (New York: Public Affairs, 2012), 274.

243. Gabe Collins and Andrew S. Erickson, "Implications of China's Military Evacuation of Citizens from Libya," Jamestown Foundation, *China Brief,* 11/4–10 (March 2011): 8–10, http://www.jamestown.org/programs/chinabrief/single/?tx_ttnews%5Btt_news%5D=37633&tx_ttnews%5BbackPid%5D=25&cHash=c1302a9ecaddfc23450fb6ec13a98136.

244. Jiang Shixue, "Closer Ties on Agenda as Sarkozy Cozies up to China," *China Daily,* September 1, 2011, http://www.china.org.cn/opinion/2011-09/01/content_23332770.htm.

245. IMF, *Libya Beyond the Revolution: Challenges and Opportunities* (Washington, D.C.: IMF, 2012).

246. Ivo H. Daalder and James G. Stavridis, "NATO's Victory in Libya: The Right Way to Run an Intervention," *Foreign Affairs,* March/April 2012.

247. Ivo H. Daalder and James G. Stavridis, "NATO's Success in Libya," *New York Times,* October 31, 2011, http://www.nytimes.com/2011/10/31/opinion/31iht-eddaalder31.html?ref=global.

248. Dirk Vanderwalle, "After Qaddafi: The Surprising Success of the New Libya," *Foreign Affairs,* November/December 2012.

249. Amitai Etzioni, "The Lessons of Libya," *Military Review,* January–February 2012. See also Adrian Johnson and Saqeb Mueen, eds., *Short War, Long Shadow: The Political and Military Legacies of the 2011 Libya Campaign* (London: Royal United Services International, 2012).

250. Scott Shane, Adam Nossiter, and David D. Kirkpatrick, "Western Companies See Prospects for Business in Libya," *New York Times,* October 28, 2011, http://

www.nytimes.com/2011/10/29/world/africa/western-companies-see-libya-as-ripe-at-last-for-business.html?pagewanted=all.

251. David D. Kirkpatrick, "U.S. Reopens Its Embassy in Libya for Business; Returning Ambassador Seeks Prospects for American Investment," *International Herald Tribune*, September 4, 2011.

252. Christopher M. Blanchard, "Libya: Transition and U.S. Policy," Congressional Research Service, Washington D.C., October 18, 2012, http://www.fas.org/sgp/crs/row/RL33142.pdf.

253. Libya Country Profile, USAID 2012, http://photos.state.gov/libraries/libya/19452/pdfs/libya_country_profile_2012.pdf.

254. Ibid., 1.

255. "Libya: Transition and U.S. Policy," Congressional Research Service, Washington, D.C.

256. Samir Amin, *The Liberal Virus: Permanent War and the Americanization of the World* (New York: Monthly Review Press, 2012).

257. Barry Gills and Joel Racomara, "Low Intensity Democracy," *Third World Quarterly*, 13/3 (1992): 501–523. See also by the same authors, *Low Intensity Democracy: Political Power in the New World Order* (London: Pluto Press, 1994).

258. Noam Chomsky, "The Struggle for Democracy in the New World Order," in Gills and Racomara, *Low Intensity Democracy: Political Power in the New World Order*.

259. William Aviles, "Paramilitarism and Colombia's Low-Intensity Democracy," *Journal of Latin American Studies*, 38/2 (May 2006): 379–408.

260. Oliver Villar and Drew Cottle, *Cocaine, Death Squads and the War on Terror: U.S. Imperialism and Class Struggle in Colombia* (New York: Monthly Review Press, 2011).

261. Human Rights Watch, *Death of a Dictator: Bloody Vengeance in Sirte* (New York: Human Rights Watch, 2012), 17–19.

262. "Armed Groups in Libya: Typology and Roles," *A Small Arms Survey*, June 2012, www.smallarmssurvey.org/fileadmin/docs/H-Research_Notes/SAS-Research-Note-18.pdf. See also Jacob Mundy, "Militia Politics in Libya's National Elections," *Foreign Policy Magazine: Middle East Channel Blog*, July 5, 2012, www.mideast.foreignpolicy.com/posts/2012/07/05/militia_politics_in_libyas_national_elections; Frederick Wehrey, "The Struggle for Security in Eastern Libya," Carnegie Endowment for International Peace, September 2012, http://carnegieendowment.org/2012/09/19/struggle-for-security-in-eastern-libya/dvct; Wolfram Lacher, "Families, Tribes and Cities in the Libyan Revolution," *Middle East Policy*, 18/4 (2011): 140–154.

263. BBC, "Disarming Libya's Militias," September 18, 2012, http://www.bbc.co.uk/news/world-middle-east-19744533.

264. Freseric Wehrey, "Libya's Militia Menace, The Challenge after the Elections," *Foreign Affairs*, July 12, 2012.

265. Peter Bergen, "How Petraeus Changed the U.S. Military," CNN, November 11, 2012, http://www.cnn.com/2012/11/10/opinion/bergen-petraeus-legacy/index.html.

266. Amnesty International, "Militias Threaten Hope for a New Libya," February 15, 2012, http://www.amnestyusa.org/research/reports/militias-threaten-hope-for-new-libya.

267. Amnesty International, "Libya: Rule of Law or Rule of Militias?"

268. Kate Dourian, "Libya Targets Oil Output Increase, Refining Expansion," *Platt's Oilgram News*, September 25, 2012.

269. Robert F. Worth, "Walling Off the World," *New York Times*, November 18, 2012.

270. Ibid.

271. David Galula, *Counterinsurgency Warfare: Theory and Practice* (New York: Praeger, 2006).

272. U.S. Department of Defense, *Counterinsurgency Manual*, 2006, reproduced under the name of General David Petraeus with Lieutenant General James F. Amos (2006), FM 3-24/MCWP 3-33.5 Counterinsurgency, li-liv., http://www.fas.org/irp/doddir/army/fm3-24.pdf.

273. Ibid., chapter 2.

274. Ibid., chapter 2, 5.

275. See Testimony of Sharon Cromer, USAID Senior Deputy Assistant Administrator, before the Foreign Affairs Subcommittee on Africa, on hearings relating to USAID and U.S. Africa Command, Global Health, and Human Rights, Washington, DC, http://www.state.gov/p/af/rls/rm/2011/169224.htm/.

276. Philip Ewing and Jonathan Allen, "Ambassador Stevens Killed at Site with No Marines," *Politico*, September 12, 2012, http://www.politico.com/news/stories/0912/81134.html#ixzz2AeQRtisx.

277. Margaret Coker, "Miscues before Libya Assault Limited Security in Benghazi, Secrecy over Safe House, Contributed to Tragedy," *Wall Street Journal*, September 21, 2012, http://online.wsj.com/article/SB10000872396390444165804578008411144721162.html.

278. Eric Schmidt, "C.I.A. Played Major Role Fighting Militants in Libya Attack," *New York Times*, November 1, 2012. See also, Eric Schmitt et. al., "Deadly Attack in Libya Was Major Blow to C.I.A. Efforts," *New York Times*, September 23, 2012.

279. David Ignatius, "Charting a Post-Petraeus Era," *Washington Post*, November, 18, 2012.

280. Anthony H. Cordesman, "The Death of Ambassador Chris Stevens, the Need for Expeditionary Diplomacy, and the Real Lessons for U.S. Diplomacy," Center for Strategic & International Studies, http://csis.org/publication/death-ambassador-chris-stevens-need-expeditionary-diplomacy-and-real-lessons-us-diplomac.

281. Dana Milbank, "Letting Us In on a Secret," *Washington Post*, October 10, 2012.

282. Jan Angilella, "The Martyr Factory: Libyan Town Became Pipeline for Suicide Bombers in Iraq," *Newsweek*, April 20, 2008.

283. Robert Fisk, "Al-Qa'ida Cashes in as the Scorpion Gets in Among the Good Guys," *Independent* (UK), September 26, 2012, http://www.independent.co.uk/voices/commentators/fisk/robert-fisk-alqaida-cashes-in-as-the-scorpion-gets-in-among-the-good-guys-8143267.html.

284. Ethan Chorin, *Exit the Colonel: The Hidden History of the Libyan Revolution* (Washington DC: Public Affairs, 2012), 283.

285. U.S. National Security Strategy 2002, announced September 20, 2002.

286. Douglas J. Feith, *War and Decision: Inside the Pentagon at the Dawn of the War on Terrorism* (New York: Harper Books, 2008).

287. Amitai Etzioni, "The Lessons of Libya," *Military Review*, January–February 2012.

288. Jacob Heilbrum, *They Knew They Were Right: The Rise of the Neocons* (New York: Anchor Books, 2009). See also James Mann, *Rise of The Vulcans: The History of Bush's War Cabinet* (New York: Penguin Books, 2004) and Ivo H. Daalder and James M. Lindsay, *America Unbound: The Bush Revolution in Foreign Policy* (Washington, D.C.: Brookings Institution, 2003). In the context of the NATO intervention in Libya, Ivo H. Daalder became important, becoming the U.S. Permanent Representative on the Council of the North Atlantic Treaty Organization (NATO) in May 2009, and was a prominent spokesperson for the success of the Libya intervention.

289. Sreeram Chaulia, "One Step Forward, Two Steps Backward: The United States Institute of Peace," *International Journal of Peace Studies*, 14/1 (Spring/Summer 2009): 68.

290. Kylie Tuosto, "The 'Grunt Truth' of Embedded Journalism: The New Media/ Military Relationship," *Stanford Journal of International Relations* (Fall/Winter 2008): 30.

291. www.politico.com/news/stories/1112/84281_Page2.html#ixzz2DWlczL96.

292. Andrew Bacevich, *The Limits of Power: The End of American Exceptionalism* (New York: Metropolitan Books, 2008).

293. Jennifer Griffin and Adam Housley, "Petraeus Mistress May Have Revealed Classified Information at Denver Speech on Real Reason for Libya Attack," Fox News, November 12, 2012, http://www.foxnews.com/politics/2012/11/12/petraeus-mistress-may-have-revealed-classified-information-at-denver-speech/#ixzz2DU8VFuQ6.

294. Gil Ronen, "Broadwell: Petraeus Knew of Benghazi Plea for Help," *Israel National News*, November 11, 2012, http://www.israelnationalnews.com/News/News.aspx/161964

295. Rachel Maddow, *Drift: The Unmooring of American Military Power* (New York: Crown Books, 2012).

296. Rahul Mahajan, *The New Crusade: America's War on Terrorism* (New York: Monthly Review Press, 2002), 71–74.

297. Mat Kennard, *Irregular Army: How the U.S. Military Recruited Neo-Nazis, Gang Members, and Criminals To Fight the War on Terror* (New York: Verso, 2012).

298. "SPLC Testifies to U.S. Senate about Rising Extremist Threat, Urges Vigilance," Southern Poverty Law Center, September 19, 2012, http://www.splcenter.org/get-informed/news/splc-ttestifies-to-us-senate-about-rising-extremist-threat-urges-vigilance.

299. Tim Cohen, "Wisconsin Gunman's Army Base Had White Supremacists," CNN, August 8, 2012, http://www.cnn.com/2012/08/08/us/military-white-supremacists/index.html.

300. "Nebraska Professor Studied Wade Page," WISN Milwaukee, August 9, 2012, www.wisn.com/news/south-east-wisconsin/milwaukee/Nebraska-professor-studied-Wade-Page/-/10148890/16044308/-/gm54d6z/-/index.html .

301. Lolita C. Baldor, "4-Star General Investigated Over Spending," *The Associated Press*, August 15, 2012, http://www.armytimes.com/news/2012/08/ap-army-four-star-general-africa-command-investigation-081512/.

302. Horace Campbell, "U.S. Military and Africom: Between the Rocks and the Crusaders," *Pambazuka News*, March 31, 2011. http://pambazuka.org/en/category/features/72174.

303. Blake   Hounshell,   http://blog.foreignpolicy.com/posts/2011/01/18/seymour_hersh_unleashed.

304. John Barry, "America's Secret War in Libya," *Daily Beast*, August 2011, http://www.thedailybeast.com/articles/2011/08/30/america-s-secret-libya-war-u-s-spent-1-billion-on-covert-ops-helping-nato.html.

305. Nick Turse, *The Changing Face of Empire: Special Ops, Drones, Spies, Proxy Fighters, Secret Bases, and Cyberwarfare* (Haymarket Books, 2012).

306. Nick Turse, "Obama's Scramble for Africa: Secret Wars, Secret Bases, and the Pentagon's 'New Spice Route' in Africa," *TomDispatch*, July 12, 2012, http://www.tomdispatch.com/blog/175567/tomgram%3A_nick_turse,_america's_shadow_wars_in_africa_.

307. Nick Turse, "U.S. Africa Command Debates," *TomDispatch*, July 26, 2012, http://www.tomdispatch.com/blog/175574/.

308. Craig Whitlock, "U.S. Expands Secret Intelligence Operations in Africa," *Washington Post*, June 13, 2012, http://www.washingtonpost.com/world/national-security/us-expands-secret-intelligence-operations-in-afica/2012/06/13/gJQAHyvAbV_story.html.

309. http://topics.nytimes.com/top/reference/timestopics/people/p/david_h_petraeus/index.html.

310. Paula Broadwell, *All In: The Education of General David Petraeus* (New York: Penguin Press, 2012), 218.

311. Malcolm Gladwell, *The Tipping Point: How Little Things Can Make a Big Difference* (New York: Little Brown, 2000).

312. "General: CIA Responded Quickly to Benghazi Attack," *All Things Considered*, NPR News, November 2, 2012, http://m.npr.org/news/World/164207549.

313. *War and Decision: Inside the Pentagon at the Dawn of the War on Terrorism*, 108.

314. *All In: The Education of General David Petraeus*, 17.

315. Col. Douglas MacGregor, Ret., "The Petraeus Saga: Epitaph for a Four Star," *Counterpunch*, November 14, 2012, http://www.counterpunch.org/2012/11/14/epitaph-for-a-four-star/.

316. Walter Pincus, "Afghan Corruption, and How the U.S. Facilitates It," http://www.washingtonpost.com/world/national-security/afghan-corruption-and-how-the-us-facilitates-it/2012/11/05/d7fbce5c-2520-11e2-ac85-e669876c6a24_story.html.

317. Alfred McCoy, "Can Anyone Pacify the World's Number One Narco-State? The Opium Wars in Afghanistan," *TomDispatch*, March 30, 2010, http://www.tom-

dispatch.com/post/175225/tomgram:_alfred_mccoy,_afghanistan_as_a_drug_war__/.

318. Scott Shane and Sheryl Gay Stolberg, "A Brilliant Career with a Meteoric Rise and an Abrupt Fall," *New York Times*, November 10, 2011, http://www.nytimes.com/2012/11/11/us/david-petraeus-seen-as-an-invincible-cia-director-self-destructs.html?pagewanted=all&_r=0.

319. http://topics.nytimes.com/top/reference/timestopics/people/p/david_h_petraeus/index.html.

320. Fred Gardner, "It's More than a Sex Scandal: Paula Broadwell, Whistle-blower," *Counterpunch*, November 27, 2012, http://www.counterpunch.org/2012/11/27/paula-broadwell-whistleblower/.

321. Rebecca Shapiro, "Thomas Ricks Accuses Fox News as Operating as a Wing of the Republican Party," *Huffington Post*, November 26, 2012, http://www.huffingtonpost.com/2012/11/26/fox-news-interview-guest-network-wing-republican-party_n_2192506.html?utm_hp_ref=media.

322. Michael D. Shear, "Petraeus Quits; Evidence of Affair Was Found by F.B.I.," *New York Times*, November 9, 2012, www.nytimes.com/2012/11/10/us/citing-affair-petraeus-resigns-as-cia-director.html?pagewanted=all.

323. Ami Angell and Rohan Guraratna, *Terrorist Rehabilitation: The U.S. Experience in Iraq* (Boca Raton, FL: CRC Press, 2011), 69.

324. "Petraeus Mistress May Have Revealed Classified Information at Denver Speech on Real Reason for Libya Attack."

325. http://www.ohchr.org/EN/HRBodies/HRC/WGMilitary/Pages/OEIWG-MilitarySession2.aspx.

326. Patrick E. Tyler, "A New Power in the Streets," *New York Times*, February 17, 2003, http://www.nytimes.com/2003/02/17/world/threats-and-responses-news-analysis-a-new-power-in-the-streets.html.

327. Horace Campbell, "Kony 2012: Militarization and Disinformation Blowback," *Pambazuka News*, March 22, 2012.

328. Leonardo Maugeri, "Oil: The Next Revolution," Discussion Paper 2012–10, Belfer Center for Science and International Affairs, Harvard Kennedy School, June 2012.

329. "Wikileaks Documents Shed Light on U.S.-Backed Intervention in Libya," *African Globe*.

330. *Predator Nation: Corporate Criminals, Political Corruption and the Hijacking of America*.

331. Matt Taibbi, "The Great American Bubble Machine," *Rolling Stone*, April 5, 2010, http://www.rollingstone.com/politics/news/the-great-american-bubble-machine-20100405.

332. "Curious Victory for NATO in Libya," RUSI Analysis. See also by Clarke, "The Making of Britain's Libya Strategy," in *Short War, Long Shadow: The Political and Military Legacies of the 2011 Libya Campaign*, ed. Adrian Johnson and Saqeb (London: Royal United Services Institute for Security Studies, 2012).

333. See Samuel P. Huntington, "The Clash of Civilizations?" *Foreign Affairs* 72/3 (Summer 1993): 22–49. Responses by Fouad Ajami, Kishore Mahbubani, Rob-

ert L. Bartley, Liu Binyan, and Jeane J. Kirkpatrick, among others, were published in the next issue, *Foreign Affairs* 72/4 (September–October 1993): 2–22.

334. Huntington, "The Clash of Civilizations?," 22.
335. Ibid., 39.
336. Ibid., 40.
337. Ali Al Mazrui, *Africa's International Relations: The Diplomacy of Dependency and Change* (London: Heinemann, 1979), 301.

INDEX